Food Culture in the
Pacific Islands

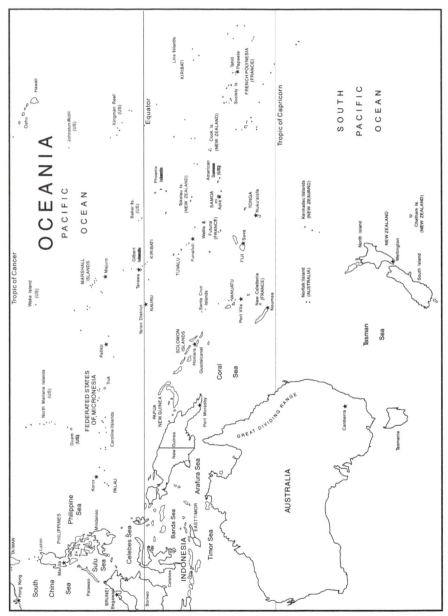

The Pacific Islands.

Food Culture in the
Pacific Islands

ROGER HADEN

Food Culture around the World

Ken Albala, Series Editor

GREENWOOD PRESS

An Imprint of ABC-CLIO, LLC

A B C  C L I O

Santa Barbara, California • Denver, Colorado • Oxford, England

Library of Congress Cataloging-in-Publication Data

Haden, Roger.
    Food culture in the Pacific Islands / Roger Haden.
       p. cm. — (Food culture around the world)
    Includes bibliographical references and index.
    ISBN 978-0-313-34492-3 (hard copy : alk. paper) — ISBN 978-0-313-34493-0
(ebook) 1. Cookery, Pacific Island. 2. Cookery—Islands of the Pacific. 3. Cookery—
Oceana. 4. Food habits—Oceana. 5. Food habits—Islands of the Pacific. I. Title.
    TX724.5.P28H34 2009
    641.5996.5—dc22   2009019969

13 12 11 10 09   1 2 3 4 5

This book is also available on the World Wide Web as an eBook.
Visit www.abc-clio.com for details.

ABC-CLIO, LLC
130 Cremona Drive, P.O. Box 1911
Santa Barbara, California 93116-1911

This book is printed on acid-free paper ∞
Manufactured in the United States of America

The publisher has done its best to make sure the instructions and/or recipes in this
book are correct. However, users should apply judgment and experience when
preparing recipes, especially parents and teachers working with young people.
The publisher accepts no responsibility for the outcome of any recipe included
in this volume.

All photos courtesy of the author unless otherwise noted.

Contents

Series Foreword   vii

Introduction   ix

Timeline   xxi

1. Historical Overview   1

2. Major Foods and Ingredients   57

3. Cooking   85

4. Typical Meals   117

5. Regional Specialties   131

6. Eating Out   151

7. Special Occasions   183

8. Diet and Health   197

Glossary   217

Resource Guide   223

Selected Bibliography   225

Index   233

Series Foreword

The appearance of the Food Culture around the World series marks a definitive stage in the maturation of Food Studies as a discipline to reach a wider audience of students, general readers, and foodies alike. In comprehensive interdisciplinary reference volumes, each on the food culture of a country or region for which information is most in demand, a remarkable team of experts from around the world offers a deeper understanding and appreciation of the role of food in shaping human culture for a whole new generation. I am honored to have been associated with this project as series editor.

Each volume follows a series format, with a chronology of food-related dates and narrative chapters entitled Introduction, Historical Overview, Major Foods and Ingredients, Cooking, Typical Meals, Regional Specialties, Eating Out, Special Occasions, and Diet and Health. (In special cases, these topics are covered by region.) Each also includes a glossary, bibliography, resource guide, and illustrations.

Finding or growing food has, of course, been the major preoccupation of our species throughout history, but how various peoples around the world learn to exploit their natural resources, come to esteem or shun specific foods, and develop unique cuisines reveals much more about what it is to be human. There is perhaps no better way to understand a culture, its values, preoccupations, and fears, than by examining its attitudes toward food. Food provides the daily sustenance around which families and communities bond. It provides the material basis for rituals through which people celebrate the passage of life stages and their connection to divinity. Food preferences also serve to separate individuals and groups from each other and, as one of the most powerful factors in the construction of identity, we physically, emotionally, and spiritually become what we eat.

By studying the foodways of people different from ourselves, we also grow to understand and tolerate the rich diversity of practices around the world. What seems strange or frightening among other people becomes perfectly rational when set in context. It is my hope that readers will gain from these volumes not only an aesthetic appreciation for the glories of the many culinary traditions described, but also ultimately a more profound respect for the peoples who devised them. Whether it is eating New Year's dumplings in China, folding tamales with friends in Mexico, or going out to a famous Michelin-starred restaurant in France, understanding these food traditions helps us to understand the people themselves.

As globalization proceeds apace in the 21st century, it is also more important than ever to preserve unique local and regional traditions. In many cases, these books describe ways of eating that have already begun to disappear or have been seriously transformed by modernity. To know how and why these losses occur today also enables us to decide what traditions, whether from our own heritage or that of others, we wish to keep alive. Thus, these books are thus not only about the food and culture of peoples around the world, but also about ourselves and who we hope to be.

Ken Albala
University of the Pacific

Introduction

The food culture of the Pacific Islands has very much been determined by the region's historical isolation from the rest of the world. Although people originally migrated out into the Pacific from bases in Asia, bringing their foods, animals, and culinary skills with them, once in the Pacific, island food cultures then had time to develop over several thousand years, while remaining virtually unknown to and largely uninfluenced by outsiders. The tropical climate of much of the region, the unique island geology, and environmental factors also played a role in the evolution of islander cuisine, which would become based on a unique range of ingredients. Although also mostly Asian in origin, the breadfruit, yams, taro, and coconut that came to constitute the basic staples of traditional islander communities (sweet potato and cassava would come later), were incorporated into a cuisine that utilized cooking and preservation techniques unique to all three major demographic zones of the Pacific: Polynesia, Micronesia, and Melanesia. These techniques included the use of the earth, or underground, oven (*umu*) to steam-bake foods, which are typically wrapped in banana leaves or baskets woven from coconut palm. This cuisine survives today, even though much has changed in the Pacific. The arrival of Europeans, and the inexorable developments that followed, have shaped contemporary food culture in the Pacific, which is largely one of extremes. Although traditional foods and cookery survive and are highly valued, Westernization has meant that the overall diet of islanders has been transformed, and that islands have changed radically from being primary producers of foodstuffs to being net importers of foods produced elsewhere. A changing diet and lifestyle have brought many health-related problems. There is no going back to traditional ways of life, but there is a chance that islander communities can now regain some of the autonomy they once enjoyed. Ironically, the tourism industry, so symbolic of the technical, economic, and social power Western culture has unleashed in the region, has at the same time been one of the most important, relatively stable sources of revenue for islander communities. Moreover, tourism has in recent years created a demand for local produce, organic foods, and fresh ingredients of all kinds, spurred by green consumers and ecotourists who value environment, health, and authentic experiences. To some extent, tourism has thereby reengaged islander people in food production and boosted their sense of identity. It also promises to effect change at the level of the local economy, giving some productive power and management over resources back to islanders whose lives, for the last 100 years at least, have very much been shaped by outside forces.

More than 12,000 islands dot the Pacific, an ocean stretching 9,000 miles from Australia to Easter Island and that extends over almost a third of the earth's surface. In terms of land mass, all the islands of the Pacific take up a minute fraction of the ocean's vast expanse. The Federated States of Micronesia (meaning "tiny islands") are 607 in number yet, combined, only total 270.5 square miles of land. Not including Australia (a massive, dry, island continent), New Zealand (comprising two main islands), and Papua New Guinea (at 287,000 square miles, the second largest island in the world), the total land area is approximately the size of the U.S. state of Maryland (20,000 square miles). Less than 1,000 islands are populated today, but these support a multicultural mix of 2.5 million people representing diverse backgrounds and ethnic origins.[1]

The Portuguese explorer Ferdinand Magellan (1480–1521) was not only the first European to traverse the great expanse of the Pacific, but was also certainly one of the first outsiders to make contact with Pacific Island people (in his case, the Chamorro people of the far Western Pacific). Magellan took three and a half months to sail across the Pacific Ocean in 1521. Up until this point in time, the islands in the region were more or less unknown to outsiders, as were the largely self-sufficient communities of people who lived and largely prospered there in secure isolation. Magellan's crossing symbolically marked the end of this cultural evolution. Thenceforward, with growing intensity, island cultures were opened up by contact with the Western world. Immigration and migration, globalization, tourism, new technologies, rapid communication, and efficient transportation systems have also reshaped how people live in the Pacific Islands over time. Currently, it takes about 15 hours to fly from Los Angeles to Sydney, Australia, via Hawaii. All the main Pacific island groups are, and have been, easily accessible by cargo and passenger jet for decades. This exposure of the islands has also had a huge impact on Pacific communities and their ways of life. This is perhaps nowhere more noticeable than when considering food culture. From the first contact with Europeans, unusual foods began to enter the diet of islanders. As time went on, with each wave of change, the food culture was affected more and more, at every stage from production through to consumption. Today, food culture in the Pacific Islands reflects this significant altera- tion. Fast, junk, and snack foods are consumed by islanders, just as readily, if not more so, than are their traditional staple foods like taro, yam, and breadfruit, which have tended to become sidelined as special occasion foods. One of the major underlying forces of change in this context has been urbanization, part of the broader process of Westernization. Genera- tional changes in attitude also erode traditional lifestyle as younger people grow up more accustomed to Western cultural norms. In the pre-West- ern contact period, all islanders lived in villages and produced, caught or gathered, processed, and cooked their own food. Today, more than 35 percent of Pacific Islanders have moved from rural villages to live and work in towns or cities, of which Suva (the capital of Fiji) is the region's largest. About one-fifth of Fiji's total population, 178,000 people, live in the greater Suva urban area. Region-wide, urbanization has been abetted by stagnating rural economies that attract negligible investment and have little infrastructure, therefore having poor access to markets. By contrast, high levels of urban population growth (between 2 and slightly in excess of 8 percent per annum) have been driven by job opportunities and wealth creation through business investment. Urban areas, including those in the Solomon Islands, Fiji, and Vanuatu, now provide up to 60 percent of the country's GDP (Gross Domestic Product). Eight of the twenty-two Pacific countries are classified as urban, but by 2020, more than half the popula- tion of most Pacific countries will live in towns or growing cities like Suva (Fiji), Noumea (New Caledonia), Honolulu (Hawaii) and Port Moresby (Papua New Guinea [PNG]). Urbanization has had serious flow-on effects for the diet and, consequently, the health of islanders. Historically, this trend has meant the demise of subsistence agriculture and its substitution by food retailing. Some islands, like Hawaii, Samoa, and Guam, import between 80 and 100 percent of their food, including fast and junk foods. But urbanization also often means a decrease in physical activity for is- landers who now find themselves working in sedentary jobs, driving cars, using public transport, watching television, and, in general, getting less exercise. Making matters worse, an overall increase in calorie intake is also prevalent in urban areas, reflecting both the easy availability and affordability of high-calorie foods, as well as changing tastes. While many of the new urban lifestyle options represent benefits for islander people, the increasing and potentially life-threatening consequences of combined dietary and lifestyle change has become a major issue, one that so far has proved very difficult to counter through public education programs or the involvement of experts and academics in the fields of agriculture, diet, and nutrition. This is primarily because consumption habits are very much the product of particular cultural attitudes toward food and eating that are deeply embedded in Pacific Island culture. These attitudes can facilitate transvaluation, whereby Western foods are found to be highly attractive according to rules pertaining to consumption in most Pacific island cultures. Pacific Islanders (and particularly Polynesians) perceive larger body mass as esthetically pleasing (beautiful); foods that by Western standards are considered too fatty are much enjoyed as a delicacy; the consumption of large quantities of food is seen as polite, particularly in the context of a communal feast, a common occurrence; and inactivity, now coincident with aspects of the adopted Western lifestyle, can be regarded as a social virtue. Such culturally-inscribed food-related values help to explain the crisis that has befallen Pacific peoples and their food culture today.

The rapid uptake of Western foods and a Western lifestyle, however, still contrasts markedly with the consumption of traditional foods and the traditional cooking and feasting that remains so strongly a part of the Pacific Island life.[2] Some of the oldest Pacific-wide traditions still practiced pertain to cooking and feasting; they are considered sacred to the many separate although closely related cultures of the Pacific region, and are widely respected. Every islander feels a sense of duty to take part in and, at the same time, show due respect for, these traditions. With regard to traditional island diets and their impact on health, the values that have facilitated the easy incorporation of Western foods and food habits do not have the same implications because the island foods are low in fats, salts, and sugars, as well as being high in fiber. The situation is thus greatly affected by the significant imbalance between the amount of Western and traditional foods consumed. While families will meet on a Sunday and celebrate in the traditional way, typically eating local foods like taro, coconut, and breadfruit cooked in an *umu*, during the working week these same families maintain modern, urban lifestyles and consume Western-style foods.

Much of the food consumed has been the worst kind of imported fast food, precooked convenience and frozen foods, fatty cuts of meat like turkey tails and lamb flaps, deep-fried foods (fried chicken is a favorite), and many forms of processed and snack food products, primarily because these have appealed most to the taste of many islanders. Islanders are today among the most obese people in the world, and suffer from a growing number of diet and lifestyle-related Western diseases, including diabetes, heart disease, hypertension, and stroke, which are thought to have been more or less unknown in the pre-Westernized Pacific. The real problem here is that cultural values in part drive this pattern of consumption. Even while, to some extent, both cultures, traditional and Western, still exist side by side (either in the context of an individual's own weekly or monthly timetable, or more broadly in the region as a whole), any potential balance has become a marked imbalance in reality. Although a simpler village way of life based in part on subsistence agriculture and fishing still exists on larger islands, on outer islands and on thousands of tiny atolls remote from the urbanized areas, this lifestyle is being inexorably eroded by the lure of the towns and cities, by global climate change (heightened storm activity, drought, rising sea levels), and by rising soil salinity levels threatening agricultural production.

What characterizes Pacific food culture today is this stark contrast between traditional foodways and Western consumption patterns. On one hand, local foods and food-related practices remain extremely important because they confirm and reinforce islander identity and communal and familial obligations. On the other hand, Western foods have also assumed importance because they have replaced the home-grown, or locally caught, with convenient store-bought goods that also represent prestige and thereby cultural capital. More and more, these foods have become the available (and affordable) choice, particularly for urban populations, and are also associated with traditional values (large body mass, food intake, and a predilection for fat), making them attractive for culturally specific reasons. Moreover, they represent being modern and Western, both notions carrying some prestige for islander consumers.

Western foods also come in novel and diverse forms. Islanders, like Westerners, naturally enough find this aspect appealing. Powerful forces like the media have played a part in boosting this type of consumption. Funded by food manufacturers and retailers, media culture exclusively supports advertising and marketing campaigns for imported, processed, Western-style foods.

Given this situation, what of Pacific cuisine? Taro, yam, breadfruit, sweet potato, coconut, pandanus, sago, fish, seafood, and pork, taro greens, various other shoots and leaves, and some fruits, are the classic ingredients of island cookery.[3] Principle among traditional foods still consumed in the islands are the staple root crops of taro, yam, sweet potato, bread-fruit and of course coconut, which is perhaps the most gastronomically versatile ingredient in Pacific-style cuisine. The term cuisine not only implies the foods, but also the cookery, dishes, and foodways of a country, region, or locale. Does the Pacific have its own cuisine? The answer is yes, although it would be fair to say that not many, other than the Pacific Islanders themselves, know very much about Pacific Island cuisine. Travelers, discoverers, migrants, and most recently, tourists, have all had the opportunity to get to know and to enjoy island cuisine over the last 200 years, yet very little of the knowledge related to the cuisine, or the foods themselves, has been exported outside the Pacific.

Within the Pacific, the same broad similarities exist between the cuisines of Micronesian, Polynesian, and Melanesian peoples: the universal employment of the *umu* in cooking, the foods themselves, and the manner in which they are cooked. Variations in taste apply more to simple seasonings and local variation in terms of ingredients like seafood and fish, of which there are thousands of kinds. The main ingredients of island cuisine can appear limited to Western tastes, and the cooking techniques could also be judged rudimentary. Seasoning can take the form of seawater (if needed) or coconut cream; today, chili is also favored in Fiji, for example. Yet, by Western standards, the foods are very plainly prepared. This simplicity of style and taste has been of lasting significance for islander people. It suggests humility, an acceptance of nature as it is, and an attitude to eating that is not focused on change for change's sake, as Western food fashion might dictate. The cuisine that exists in the Islands is indigenous, even while many of the ingredients—particularly taro, yams, breadfruit, and sweet potato—originally came from elsewhere (Asia and South America). The marvel of this apparently simple cuisine of the Pacific is that, given the seemingly limited range of ingredients, there is a great variety of tastes and textures among the many different regional varieties of fish, shellfish, plants, and animals.

Even the coconut, which Westerners know more commonly as a canned or dried product, the islander knows according to a whole spectrum of flavors and textures that it acquires as it matures over six months. In addition, taro, yam, and sweet potato are all complex carbohydrates that develop particular characteristics of their own even though, in terms of Western taste, they can seem bland. Islanders have retained their taste for this largely unadorned style of food.

Another reason for the lack of interest in Pacific cuisine stems from the fact that islander foods and methods of cookery are quite unique to the region, a largely tropical zone where only certain types of food can be grown easily and well. The raising of beef cattle and sheep, as well as grain crops, for example, simply cannot be sustained in the island environment. Conversely, the concept of the underground oven has not been taken up in other countries, less for its obvious impracticality in urban areas than because it represented an already outdated technology requiring labor to dig large holes and hot stones for heating. More significant is the fact that the types of foods the islanders like to eat, particularly the starchy vegetables (taro, cassava, sweet potato, yam, and breadfruit) suit the long, very slow method of steam-baking that the *umu* provides. The *umu*'s export and use elsewhere, therefore, would seem to depend on the exportability of the foods it cooks best. As this is predominantly fresh produce indigenous to the region, it does not travel well either. The only real indicator of the influence of Pacific food culture on the wider world is the frequency of use of certain ingredients like coconut milk or tropical fruits, like pineapple, both largely in processed forms. Indeed, millions of recipes printed on can labels attest to a largely invented Pacific cuisine tailored to Western tastes. Consequently, there have been very few Pacific-themed cookbooks of any authentic quality published, but there are hundreds of clichéd accounts themed around cocktails and beach parties.[4]

Perhaps the most profound reason why Pacific cuisine is largely ignored is because of the historical domination of the islands by Western culture. Ethnic foods are greedily consumed when those foods belong to cultures that represent exotic others, whose lives are sufficiently removed as to make eating their style of food all the more of an escape from the everyday world, or an exercise in cultural interaction. Naturally, food as a fantasy of (consuming) otherness is a well-known and exploited aspect of contemporary food tourism. Values like authenticity, tradition, and heritage can readily be expressed as an exoticized food experience, represented in part by watered-down versions of dishes that satisfy the tourists' desire for a supposedly real island experience, but which diverge almost entirely from any actual island cuisine. Such food is served in combination with lively sociality, and island ambience (including music and dance) to help create a sense of occasion. In stark contrast, any latent desire to eat the indigenous foods of particular peoples (such as Native Americans, Australians, New Zealanders, and Pacific Islanders) is far less often expressed. It is repressed, if it exists at all, in the sense that such desires can arouse feelings of guilt, and risks reminding the nonindigenous of their role in, or links to, however indirect, the marginalization and exploitation of indigenous peoples. There are as a consequence very few dedicated Pacific Islander, Maori, or Aboriginal restaurants as such.[5] What these cultures have had to offer the West, in terms of *culture*, has mostly been rejected long ago. In this context cuisine has retained little kudos. Only the Westernized makeover of Pacific Island food culture in the image of the beach party barbecue, allows for the appropriation and incorporation of some the Pacific's culinary themes and foods, that otherwise would be rejected out of hand.

Ritual events such as the *umu* and the cuisine to which it is suited have continuing importance in the islands, but are virtually unknown elsewhere. The *umu* is vital in island food culture because it is one of the last vestiges of the traditional way of living and reinforces the social contract in a context of celebration, feasting, and commensality. This is probably because islanders have not migrated far historically, and have seldom moved outside the Pacific region, unlike the Chinese, for example, who have migrated to work elsewhere, taking their cuisine with them. In this postcolonial world, the term "islanders" must include many people of culturally diverse backgrounds, including Indian, Chinese, Japanese, Korean, French, Australasian, American, and Filipino people. Each of these cultures has influenced island foodways. Hybridized versions of Western dishes and dishes that are the product of various ethnic traditions coexist alongside islander food culture, which, in turn, has been shaped by the foods and foodways of numerous other cultures. The islands have also become home to an international community of travelers, tourists, and migrants who have given island food an image of casualness and simplicity, one borrowed but adapted from traditional island feasts. The barbecue, Hawaiian luau, and beach party have ongoing appeal for the tourist, who often thinks or dreams of the islands as a paradise typified by cocktails at sunset, dainty nibbles, and a view overlooking the beach. Tourism has also brought the international cuisine of the hotels and resorts, which has capitalized on the relaxed mood of island living by providing simple foods like salads, freshly grilled seafood, and tropical fruits as typical fare. The easy-going, happy-go-lucky islander personality brings consistency to this theme, thereby connecting the visitor, however vicariously, to local and traditional island values. For the visitor or tourist, the seemingly plentiful supply of fresh coconut milk, seafood, and tropical fruits, the ritual use of the earth oven, and the convivial, communal feasts that often take place against the brilliant backdrop of a tropical sunset, keeps the image of traditional hospitality alive. Today, there is a palpable sense of casual living for anyone visiting the islands, a relaxed attitude that has as much to do with the tropical climate as it does with the traditionally unambitious approach to life taken by islanders. This attitude is now synonymous with an easy-dining style in the islands. Today's Pacific cuisine is a complex expression of the ongoing blend of local, regional, and global adaptations, and between traditional and changing contemporary values.

What remains extraordinary is that the main cultural groups—Micronesian, Polynesian, and Melanesian—still retain some of the essential elements of their food traditions: foods themselves, specific combinations of ingredients, cookery techniques, eating practices, food-related terms and expressions, and, importantly, food rituals and symbolism. Whether it is the Tokelau Islands, three tiny atolls in Polynesia with a total land area of nine square miles, and home to 1,600 people, or giant Papua New Guinea (PNG), with over six million inhabitants, common aspects of food culture can easily be identified. Among the most significant of these would be the use of the *umu*, the myriad applications of the coconut (nut and palm), ritual feasting and its social significance, and the expression of family bonds and relationships communicated through food practices, including consumption, and the highly significant symbolic value placed on starchy vegetable crops like taro, sweet potato, and breadfruit. Although these traditionally high-status foods are consumed less and less frequently as daily fare, and are currently are more expensive than substitutes like cassava, rice, or noodles, the traditional starchy foods are still mandatory at special events and collectively held in high esteem. The reason for this cultural resilience against pressure to change is a theme in Pacific food culture. In spite of being small and therefore vulnerable oases of humanity, having experienced massive cultural upheaval, loss of life, huge economic pressures, the coming of the cash economy, agribusiness, and the consequent breakdown of village food economies and urbanization, traditional beliefs and values regarding food still matter to islanders because they represent their sense of self. Food remains manifestly expressive of their most deeply held views about life, family, friends, and neighbors.

The discussion of Pacific Island food culture in this volume includes that of Australasia, that is, Australia (including Tasmania) and New Zealand. Both countries have had a major influence in the Western Pacific, as well as sharing Polynesian and Aboriginal (Australian) cultures that have common historical origins. The book covers food culture in Micronesia, Polynesia (including French Polynesia), and Melanesia (which includes Samoa, Fiji, Tonga, the Cook Islands, Vanuatu, and the Mariana Islands, among many other island groups), but excludes the Philippines, Indonesia, and Japan, all of which require book-length studies themselves. The same is perhaps true of Australasia, but the relationship between Australia and New Zealand and the Pacific region makes its inclusion significant. Clearly, in this context, not one but several food cultures coexist in the region. A brief account of some of the major aspects of island food cultures follows; these cultures exist in many forms across the Pacific, and all of these have been subject to different historical forces and influences. Among those places representative of both tradition and change are Hawaii, Samoa, Tonga, the Cook Islands, French Polynesia and New Caledonia, the Federated States of Micronesia, New Zealand, Fiji, Vanuatu, the Solomon Islands, Papua New Guinea, and Kiribati and Tuvalu (formerly the Gilbert and Ellice Islands). Australia, although it has become home to numerous islander people (including natives of the Torres Straight islands), since it was settled by Europeans in the early 1800s, has been less significant in terms of Polynesian islander migration than New Zealand, its close neighbor. New Zealand is home to the greatest number of Polynesians (Samoan, Tongan, Cook Islander, Niue Islander, Tokelau Islander) in the world. New Zealand and Australia are technically advanced Western countries with powerful economies, and have fulfilled a significant political and economic role in the Pacific region. The food culture of Australia and New Zealand is Western (defined in terms of having industrialized food production and processing). The cuisine is clearly multicultural in both countries, reflecting immigration patterns. Australasia has certainly exerted an influence on island foodways, both in terms of production and consumption, but the same could not be said of the islands, whose cultural and economic influence has been slight.

NOTES

1. Population estimate excludes Australia (21 million), New Zealand (4 million), and Papua New Guinea (6.3 million).

2. Nancy J. Pollock, *These Roots Remain: Food Habits in Islands of the Central and Eastern Pacific since Western Contact* (Honolulu: University of Hawaii Press, 1992).

3. Secretariat of the Pacific Community (SPC), *The Staples We Eat* (Noumea: Secretariat of the Pacific Community, 1999); John M. Bailey, *The Leaves We Eat*, Handbook 31 (Noumea: South Pacific Commission, 1992); Secretariat of the Pacific Community (SPC), *The Fruits We Eat* (Noumea: Secretariat of the Pacific Community, 2001; Annie Walter et al., *Fruits of Oceania*, Aciar Monograph 85 (Canberra: ACIAR/IRD Editions, 2002).

4. See, for example, Rachel Laudan, *The Food of Paradise: Exploring Hawaii's Culinary Heritage* (Honolulu: University of Hawaii Press, 1996); Rafael Steinberg, ed., *Pacific and Southeast Asian Cooking*, Foods of the World Series (New York: Time-Life Books, 1970); Jennifer Brennan, *Tradewinds and Coconuts: A Reminiscence and Recipes from the Pacific Islands* (Boston, MA: Periplus Editions, 2000); Gwen Skinner, *The Cuisine of the South Pacific* (London: Hodder and Stoughton, 1983); Susan Parkinson, Peggy Stacy, and Adrian Mattinson, *Taste of the Pacific* (Auckland, NZ: David Bateman, 1995). For examples of stereotypical cookbooks that appropriate elements of Pacific islands' culinary culture and style, see Rich-

ard Perry, *Retro Luau: Planning the Perfect Polynesian Party* (Tigard, OR: Collector's Press, 2004); Donald Frank FitzGerald, *The Pacifica House Hawaii Cookbook* (Toluca Lake, CA: Pacifica House, 1965); *Tropical Drinks and Pupus from Hawaii* (Honolulu: Island Heritage, 1986).

5. See Carolyn Morris, "On the Absence of Maori Restaurants: The Politics of Food and Indigeneity in Aotearoa/New Zealand," *Appetite* 47, no. 3 (2006), 395.

Timeline

60,000 BCE	Groups of humans enter Sahul, comprising Australia, Tasmania, and New Guinea, then joined as a single land mass.
32,000 BCE	Buka Island in the west Solomon Islands is settled.
28,000 BCE	Evidence of human use of taro dates in the Solomon Islands.
6,000 BCE	Tasmania and New Guinea are cut off by sea from mainland Australia.
1000–2000 BCE	Ancestors of today's Pacific peoples develop sophisticated sailing technology.
1400 BCE	Emergence of Polynesian people as a distinct ethnic group (in Tonga).
1000 CE	Polynesian-speaking settlers (Maori) reach New Zealand from the Cook Islands.
400 CE	Marquesan islanders settle the Hawaiian Islands.
1200 CE	Tahitians conquer Hawaii and instill Tahitian culture.
1521	Portuguese maritime explorer Ferdinand Magellan (1480–1521) succeeds in crossing the Pacific and anchors off modern-day Guam.
1642	Tasmania is first sighted by Dutch explorers.
1774	Iberian (of Spanish origin) pigs are introduced to Tahiti, replacing the island breed; they later become an important source of

	protein for the convicts of the Australian colony of New South Wales (NSW).
1769	English explorer and navigator Capt. James Cook (1728–1779) and crew, aboard the *Endeavour*, arrive in Tahiti. Tahitians in canoes surround the ship, offering breadfruit, bananas, and coconuts.
1788–90	Penal colony is established in NSW and depends on imported food.
1792	Breadfruit is transported successfully from Tahiti to the West Indies and first shipment of 80 live pigs arrives at NSW as breeding stock.
1796	Famine threatens Australian colony. Beer is made from corn and the Cape gooseberry.
1800	Cassava moves east to Melanesian and Polynesian island groups.
1802–03	300,000 pounds of salted Tahitian pork meat is sold through the Sydney merchants.
1817	First printing press in the Pacific Islands is set up in Tahiti.
1830	Greek settlers arrive in NSW and influence the scale of wine production.
1833	Sheep are brought to New Zealand (NZ). Lamb will eventually be a major export commodity for NZ.
1840	First market gardens are established in the Australian colonies.
1850	Hawaii exports 375 tons of sugar to the United States.
1850s	Importation of labor begins. Eventually, workers from China, Japan, Portugal, the Philippines, and Puerto Rico are employed to man Hawaii's sugar, and later, its pineapple, plantations and processing plants.
1853	New Caledonia is made a French possession.
1864	Publication of first Australian cookbook, by Edward Abbott (1801–1869), *The English and Australian Cookery Book*, in London, by publishers Sampson Low.
1874	Fiji is annexed by the British Empire.
1875	Gas cookers are available in Australia.

1876	Last full-blooded Tasmanian Aborigine dies.
1882	The refrigerated ship *Dunedin* leaves from NZ for London with first frozen meat shipment.
1890	There are 10 million cattle and 100 million sheep in Australia.
1893	Author Philip E. Muskett (d. 1909) declares meat and tea to be consumed in excess in Australia.
1899	American entrepreneur and major pineapple exporter James Drummond Dole (1877–1958) arrives in Hawaii, following its annexation by the United States.
1906–07	New Zealand suffers a potato blight.
1920	Hawaii exports over half a million tons of sugar to the United States.
1923	James Dole buys the island of Lanai for pineapple production.
1933	Australia's first milk bar, a shop serving milk-based drinks (shakes), soda pop, and ice cream opens in Sydney. The cities of Melbourne and Brisbane follow suit in opening their own milk bars.
1936	Cassava (Fijian *tavioka*) is introduced into Fiji's Lau group to help increase the food crop harvest in the islands' poor soil.
1939	Australians eat 248 lbs per head of meat annually (not including meat from wild animals).
1939–45	World War II. Changes include technological improvement and mechanization of processes in industrial food manufacture, including drying, canning, condensing (milk), and powderizing (custard powder).
1942–45	Australia supplies American troops with 1.5 billion lbs of foodstuffs. Americans send experts to Australia to improve production and safety standards in the food industry.
1945	New Zealand has 200 acres under grape vine.
Post-1950	Human consumption of cassava increases across the Pacific region.
1962	Samoa gains independence from NZ.
1967	Era of the 6 o'clock closing time of public houses in Australia ends.

1970	Fiji gains independence.
1974	"Kiwifruit," previously known as Chinese Gooseberry, becomes a brand name (NZ).
1975–85	Australian "East-West fusion" cuisine, an experimental culinary style, develops.
1978	Ellice Islands become Tuvalu.
1979	Gilbert Islands become the major part of the renamed nation of Kiribati.
1990	Cyclone Ofa hits Samoa. Half of the homes on Savaii Island are destroyed. Food aid is called for.
1995–97	Healthy Weight Loss Program is instigated in Tonga.
2000	West exports US$30 million worth of low-grade meat to the Pacific Islands.
	Fiji imposes ban on mutton flaps.
2002	Illegal live fish trade in the Pacific is estimated to amount to US$500 million. Fiji's production of rice is less than half what it was in 1993.
2003	Cyclone Ami causes an estimated US$66 million worth of damage to farms, infrastructure, and cash and food crops in Fiji.
2004	American Samoa School Lunch Programme orders 19,000 fast food meals from KFC and McDonald's to feed all school children in honor of National School Lunch Week.
	Slow Food (Italian, now global, organization that champions local foodways) is established in Hawaii.
2007	New Zealand has 23,000 acres under grape vine.
	Forbes Magazine lists 9 Pacific nations among the world's 10 fattest countries.
	Australian food company Goodman Fielder buys major stake in Arnott's biscuit company in PNG, as a result of increasing demand for biscuits in the Pacific region.
2008	Spike in world food prices for rice, wheat, chicken and cassava (the latter as a source of biofuel) puts pressure on islander food security.

34 percent of Fiji's population reportedly lives in poverty. Fiji's interim Minister of Agriculture encourages islanders to grow their own food.

2009   Program established to promote food safety in the supply chain (from "farm to plate") that is intended to protect up to 5,000 Hawaiian farm-based producers by decreasing spoilage.

United Nations Food and Agriculture Organization encourages more Pacific states to make their own flour from traditional root crops instead of importing expensive alternatives like wheat flour.

1

Historical Overview

The food culture of the Pacific region reveals a history of extremes: happiness but also hardship; plenty as well as dearth. With basic technologies, yet ingenious application, the people who settled Oceania overcame the geophysical and climatic shortcomings of their adopted island environments and flourished despite many difficulties. They originally migrated out into the Pacific via South Asia, taking with them the food plants and animals they already knew, successfully adapting most of these to island locales, which in many cases were quite different from what these intrepid migrants had previously known. While the coastal and tropical conditions of the islands may have been similar to parts of Southeast Asia, different island and atoll soils, extreme weather events (hurricanes, droughts, tsunamis), access to resources including water supply, and different types of flora and fauna would surely have challenged the new inhabitants, forcing them to adapt by being innovative and inventive. No one should doubt the difficulty of surviving in the island environment. Indeed, it took thousands of years of cultural evolution, in relative isolation, separated from most of humanity, to produce the Pacific Islands' unique food-provisioning system, so perfectly adapted as it traditionally was to particular island conditions.

Pacific food cultures more than coped with the limits of what poorly resourced, tiny tropical islands in a vast expanse of ocean could deliver. Some locales were naturally better provisioned than others, with access to fresh water, fish, and various other sources of food. Nonetheless, the region-wide demands of the environment and climate were substantial, to the extent that, over the centuries, invention, ingenuity, strength, and tenacity were needed to survive and to prosper. This application of knowledge would mark Pacific Island food culture out as one that was finely tuned to available resources and local conditions. The robust and efficient provisioning system that developed would be more than merely expressive of a deep knowledge of how to realize the potential of island environments. Pacific island foodways were also holistic, in so far as the spiritual, political, and familial life of the community were given social expression through obtaining, producing, processing, cooking, presenting, and eating food. All such food-related activities were experienced as integrated social events. The deepest-held beliefs and values of Pacific Island societies were thereby given social and cultural expression via an everyday involvement with food that touched everyone's life. A reciprocity existed whereby the meaning attributed to food—to gestures, actions, processes and transformations associated with it—supported and strengthened the system of provisioning by making even the most commonplace, necessary aspects of food profoundly meaningful. As in other cultures, food culture in the Pacific Islands evolved as a powerful means of social communication. Out of a difficult environment, one that had initially set absolute limits on the likelihood of human survival, solidarity, abundance, and generosity were grasped and championed as central cultural values. The public display of plenty and the offer of food without reserve were to become spectacular signs of social well-being as much as they were tributes to visitors and special guests, or to those being honored in some particular way. The offer of the gift of food (*always* more than enough food to satisfy physical needs) showed to the gods, the chiefs, the people, and the guests that the community's well-being was assured and was being celebrated. By virtue of lavish display, the system of order and social hierarchy were reinforced. Abundance produced happiness, and collective happiness in the form of a feast was the ultimate endorsement for any society.

Eventually, into a world hitherto shielded from the outside by mile upon mile of ocean, came a succession of shaping influences that represented a new set of extremes, this time less physical or geographical than cultural. In little more than 200 years, Western explorers, followed in succession by traders, businessmen, missionaries, colonizers, the modern military, and most recently by multinationals and tourists, would bring waves of radical change to the islands and their food culture. Extreme isolation, extremes of environment and climate, and the extreme influence of Western cultures and economies on traditional island values and ways of life shaped island food culture as it is today.

EARLY MIGRATION

The movement of people out into the Pacific marks the start of what many experts say was the greatest of all major human migrations.[1] The claim is based on simple facts: the region is immense and the islands that it contains are difficult to find and hard to access. Sophisticated sailing and navigation skills and technically advanced ocean-going sailing craft (outrigger canoes) were developed for the greatest migration phase: out into the far Eastern Pacific, beyond what are today the Solomon Islands, and into Polynesia. It is unknown what seacraft were used in the first phase of migration, in and around Papua New Guinea (PNG) and what is called Near Oceania. But certainly, adequate supplies of food and drink were required for the voyages, together with stocks of plants that these people could propagate once ashore in their new island environments. Taro, coconut, yam, breadfruit, pandanus (of which the juicy fruit is eaten—see chapter 2), sago, rice, and arrowroot (a starch) were some of the main food plants taken along that would become staples of the wider Pacific region, or parts of it (rice would be propagated in Micronesia, but would eventually be abandoned in favor of the more successful root crops and breadfruit).

Between 30,000 and 8,000 years ago, peoples of two distinct groups of modern humans (*Homo sapiens sapiens*), Australoids and Mongoloids, populated various islands in the southwest corner of the Pacific: in and around Papua New Guinea, parts of the Bismarck Archipelago, the Solomon Islands, and western Micronesia, in the region that borders the Celebes Sea. In addition, perhaps as early as 60,000 years ago, Australoid groups moved into what is now Australia, but what was then a mega-continent, Sahul, an ancient land formation that included the then conjoined PNG and Australia (only in the post-Ice Age period, beginning 6,000 years ago, would rising sea levels create the two countries more or less as they are today). Migration south was thereby made much easier because of virtual landbridges (or shallows), as it was eastward, in Sunda, the name given to the Southeast Asian mega-landmass that included what is today the Philippines and parts of Indonesia.

Parts of the Solomon Islands were settled by 30,000 years ago. Subsequently, voyages of greater length were required to reach islands further eastward (including outlying eastern islands in the Solomon group, Vanuatu, and New Caledonia to the southeast, and further east again to Fiji, Tonga, and Samoa. The voyages that were eventually made demanded ingenuity and great technical ability. The people who settled these islands farther to the east, making up the greater part of contemporary Polynesia (including the Hawaiian Islands, French Polynesia (the Society Islands), Easter Island, the Cook Islands, Tokelau, Niue, Tonga, Samoa, and New Zealand) left in waves from bases in the region of far-western Micronesia and also from Taiwan, about 5,000–6,000 years ago, forming part of a wider movement called the Austronesian expansion. Evidence also indicates that, around 4,000 years ago, Austronesian people spread north from what is now the Philippines (Palau) to the Mariana Islands and from there, southeast, to Fiji (3,500–3,300 BCE); to Tonga and Samoa (3,000 BCE); to Tahiti (the Society Islands, now French Polynesia), in 750 CE; to Hawaii (in the far north-central Pacific, 600 CE); to the Marquesas and the Tuamotu Archipelago (northeast and southeast of Tahiti, respectively) between 300 and 600 CE; to Easter Island (the far-easternmost Polynesian island, in 400 ce); and to New Zealand (the island group farthest south in Polynesia) around 1000 CE.[2]

The eastern movement of peoples may have reached as far as the Americas, and recent archaeological evidence supports this theory. Chicken bones, related genetically to chicken species thought to be of Polynesian origin, have been found in South America.[3] The sweet potato (*Ipomoea batatas*), thought to have been introduced by Spanish ships traveling westward from the Americas in the 16th century, could also conceivably have been carried earlier into the Pacific region by islanders who had reached the coast of South America (Chile). Generally, however, the pattern was very much from west to east. The other point to make here is that the biodiversity of island flora and fauna also tends to decline from west to east, across the Pacific. Nonetheless, the migrating people were accomplished agriculturalists, skilled in the arts of producing and cooking their own food and so, to some extent, were ready to face the new challenges of island living. Gradually, as migrations continued out into the Pacific over several thousand years, food culture developed with it.

The precise dates for the first migrations are not absolutely certain, although, with DNA testing becoming more accurate all the time, the general movement and pattern of the migrations is now fairly clear.[4] It was an amazing achievement for these self-sufficient explorers and their families, who went in search of new places to settle and established a vital food culture in the islands. Many aspects of that culture continue to be traditional today. In bringing with them varieties of taro, yams, bananas, sugarcane, breadfruit, coconut, sago, pandanus, arrowroot, and initially, rice (at the time of Western contact, rice was only found to be growing in the Mariana Islands), they also either brought or later developed unique techniques that allowed them to cultivate, cook, and preserve foods in the ways best suited to their new environment.

These food plants were already part of Asian food culture, of which the Chinese was the most advanced at the time of the early migrations. Chinese food culture was already well developed, even 3,500–4,000 years ago. Its influence on agriculture, technology, and cultural symbolism would also shape the future food culture of the Pacific and the social beliefs and values associated with food and foodways. The Chinese valued *fan*, in particular, which was conceived of as the all-important starchy component of a meal (and traditionally, this food is still rice), complemented by *ts'ai*, meaning all other dishes, whether comprised of vegetables or meat. The starch was central, while the complementary dishes provided the means to vary the taste and texture of that core component. These same values would, in essence, be transposed, and have an ongoing and fundamental role to play in the development of Pacific island food culture.

Archaeologists and others have worked hard to put together the history of prehistorical times and what the cultures that emerged in the wider region were like. Without written records, and with little in the way of permanent architecture, what remains of these ancient ways of life is minimal. Nonetheless, items like volcanic rock cooking stones, platforms for snaring pigeons, shellfish hooks, kitchen middens (ancient fire sites where shells and other remains of foods, like bones, accumulate and are preserved in the ground over time), grinders, pounders, cutting tools, and pottery have provided insights into food culture and everyday life in the early period of settlement. Of the earliest of the these cultures, the Lapita (known as the Lapita cultural complex) is the most significant, because it is the first culture that developed over a wide area of the Pacific, and is so named after the distinctive, decorated clay pots it produced (of which many were found at the village of Lapita in New Caledonia). The Lapita represented an important culture in Melanesia and Micronesia, not only because of the unique pots (used—it is thought—for cooking and storage) but also because they continued pig husbandry and gardening, particularly of taro, that had been a feature of PNG life as early as 9000 bce. Lapita culture spread from the Bismarck Archipelago off northwest New Guinea, beginning about 3300 bce (Lapita artifacts were first discovered by archaeologists on Watom Island, north of New Britain, in 1909). The culture reached Fiji 300 years or so later, via the Santa Cruz Islands, New Caledonia, and Vanuatu. Lapita culture also spread to the Kingdom of Tonga (160 islands spread in a wide archipelago), which represented the eastern fringe of the Lapita complex's presence in the region, although examples of their pots have been found as far East as the Marquesas Islands, which gives an indication of their widespread use if not of manufacture. Lapita culture flourished in Tonga between 2850–1550 bce and represents the best early example of how the challenge of living in the new island environment was met. Within the Tongan islands, Lapita culture spread out, but eventually halted east of Fiji. It declined more rapidly, as clay was not available on many of the islands and atolls. But importantly, Lapita culture modified itself in response to the environment and to population pressures. The demise of its pot culture could have been due to a number of factors.[5] But change was certainly forced upon the Lapita as the basic food provisioning system of fishing and collecting wild foods were put under pressure by the expanding population. Adaptation took the form of outward migration to other islands and the development of agriculture. Lapita culture diversified at the local level as groups migrated, probably using the outrigger sailing canoe as a means to do so. To some extent, this means of transportation ensured the continuity of the culture. Plants or seedlings, animals and technologies could be relocated. When Dutch explorers discovered Tonga in the early 1600s, they noted large twin-hulled canoes off shore. Canoes as long as 62 feet have been built and sailed in order to verify the possibility of long-range migration by this means. The Hawaiian double-hulled canoe, *Hokule'a*, has made several successful voyages between Hawaii, Tahiti, and New Zealand.

Pottery culture survived in Melanesia, but died out entirely to the east. Beyond Fiji, the modified "potless" Lapita cultures of Polynesia would come to rely exclusively on agriculture and fishing, the *umu* (as it is known in Polynesia), or underground oven, and the drying and pit storage of food (fermentation). The distance from Melanesia and Micronesia (440 miles from Vanuatu to Fiji) also isolated the inhabitants of the more remote region from traditions like pot making, and so their own distinctive food culture developed as a result. About 2,500 years ago, a distinctive Polynesian culture began to emerge in the Western Pacific and continued to diversify without outside influence. In the Hawaiian Islands, there was a substantial development of horticulture, including irrigated gardens in which taro were grown, and dry-cropping of sweet potato. Coconut, sugar cane, banana, breadfruit, and yam were also grown. Pigs and dogs were raised for food, and fish (mullet and milkfish) were farmed in constructed coastal ponds. Hawaii's population had grown to an estimated 200,000 at the time of the arrival of Europeans. A hierarchical leadership had also emerged, leaving a huge number of commoners without rights or land. King Kamehameha I (1758–1819) was the equivalent of an absolute ruler. He established the Kingdom of Hawaii in 1810. By contrast, at the other extreme of Polynesia, the Maori culture of New Zealand developed (from approx. 1000 ce); this did not have the same hierarchy, but rather included many local chiefdoms, often at war with each other over valuable

Early Lapita pot, New Caledonia.

food-producing lands. The population was spread out and land was much more plentiful, even if the temperate climate was not as productive as that in the tropics; however after the annihilation of much native fauna (varieties of flightless birds, for example), arable land became a premium asset. About 100,000 Maori were present at the time of contact with Europeans.

Three broad subregions of the Pacific were eventually identified (in the 19th century), distinguished by the use of terms that, when coined, referred to racialized physiological features. Although the indigenous peoples shared common ancestry and cultural traits, including their food culture, social system, and traditional beliefs, these same three terms are still used today, but more to designate broad geographical zones than physiological differences: Micronesia (*micro*, "tiny") is an area of the far Western Pacific, spreading north of PNG, and includes the regions of Palau, Yap, Truk, Pohnpei, Kosrae (all states within the Federated States of Micronesia), furthermost east, Kiribati (pronounced, kee-ree-barce), and, to the far northeast, the Marshall Islands. The Mariana and Northern Mariana Islands are also geographically part of Micronesia, but are today largely administered by the United States; Melanesia (*mela*, "black") covers the region encompassing New Guinea, the Solomon Islands, and Fiji (the people of Kiribati are also of Melanesian descent); and Polynesia (*poly*, "many"), roughly covers everything east of the international date line, but includes New Zealand to the southwest, Tonga, Wallis and the Futuna Islands (both French territories), Tahiti (French Polynesia), Pitcairn Island, and Easter Island (administered by Chile as a "special territory") in the extreme far-eastern Pacific, and the Polynesian Hawaiian islands in the central-north Pacific. The three major ethnic groups of people, so defined, are therefore known as Melanesians, Micronesians, and Polynesians. All of these bear the genealogical traces of their genetic ancestry: Mongoloid, Australoid, and Lapita (a mixture of both). Today, the old boundaries still exist, even though the demographic and geographic determinations do not equate exactly. Currently, the demographic profile of the region is decidedly multicultural. The history of Pacific food culture is also a history of this now diversely populated region that, over many centuries, evolved with negligible contact with the outside world.

What the original inhabitants found when they reached the Pacific Islands was vastly different, in some cases, to what they might have known in the far-western Pacific or in mainland Asia. Technology requires adaptation to new conditions, or is rejected if it cannot be adapted, as the case may be. While the Lapita are famous for their pots, as Pacific Islanders they would not need them for cooking as their culture developed. They almost exclusively used both fire (or "hearth cookery") and the earth oven (*umu*), a device perfectly suited to both the environment and to the type of foods that the islands and atolls produced. Taro, breadfruit, yams, then later sweet potato, and, more recently still, cassava, all steam-bake beautifully in the *umu*, which utilizes fire-heated hot rocks to cook food. Briefly (see chapter 3 for details), a pit is dug and hot rocks are positioned inside; food is placed on the rocks, usually wrapped in leaves. The pit is sealed with earth and left for some hours to allow for adequate cooking. The *umu* was a brilliant adaptation to the island environment because it could also cook a great deal of food at once, was fuel efficient, and was able to concentrate the flavor of the foods, a taste factor that should not be underestimated when considering the evolution of island cooking. Such technical adaptation naturally followed from the fact that the islands were far less well-provisioned in terms of native flora and fauna (and deposits of clay for making pots) than Southeast Asia, New Guinea, the Solomon Islands, and the broader region from where eastward migrations took place. Many Pacific islands and atolls became home to a number of vegetables and animals that the migrants had brought with them, but these would need special treatment and technical adaptations like the *umu*. The need to develop a food supply system that could provision islander populations in the long term also made the development of a sustainable island vegeculture system all-important.

But the Pacific islands themselves vary a great deal, both geologically and ecologically, making for considerable differences in the modes and means of adaptation in different locales. The ability to sustain particular crops and creatures was partly dependent on geography. Breadfruit did not grow well in the northern climes of Hawaii, and taro cultivation in New Zealand was hampered by the colder climate (the northernmost point of the country is 700 miles south of the tropics). Brought during the Maori migration from the Cook Islands, around 1000 CE, taro was grown in the north, but it did not thrive (the great British navigator, Captain James Cook, mentions it being cultivated at Tolaga Bay). It would be the *kumara*, or sweet potato, that would become one of two staple crops of the Maori. Throughout the year, Maori also harvested many other edible plants, or parts thereof, including bracken fern root, called *aruhe*. Cook also noted stocks of this food, along with dried fish, on one of many visits to Maori villages in New Zealand during 1769. A rhizome, *aruhe* was nearly always found wherever bracken (*Rarauhe, Pteris aquilina*) grew wild, which was in most parts of New Zealand, and its roots grow up to an inch thick. It was also cultivated in special grounds from ancient times. Roasted on embers, *aruhe* was then pounded on a wooden or stone block with a pestle (*patu aruhe*), then peeled and eaten. Its starchy contents taste something like arrowroot, and the starch could also be used to make flat loaves. A favorite traditional accompaniment was *inanga*, a small lake fish. New Zealand's climate was too cold to support sweet potato production all year round, so fern root supplied the staple, which was a unique circumstance in the region.[6]

Such regional differences are characteristic of Pacific food culture. Even the hardy coconut, so often associated with images of the Pacific Islands is not ubiquitous, and diminishes as one moves eastward or too far south. Coconut palms will not grow on high islands at altitudes above 3,280 feet (over half a mile); pandanus and coconut proved to be lifesavers on atolls where poor soils did not always sustain root crops; and sago, requiring swamps, became very important in PNG and its immediate region, but not always elsewhere in the region. Importantly, throughout Oceania, sustainable food-provisioning systems developed that were adequately adapted to the local conditions.

Melanesia, which geographically includes PNG, Fiji, New Caledonia, and the Solomon Islands, is mostly made up of what are called island-arc islands (formerly continental islands) that have fertile soils and contain continental rock. These can support an abundance of vegetation. New Caledonia also has a drier "savannah" on its leeward side, where Kanaka people planted yams and sweet potato. A second group is made up of high islands, which are volcanic, with central mountains, steep cliffs, and reasonably fertile soils, and are usually surrounded by coral reefs (Tahiti and Rarotonga). A third group is made up of coral atolls (made from coral formed out of the skeletons of tiny marine animals), which are what remains, virtually at sea level, after volcanic islands subside. They provide an, at times, tenuous habitat, typically supporting coconut palms and pandanus (an important atoll food); nonetheless, they have sustained human communities for upwards of 2,000 years (examples include most of eastern Micronesia and, further west, Tokelau and the Tuamotu Archipelago). Coral atolls are usually surrounded by barrier reefs enclosing a lagoon. Other fringing reefs can be in contact with the atoll itself. Naturally, reefs are home to the fish, shellfish, and crustaceans that traditionally added significantly the diet.

The provisioning, production, and consumption of food became central to island life, and it would not be an exaggeration to state that island community life is everywhere touched by food culture. In the first place, so much of the daily routine evolved around one kind of food-related activity or another: gathering, fishing, hunting, basket or net-making, planting,

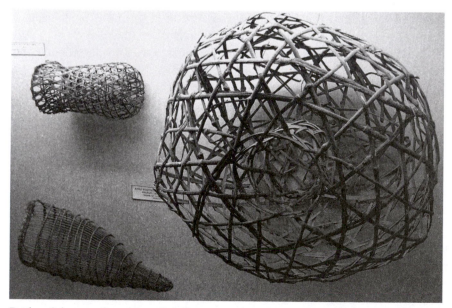

Basket fish traps from New Caledonia.

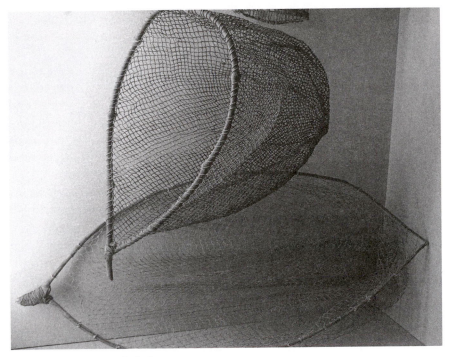

Fish nets from New Caledonia.

gardening, processing, fire-making and cooking, daily consumption, and feasting. As such, food culture emerged as an expression of island life itself and, consequently, of the values that assumed importance along the way. Community and family relationships (kinship ties), allegiance to chiefs, elders, and leaders, religious and spiritual beliefs, and all manner of social rules were expressed through food-related practices or ideas. Indeed, in so far as social hierarchy and the rule-following that this demands are fundamental to islander societies, these are constantly played out in relation to food culture, thereby being both affirmed and reinforced. Fundamental beliefs inherited from ancient Chinese culture (the notions of *fan* and *t'sai*) were transposed into island foodways, making the starchy staples (taro, breadfruit, and yam) far more significant, in general, than meat, fish, other vegetables, or fruit. Taro also signified generation, family ties, and abundance. A bountiful harvest, the display of plenty, and, finally, the consumption of much taro, demonstrated to all the robustness and well-being of the community. There were exceptions to this rule about the staple starches, expressive as they were in many ways of community itself. Special foods like dog, pig, lobster (crayfish), and turtle also had ceremonial significance, but the staples had by far the greatest everyday importance, both as food and as symbol.

Some foods, deemed special, were eaten in greater quantity by elites. Powerful social minorities developed in the Hawaiian and Society Islands (of which Tahiti is the most famous), which elevated the material and symbolic role of some foods as a means of reinforcing rank because like taro, some foods were regarded as being virtually sacred. Certain foods could only be prepared by women. Others, like poi (Hawaii's fermented taro paste), were prepared by specially designated males. Furthermore, foods often had to be served to men first, which was a very common custom throughout the region. Women often tended gardens. Men fished. All rules associated in one way or another with the getting, production, preparation or consumption of food gave an infinitely nuanced expression to the rigid social organization of Pacific island society. As the anthropologists understand it, food functions symbolically, as does language; as such, food communicates through activities as diverse as gathering, gardening, fishing, weaving, fire-making, cooking, presentation, and eating.

Overall, islanders made excellent use of the limited land available to them by propagating plants that were well adapted to the conditions: taro, which with due care (the Hawaiians were accomplished taro cultivators) thrived in the tropical conditions of many islands; the long-living coconut (Cocos nucifera), perhaps the hardiest of all island species, which is still widespread in the region and largely looks after itself, fruiting twice a year and peaking in its production between 15 and 30 years of age, but living up to 100 years; and pandanus, which is also a hardy species that produces a sought-after fruit and a nutritious starch, extracted from its trunk. Crucially, pandanus grows well in the poor soils of atolls. How the various introduced plants and animals used for food initially fared in the new environment depended on soil and rainfall, on the degree of care taken in propagation, and on how much variety and the amount of both flora and fauna a particular island could support. But the dietary staples of taro, breadfruit, yams, sago, and pandanus (particularly valuable on arid low-lying atolls), together with the technology of preservation and cooking (underground), became the key features that would sustain a uniquely Pacific cuisine.

Dogs, pigs, chickens, and rats (Rattus exulans) were the main animal species brought into the Pacific during the migrations, and all were eaten as a source of food. Hawaiian chiefs were particularly fond of dog, the animals first being fattened on a special diet, including taro. Dogs were also used for hunting. The largest animals eaten by islanders were pigs, omnivorous foragers that dig up roots, eat scraps, and do not require grazing. Pigs have long been a highly valued and prestigious animal in island cultures. They are still hunted wild in the mountains of Fiji and on outer islands elsewhere in the region, as well as being farm-raised and imported frozen, as pork. Two generic types of pig were originally introduced into the Pacific. From what is now Indonesia, pigs were taken to PNG, 5,000 (but some say as late as 2,500) years ago. From there, this long-snouted, long-legged razor back variety of pig (*Sus scrofus*) was carried into the Pacific as far as Easter Island, Hawaii, Tonga, and possibly New Zealand, although no pigs were observed there at the time of first contact with Europeans. Captain Cook introduced the second type of pig on his explorations in the Pacific, and European breeds were subsequently mixed with the wild variety. Currently, feral pigs cause damage to the environment (particularly in NZ), but are nonetheless highly prized by gourmets for their flavorful flesh.

Broadly speaking, island food culture thrived, while always being subject to unpredictable natural disasters (floods, droughts) and poor weather that prevented fishing, hunting, gathering, or planting, so techniques including fermentation, smoking and drying were developed and refined in order to overcome food shortages when they did arise. In time, fermented breadfruit and taro both became much-esteemed staple—but also sacred—foods. Techniques like these, together with the abundance of sea food and a tropical ecology that could support the speedy growth of many food plants, helped to ensure food security for the first Pacific Islanders.

Obvious differences exist between this typically Pacific cuisine and its Western counterpart. Modes of agriculture and the types of livestock preferred also differ markedly. Staple Western crops like wheat, barley, oats, rye, and other grains simply do not fare well in the humid conditions. The tropics suit the propagation of leafy green and root vegetables, gourds, fruits, and coconut. Similarly, larger grazing animals like cows and goats, even if they had been transported by canoe, would not have suited the tropical island habitat. Aside from the fact that these animals are not physiologically suited to the tropics (dairy cows and goats do not readily lactate in the tropical heat), tracts of land needed for grazing or feeding were simply not available on small islands given over to plantings of taro and breadfruit.

Of course, migration and settlement did not take place without month to month hardships, or without causing longer-term changes to the environment and ecology. It is often thought that ancient peoples once lived, or still live, in harmony with nature. The truth is that environments are in a constant state of change through natural forces and through the effects of living things, including humans. The dogs, rats, chickens, and pigs brought to the islands would no doubt have had an almost immediate effect on existing plants and animals already inhabiting the islands. Seeds present in soil attached to introduced vegetables like taro, for example, would potentially have introduced pest species into the new environment. As with introduced fauna, exotic plants had the potential to disrupt or damage the local ecosystem, one originally fairly free from such change due to the region's long period of isolation. The introduction of cattle, horse, goats, sheep, and deer in New Caledonia would inevitably cause serious erosion and displace traditional taro plantations.[7] In PNG, introduced cattle have also put strain on land use. More recently, reports have indicated that Hawaii's native habitat and traditional ecosystem are in serious decline due to centuries of infestation by insect pests, the introduction of exotic species, plant diseases, soil erosion, pollution, and damage to waterways.[8]

Not surprisingly, the more remote islands and atolls, like those of Tuvalu (previously called the Ellice Islands), appear to have been populated last in the extended period of migration. Some 450 years ago, people from Samoa, Tokelau, and other central Polynesian islands inhabited Tuvalu. An ongoing regional ethnic diversification that took place over millennia can be understood using a single example. When the northern neighbors of the Tuvaluans, the often hostile I-Kiribati (of Micronesian descent), intermixed with their new neighbors, Melanesian and Polynesian traits were combined, affecting the physical traits of Tuvaluans, while the latter's culture remained predominantly Polynesian. There was also, however, some cross-fertilization of knowledge. Food preparation techniques like toddy making (toddy is a fermented drink derived from the sap of coconut palm's inflorescence, or flower head) were passed on as a result of social contact between the two cultures, which amounted to the spreading of technology and techniques from Kiribati to Tuvalu. This process of knowledge exchange is a feature of Pacific island food cultures, which is perhaps true of food cultures everywhere. New techniques and foods are gradually incorporated from elsewhere. Thus, local traditions can remain strong while, at the same time, generically similar culinary traditions and food habits can be common to a number of Pacific foodways.

Over time, the food value of most edible substances, plants and animals, birds and fish came to be understood and incorporated into island food culture. Food was understood in the primary sense of being a substance that could help sustain life, which meant that most if not all potential food sources were explored by virtue of necessity. Therefore, all manner of collectable seafood were utilized, including mollusks, crabs, seaweed, and fish, as well as bats, lizards, insects, larvae and pupae, bird and turtle eggs, buds, berries, nuts, leaves, and fruits. In many ways traditional Tuvalu food culture, which remained relatively intact until very recent times, exemplifies the kind of meticulous resourcefulness that the initial need to survive inspired. Prediscovery, the atolls comprising Tuvalu constituted a finely tuned yet robust subsistence food economy.[9] Traditional lore cemented knowledge that was gained through long experience. The lunar calendar was used as a guide for planting, and the values of plants and other substances were affected by the subtle sense-based discernment of flavors and textures. The fishermen were experts on the weather, currents, the habits of sea-life, and how to construct nets, boats, and tools for fishing. Locals understood the variations in the taste of plants. The medicinal and pharmacological uses of flowers, shoots, buds, roots, seeds, saps, resins, bark, and leaves were understood and passed down. In this way, the coconut provided oil for cosmetic use and for medicine as well as flesh and liquid for food and drink.[10]

The regional and local variation of Pacific food culture is wide-ranging. The historical change, difference, and development in foodways relate to geo-climatic factors and, thus, to agriculture; geographical location (relative isolation); population and its impact on island ecosystems; and proximity (conflict or trade with other cultures or communities). Overall, the lush tropical rainforests of New Guinea, the volcanic Hawaiian Islands, largely temperate New Zealand (where the blasts of freezing arctic southerlies are commonplace) typify extremes: varied climates, soils and terrains that, overall, support a diverse range of food crops, sea life, and animals. Even small atolls of little more than a third of a square mile could support 1,000 people, if resourced with adequate rainfall, taro, coconut, and fishing grounds. The successful settlement of such a vast region is an astonishing feat on its own. Food shortages due to climatic forces (cyclones, tsunamis), drought, or infestation were offset by various means, including trade. The Langa Langa people of the Solomon Islands, who lived on offshore reefs, possessed no arable land of their own; however, using shell money and fish, they traded with gardeners on shore to supplement their diet.[11] This kind of reciprocity also existed between inland and coastal dwellers. Island economies of food were therefore micro-tuned to local variation in environment, ecology, and climate.

CONTACT WITH THE WEST: TRADE AND CONFLICT

A diverse population of people and cultures had developed across the many different island environments in the centuries that preceded

European discovery. The Tongans, Hawaiians, and Tahitians, all had extensive kingdoms, dynasties that maintained power for considerable periods. The Tui Tonga dynasty of Tonga has been referred to as an empire, to the extent that it was influential over a wide area, stretching from Tikopia in the west to Niue Island in the east. The Tui Tonga expansion began around 950 ce. By 1200 ce, huge monoliths that still attest today to the power of the historic Tui Tonga, had been erected near the coast of Tonga's main island, Tongatapu, at Houma, near the site of the ancient capital, Lapaha. Coral slabs were originally brought 800 miles by canoe from Uvea (Wallis Island) to be erected as carved monuments. The resulting Ha'amonga 'a Maui Trilithon, as it is called, attests to more than the architectural knowledge of the Tui Tonga, because it is supposed to have had an astronomical function as a clock, used for navigation as well as for seasonal planting. The Tui Tonga empire declined during the 13th and 14th centuries due to warfare and political intrigues, as did the Tahitian and Hawaiian dynasties at a later time. But lands stayed under the control of chiefs until much later; in Tonga, until the civil wars of the early 19th century. Until this time, the people remained obligated to till the soil and produce food, as well as to supply military service to the community. The extent of the chiefs' power would have been reflected most clearly in the feasts they held, when they would have demanded that the best of everything, including foods, be offered up. Early Western visitors to these feasts noted their scale and the numbers of visitors in attendance.

The demography of these Pacific societies is still being determined by archaeologists, so estimates vary, but a million or more people may have lived in the Pacific region at the time of European contact. Up to 50,000 people lived in the Mariana Islands alone in the 1600s. The first European crews to sail into the Pacific in the 16th century would have traversed seemingly endless stretches of water with little or no respite, to be eventually surprised, and relieved, to find that the tiny specks of land at which they lay anchor were in fact oases that supported edible plants, animals, and quantities of fresh water. No doubt most astonishingly of all, fellow humans were also found thriving in many of these remote outposts. In fact, the later, larger-scale discovery of many Pacific islands (in the 18th century) revealed to Western explorers that there were very few previously inhabited Pacific islands that were empty of humans at that time. Only the Norfolk Islands, the Kermadec, Phoenix and Line Islands, and the Pitcairn group revealed the remnants of abandoned settlements. With discovery, this pan-Pacific community of cultures was about to change forever.

Most islanders appeared happy and healthy according to many early observers of island life, including the greatest of all of the West's Pacific explorers, Captain James Cook. Cook often reported on the vitality and health of native Pacific Islanders in his journals. The Tahitians had fine teeth, Cook noted, and described the Tongans as seemingly free from disease. New Caledonians (Cook named New Caledonia) were strong, robust, active, well made people, and he found Cook Islanders to be well fed, stout, and active.[12] Captain Cook also described foods, eating, and cooking techniques like the ground oven (*umu*). But the lives of native islanders were not perfect. Seaman were often wowed by first impressions (at ceremonial welcomes), and the hardships and very substantial dangers islanders faced were thereby obscured. Life expectancy is known to have been much shorter than it is today, and has been estimated to be as low as 30 years among New Zealand Maori prior to 1769. Diet, or starvation, however, cannot be cited as the primary cause of this, although shortages did occur due to crop failure, cyclone damage, or poor harvests. Food supplies were also destroyed by man-made means: warfare. It was common practice in the islands for warring tribes to destroy the food supplies of enemies if the opportunity arose. Warfare certainly took its toll on the lives of young men as well. Practices like ritual cannibalism were also commonplace, and must have accounted for many hundreds if not thousands of lives being lost.

Foodways, including the display and gift-giving of quantities of food, as well as feasting, made a favorable impression on the first shiploads of visitors. The offer of food to strangers is an almost universal form of hospitality practiced around the world, and is of ancient lineage, but island hospitality comprised everything a guest might wish to have in the way of food, drink, comfort (including sexual favors), and entertainment. As was their custom, islanders staged great displays of food at feasts in honor of guests, something that ceremonially demonstrated their wealth, community well-being, and, only in addition, hospitality. This type of occasion would certainly have added to the impression that many early visitors had of the islands, that they had arrived in paradise, a term that is still often used to describe aspects of the Pacific Islands experience today.

But neither celebrations and generosity, nor feasts of welcome, suggest how early relations developed or the course of events that followed first contact. Ships often arrived in desperate need of refreshment and supplies of food and drink. By and large, island reserves and the tribes that managed them could accommodate such needs, although this invariably depended on good communication. The offer of food as a gesture of hospitality was one thing, but poorly communicated demands and ensuing misunderstanding was quite another. Both islanders and Europeans could be intolerant and hasty to act on such misunderstanding, sometimes resorting to hostility and violence. Traditionally, islanders in most regions of the Pacific had been involved in tribal wars. The islands of Tahiti, Tonga, Fiji, and Hawaii were all engaged in bitter localized conflicts during the time of Cook's voyages. It did not take much to start a fight between what were essentially two very different cultures with different beliefs and world views.

Islanders also recognized the income and trading opportunities that Europeans represented. Paid work brought immediate rewards and perhaps adventure, while trade had obvious rewards. As early as 1804, Maori men were participating in whaling; by the 1840s, whaleboats were being manned and operated by them. They also played a major role at the shore stations, some becoming headsman in charge of the operations of a whaleboat. Up to 40 percent of the New Zealand whalers may have been Maori. Nonetheless, in the early days, the Europeans' technology, ships, guns, clothes, and naturally their behavior and language would have all been profoundly confronting, and indeed, at times, frightening and horrifying to behold. The Polynesians, who had no concept of property rights or legal ownership of material goods, frequently encountered hostile opposition because they would regularly remove visitors' belongings or items from visiting ships without permission. This type of cultural misunderstanding could easily lead to bloody conflict.

While not always the prime commodity traded, food was by necessity a crucial part of the trading economy simply because the provisioning of visiting ships and their crews was a standard requirement. In return for this, islanders received various tradable items like tools, but also Western food and drink. What a strange experience it must have been for islanders to watch their European counterparts eating with knives and forks, or trying the sailors' fare of salt beef, rum, and hard tack (dried flour and water biscuits). This was how the primary need for food, on one side, fuelled by curiosity and covetousness (the islanders wanted their share of European culture), on the other, instigated exchanges and furthered relations between cultures for better or worse.

Exchanging foods as gifts, as provisions, or as an incidental consequence of social contact meant that, as well as ideas and techniques related to food, social values and beliefs expressed through food-related practices were communicated. The cultural divide was thereby negotiated through food culture in a way that was ongoing and, to an extent, this is still true today. Food brings people together through mutual need, as well as by virtue of hospitality, generosity, and the immediate pleasures that food can provide. The power that sharing food (commensality) invests in the idea of community also reinforces the very notion of social life in the minds of those present. Eating together gives rise to and then confirms relation-ships that subsequently grow and are strengthened by further encounters around the table; or, as in the Pacific, while communally seated on the ground in front of the platted dining mats on which the dishes of food are arranged.

This mundane backdrop—of eating a meal together—is part of the story of Pacific trade, which, in its earliest incarnation, was food-based and typified the relations that developed in the initial post-contact period. Islands were regarded as provisioning depots by the visiting ships, and with regard to provisioning islanders, fulfilled their role well. As time went on, trading diversified and was consolidated, in the process turning food into a commodity. The sociality inscribed at the heart of Pacific foodways also remained strong. In this context, islander cultures were mostly able to ab-sorb change coming from outside. They resisted, accommodated, but also at times, positively embraced, changes that proved to have a devastating effect on the traditional Pacific way of life in the longer term.

After the explorers and their crews had finished the task of mapping the region (both geographically and as a potential source of wealth), the next phase of intercultural relations was marked by the presence of a group referred to as beachcombers and castaways. These men lived uncertain, often itinerant, lives in the islands in the period following exploration (1790–1820). The opportunity to make one's fortune in the islands beck-oned in those early days, especially with fledgling colonies in both New Zealand and Australia seeking contact and commercial ties with potential trading partners. The region attracted traders, sailors, and craftsmen, as well as escaped convicts, deserters, and castaways who, having made their way to particular islands, made new lives for themselves. Many native islanders became itinerant travelers and beachcombers themselves. The trade in sandalwood (encouraged by Hawaiian chiefs, among other island leaders), sea cucumber (an aquatic animal, holothurian; Fr. bêche-de-mer), followed by whaling turned the Pacific into a region of opportunity for outsiders and explains the steady stream of individuals who sought refuge and reward in the islands.

Those involved in food provision facilitated early trading agreements between islanders, Europeans, Americans, and, increasingly, Australians, but also in some cases became producers of the foods sold to traders. Dur-ing the early 1800s, William Davies was a beachcomber on the Hawaiian island of Oahu. He reputedly rose early and worked a twelve hour day in his fields, where he grew enough food crops to trade when necessary. Other castaways lived in more remote areas, partly for reasons of security. In the Marquesas (north east of Tahiti), one castaway maintained a neat cottage and garden surrounded by breadfruit and bananas in a valley high up on the mountainous island of Hivoa, where he was helped by his native wife and children in growing potatoes and fruit, which he traded with visiting whalers. Such go-betweens were the first precommercial traders of the Pacific, and this kind of early exchange marked the beginning of a much greater transformation that would include the introduction of many Western-style foods.[13]

The sandalwood (a fragrant timber used for incense and to make furniture) and bêche-de-mer trades, followed by the much more significant whaling industry (the first to significantly change the social and material economy of the region) further served to develop cultural relations. Whereas the castaways and beachcombers were forced to abide by local island ways and laws, with the advent of larger-scale commerce and trade, the balance of power tipped toward the newcomers. This process exposed islanders and foreigners equally to the foodways of the other culture. In the early days, locals developed provisioning systems, using boats to buy and collect yams and pigs raised for the purpose of feeding traders and whaling ships' crews; meanwhile, the latter, no doubt desirous of some variety in their monotonous diets, would have happily traded some weevil-infested flour for fresh produce. In this way, a hybrid food culture was already forming while traditional island foodways remained more or less intact. The foods of the West merely added to the islanders' available food supply at this time. Islanders typically supplied food to traders or whalers in return for tools, blankets, refined sugar, tea, wheat flour, polished rice, and bully beef: a food product that would become of great importance and cultural significance in the Pacific. Originating in Ireland, the technique of salt-curing (corning) beef in kegs was developed as a way of provisioning British navy crews during long voyages. In the early 19th century, the same product was tinned for the first time as corned beef. Today, it is regarded in the West as a standby food like sardines or Spam, one of a range of commonplace canned supermarket items that are not highly regarded in terms of status or from a dietary perspective. Yet, it has never ceased to be a favorite of Pacific Islander populations. As it was designed to do so, bully beef kept well enough in the tropics, and was much liked by islanders for its taste, becoming in their eyes the quintessential food of the Western "other." After all, Westerners were regarded as fascinating and attractive. Their foods, therefore, were also objects of desire. Bully beef has enjoyed a lasting cultural kudos. It symbolizes the West in a form that can literally be consumed. Perhaps there is a hint of the old cannibalistic logic functioning here, whereby the spiritual power of the other is consumed with the food itself.

Other early-introduced consumables were more obviously addictive and life-threatening. Tobacco and alcohol, in particular, wrought havoc with the health of islanders. The coconut oil trade that developed in the Gilbert Islands (now Kiribati) followed the earlier contact and exploitation by whalers in that region. All islanders were touched in some way by the production and export of copra (dried coconut flesh), and the associated copra trade-related transactions often involved traffic in drugs like nicotine and alcohol. Gilbert Islanders were quickly transformed into tobacco addicts. Reports in the 1840s documented the relish with which they actually chewed and swallowed, rather than smoked, tobacco.[14] The Gilbert Islanders' traditional sour toddy, a drink made from coconut palm flower heads, was taken by traders and distilled into a more potent spirit that inevitably found its way back into native hands. They duplicated the process of distillation, thereby adding to their stock of tradable items; predictably, however, numbers of islanders also descended into drunkenness, which widely disrupted local life in the islands at times. Traditionally, Islanders were drinkers themselves. Excessive kava consumption was widespread, especially among the chiefly caste of Hawaii, for example.[15]

Kiribati provides a typical example of how early trade links developed. American, British, and Australian whaling ventures were all operating there by 1825. The men involved also bartered tobacco and iron in return for bêche-de-mer and turtle shell. Turtle meat proved a very palatable food for the Westerners, as much as it was enjoyed as a prestigious food at local feasts. Western foods like flour and tea, as well as tinned fish and meat, became part of the local economy. Then, as whaling diminished, a boom in local coconut oil trade extended the already established links until the islands became a British protectorate in 1892, and finally a colony in 1916. The control of law-making was relinquished, local foodways were discouraged under the rule of the British Empire, and Western culture was actively passed on, in schools as in everyday life. This period saw the increased spread of Western foods and foodways. Both diet and cookery were affected. Island cultures were gradually drawn into a cash economy that gave islanders new power and new choices while, at the same time, control over production of their own foods was weakened, subsistence agriculture undermined, and trade and commerce with the outside world encouraged. The convenience of imported, processed, and often ready-to-eat foods challenged all that had previously been of value in the islanders' food culture. Of the islands that proved more valuable than others, those with a willing local labor force were even more attractive. The arduous extraction of timber (sandalwood), the catching and processing of whales for whale oil, or the husking, splitting, and processing of coconut flesh (copra), always required plenty of able-bodied men. Many islanders volunteered to work for the traders and foreign powers, but many were also abducted, treated brutally, and forced to labor on board ship or in processing, packing, and loading the various products. The labor demands naturally grew as large-scale plantations of sugar, coconut, and pineapple developed in places like Hawaii, Fiji, and Queensland, Australia, in the latter 19th century.

In addition, as regional and global trade developed, provisioning became an important commercial enterprise in itself. Australia was one of the early players in provisioning, having brokered a deal to import meat from Tahiti in the late 1700s. The first shipment of Tahitian pork was sent to the penal colony in NSW in 1801. Islanders also became very involved in this trade, which was a precursor to the industries that would be set up in the islands in the decades to follow and that would implicate island economies not only in provisioning systems of broader scale, but in industrialization and the large-scale extraction of resources. Many hundreds of Fijians were employed in the early years in collecting (diving), boiling, smoking, and drying bêche-de-mer, and many more islanders helped to supply the sandalwood traders. After 1820, both these sources of revenue went into decline (the collection of bêche-de-mer was almost entirely confined to the Torres Straight by the 1860s), only to be overtaken by whaling, which brought thousands of men into the region over a period of 40 years and established a truly modern industry there. In 1844, at the height of the whaling boom, America had 571 vessels operating in the Pacific.[16] Whale meat was not consumed by Westerners (it was primarily the oil they were after), although islanders would customarily eat whale if they had the opportunity to catch one.

Provisioning the whaling enterprise was a major exercise on a scale never before seen in the Pacific. With the boom came the inevitable influx of people and technology, money and goods, including imported foods to offset shortages in the islands. The inevitable reduction of stocks of whale did not precipitate the collapse of this commerce in the region either; rather the opposite, since commercial activities attracted interest in whatever else the Pacific had to offer and inspired thousands in the region to look for alternative opportunities to make a profit.

Of course, islanders were relatively defenseless against Western weaponry, although this was not as one-sided as might be expected. Food culture was a part of this story, too. The 3 million pounds of salted Tahitian pork traded between 1793 and the mid-1820s to help feed the convict colony of NSW was paid for in part with muskets that were amassed and used to precipitate the outbreak of a civil war in Tahiti.[17] This trade in food and weaponry would be duplicated elsewhere. Wherever food was traded or needed by traders, guns were a convenient and sometimes politically expedient form of payment. Arms traded to a warring tribe might well serve not only the tribe in question by assuring the defeat of its rifleless rivals, but also the trader-suppliers of arms who were always looking for ways to get "on-side" with natives in order to gain access to valuable resources. As was typical, in 1864, on the island of Yap in western Micronesia, 8,316 pounds of bêche-de-mer were traded for 75 muskets, powder, lead, axes, and knives.[18]

BLACKBIRDING AND DISEASE

By the time of Cook's tragic death in Hawaii in 1779, little was left to be discovered in terms of what would be of economic use to the European nations who had financed the explorers. For the great majority of larger islands and groups, contact with the West had brought immediate and often devastating consequences. Death, abduction, and disease were all causes of social upheaval that Pacific food culture. Due to the relative paucity of their exploitable resources, some island cultures (particularly those of low-lying atolls) managed to preserve their traditional way of life and foodways relatively intact, although at the same time they were more likely, from sheer vulnerability, to be targeted by blackbirders (the name given to kidnappers active in the Pacific in the late 1800s).

Like many others, Tuvalu is a low-lying atoll group that proved perfect for the capture of laborers. Consequently, Tuvalu suffered losses at the hands of the marauding blackbirders who combed the Pacific in search of human cargo. Serious upheavals of native community life and, in more than a few cases, the annihilation of whole populations resulted from this form of contact. Blackbirding was often conducted at gunpoint, went largely unchallenged, or even unnoted, as it occurred in the remote Pacific. A few ships would anchor off shore and an armed landing party would be sent in. Hundreds of men, women, and children could then be rounded up and either lured under false pretences (the promise of a legal contract to work for good pay) or forced to leave their island home. Traders had done this to some extent since first entering the region, but on a much smaller scale. Although on the wane in the 19th century, modern slavery had been practiced and endorsed by Europeans since before the discovery of the . Inarguably, slavery had added to the West's wealth for almost four centuries. Incursions into island populations were a historical consequence of such a culture, one further encouraged by trade, whaling and plantations, all of which—at times desperately—needed labor.

Blackbirding solved the immediate labor shortages. Conditions of virtual slavery existed for most of these indentured workers. Vanuatu contributed 13,000 workers to the sugar plantations of Queensland, which between 1863 and 1904 claimed a total of 60,000 islander workers. By the mid-1880s, the Aboriginal population in Queensland had declined by almost three-quarters, to perhaps only 32,000, due to the indenture system. By 1911, the Solomon Islands had lost 30,000 men to labor elsewhere, while Japan's poor prefecture of Okinawa exported thousands to work, mostly in the Western Pacific, but as far afield as Hawaii, where Chinese and Filipinos were also indentured as sugarcane plantation workers.

Peru, which borders the Eastern Pacific, was among the most notorious of blackbirding nations, claiming thousands of Pacific islanders for its guano mines. Guano is bird dropping that, over time, is deposited in huge quantities at roosting sites; it was highly valued as a potent natural fertilizer before the invention of superphosphate. Over 6,100 Polynesians are thought to have been taken away by their self-proclaimed Peruvian masters. Only 257 of these islanders are recorded as having returned home.[19] Other blackbirding nations included Australia, the United States, and Britain. This type of exploitation reproduced and reinforced the notional categories of "savage" and "civilized," entrenching racism and exploitation as a legitimate means of gaining power and wealth. Island communities, however, were not without their own forms of slavery. Particularly in Hawaii and Tahiti, where elite classes of demigod-like chiefs and kings were established, virtual conditions of slavery existed for islanders who, according to accepted local law, were required to work without reward for their native masters. Pleasing the gods was considered payment enough. Hawaiian chiefs took an active part in selling off the islands' sandalwood forests, reaping rewards that were never shared among their fellow islanders.

Contact also meant disease, perhaps the most devastating of all the foreign imports. Influenza, measles, tuberculosis, dysentery, and whooping cough all decimated islander populations. Having lived for centuries in isolation from large human populations elsewhere, islanders had little or no immunity to common infections of all kinds. Infectious diseases accounted for thousands of lives lost among islander populations. No major island groups were spared. Fiji suffered a series of epidemics: pulmonary infection in 1791–92, acute dysentery in 1802–03, and measles in 1875, the latter wiping out an estimated one-quarter to one-third of the population.[20] In Hawaii, of the original estimated 250,000 native inhabitants at the time of first contact, this figure was reduced to 38,500 by 1910.[21] Deaths actually exceeded births during the 19th century in the Cook Islands, where the ratio was 44 to 10 in 1843. By 1856, the population of

Rarotonga was less than 2,000. Four deadly diseases, specifically tuberculosis, typhoid, influenza, and smallpox, struck the Marquesas Islands between 1791 and 1864, killing approximately 80 percent of the population. The problem was ongoing. In one of the worst recorded cases of sudden infection, at Apia, in Western Samoa, 8,500 people (22 percent of the population of the country) lost their lives to influenza carried in by a visiting ship's passengers in 1920. Disease continued to reduce the populations of Pacific island communities drastically until public health measures in the early 20th century began to arrest the trend, with life expectancy gradually increasing along with declining infant mortality.

Throughout the 19th and early 20th centuries, the Pacific region experienced enormous upheaval and change. From the early days, Western economic and political powers shaped Pacific island cultures to suit their own ends; in many cases, disease, death, and cultural devastation resulted in total chaos. This, however, did not stop islanders from willingly involving themselves in trade and taking opportunities, both of which were already part of their culture to some extent. In certain cases, islanders actively embraced an enterprising, entrepreneurial spirit. Maori were a notable example of this, and were also commercially aggressive.[22] They provided pigs, fish, and vegetables, including potato. By the 1850s, Maori were supplying tens of thousands of tons of the tuber to settlers in NSW. They also planted thousands of hectares of wheat, which effectively supplied the whole of Auckland, still leaving a surplus that could be exported.[23] Maori also introduced new foods like whitebait to pakeha (Maori for "white people"), and offered their own style of food (kai) to settlers. Today, kumara (kumala in Fiji), or sweet potato, once a staple of the Maori diet, is a quintessential New Zealand (or, in the vernacular, Kiwi) ingredient.

A mix of native foods and imported crop varieties became a source of revenue and a shaping force in Pacific cuisine. The search for bêche-de-mer represents the start of a food trade in the islands, but copra, sugar, and later pineapple, consolidated the commercial plantation system. Hawaii, Fiji, Samoa, and Tahiti were among the major producers of copra and sugarcane, two crops that earned fortunes for planters at different periods in the Pacific's history. Numerous smaller export enterprises followed, producing coffee, cocoa, tobacco, citrus, and vanilla. Many individual enterprises failed over time due to common factors such as prohibitively high production and shipping costs combined with fluctuating world commodity prices. (Vanilla is still a valuable boutique product grown on several Pacific islands, including Pohnpei, in Micronesia, and in Vanuatu.) The plantation economy that supplanted the early haphazard enterprises of the small-time traders and, later, the whalers, was set in place by well organized, international players like Burns Philp and Lever Brothers, who were among those globally positioned companies that initially sought to gain a share of the lucrative copra market. Copra was exported for use in the soap and margarine industries. Initially, Germany developed coconut plantations and, as well as using Samoan labor, imported thousands of Melanesian and Chinese workers. Trade implied offshore profits and the recruitment of often imported labor. The colonial partition of the Pacific followed in the wake of this consolidation of commercial interests, both as a way of protecting the latter and of gathering extra revenue from business via export and import taxes. The labor market was regulated for the benefit of capitalism and the colonial powers, which also taxed islanders.[24] The influence such changes had on food culture were incidental, but also incremental. As the economic interests and influence of the West largely went unchallenged in the Pacific, food habits inevitably changed as new foods were introduced, as well as because native peoples were abandoning their traditional tasks, frequently related to food provision, in order to work for pay.

One of the ironies related to changing diet was that Europeans, Australasians, and Americans never really adopted the foods of the locals, even though their own staple foods were obviously difficult to procure, and moreover, not easily grown, or their food animals, raised, in the islands. But a food culture travels with its people for other reasons. Although, principally due to climate and geography, the then food culture of the tropics and that of the northern hemisphere were entirely out of sync with each other, it was for cultural reasons related to deeply held views and specifically the fact that these are expressed through ones relations with food, that the Europeans held so tenaciously to their diet. Habit cannot fully explain this determination. Cultural pride, identity and to this extent, imperialistic attitudes expressed via food culture, meant that the newcomers held all the more strongly to their largely incompatible cuisine. Although grazing or feeding cattle could simply not be sustained on small islands given over to plantings of taro and breadfruit, the islanders nonetheless gained a liking for (canned) corned beef and later, for canned fish. Against all practical obstacles, Westerners persisted in valuing their own traditional foods; a belief that helped them prevail. As a consequence, the foods of the islands today are in many ways hardly different from those anywhere else in the Western world.

THE MISSIONARIES

There were spiritual as well as material forces at work to ease the transition of islanders to an essentially different way of life. The missionaries, who came in the name of a Christian god, had a significant effect on daily life and customs, including the food customs of the native population. In the 16th century, it was the Catholic faith that made the first impression, as Spanish and Portuguese explorers, and following them, plunderers from the same nations who were journeying toward home from the Americas, established bases in the Western Pacific, implanting their religious beliefs as they did so. The first missions in the Pacific were established in Micronesia in the 17th century, followed by the building of churches. Christianity had come to stay, although it was not until the 19th century that the missionary movement conquered Polynesia. After trade opened up the region to shipping, there was greater access for anyone with a message to spread. The London Missionary Society sent members to Tahiti and Tonga in 1797, and then moved on to the Cook Islands and Samoa. The Roman Catholics also arrived in the Society Islands, and would eventually succeed in converting the local islanders to their particular Christian persuasion. The Catholic faith spread from there to the Tuamotus and the Marquesas, while Methodists from Britain and Australia were successful in Tonga, which underwent mass conversions in 1833–34, counting king Tauf'ahau, later King George Tupou I, among the converts. Most Tongans were Christian by 1851. From Tonga, Christianity spread to Fiji, where it was also embraced. By the end of the century, much of Polynesia had been converted to Christianity, and there were many ordained native priests.

As unofficial representatives of the imperial powers of Britain and France in the Pacific, the battle for human souls was waged zealously by both Catholic and Protestant ministries. This took the form of reforming local practices, including those related to food and, especially, eating. Horrified by the feasting "to excess" of islanders, who were witnessed gorging on food for days, followed by several more of virtual fasting, missionaries, backed by colonizers put programs in place to convert islanders to the three meals a day model. Moreover, European table manners were enforced, which meant no more eating with the hands only. The exclusive use of tables, chairs, knives and forks, cups and saucers, napkins, and all the other accoutrements of the Western dining room were vehemently encouraged.

The reshaping of islander society was thus achieved through conversion to Christianity and, under its guise, conversion to civility. Cooking too, in the Western mode, was included in the plan for reeducation, and this naturally involved the use of Western ingredients, which became ever more prevalent. While the church offered religion and redemption in the name of a Christian god, modern cookery offered deliverance from a "primitive" way of life in which food culture had always been central. Thus, food-related practices became the target of a real-life battle between island tradition and Western rationality: health and hygiene were also high on the list of reasons islanders were given for abandoning their customary food habits. In this way, Christianity paved the way for the introduction of new food practices as it marked the abandonment of others: primitive traditional practices like ritual amputation (Hawaii), mutilation or scarification (the Maori *moku*, for example, is a form of tattooing that pierces the skin), and cannibalism, were all adamantly discouraged by church leaders. Atrocious acts of cannibalism certainly took place, among the worst being New Zealand's Boyd Massacre (1809), involving the slaughter and devouring of 66 crew members of the whaling vessel, *Boyd*, which had been anchored off the coast at Whangoroa in the North Island. Cannibalism was a practice that belonged to the lore of tribal societies and, as well as being carried out as an act of vengeance, also expressed beliefs about power. Eating other humans was not about hunger, but rather about demonstrating one's superiority. It was also thought to be an act whereby another's mana (spirit-power) was also consumed, thereby making the cannibal stronger. Islanders in part abandoned beliefs like these because they had been presented with an alternative belief system that made sense of their world in other, less obviously violent and aggressive ways; this must have been appealing, given the recent history of violence they had endured. Engagement with community and spirituality was strengthened by Christian morals and ethics. As a further acknowledgement of the desire to change, Western ways of life were also adopted, including new foods and methods of cooking. The use of refined flour, sugar, and other products, and techniques like baking and pot cooking, challenged the old methods.

The rapid adoption of Christian values by islanders was partly due to all the warring, disease, and distress that contact with the West had brought. Even though it was the religion of those who oppressed them, the essential Christian message of tolerance, equality, and kindness was well received by the oppressed islanders, who converted rapidly. Many of their descendents remain devout churchgoers.

Christian beliefs had ideological and material effects on how islanders lived and what they ate. For example, the significant food rituals of Christianity were embraced. Christmas and Easter, and the taking of the Eucharist, directly challenged the older traditional ritual celebrations. Traditional feasting, erroneously interpreted as profligate by influential missionaries in the region like John Williams and William Ellis, was to be replaced with Sunday lunch. Feasts remained a part of island life, but observing the events of the Christian calendar had increasing influence. In contemporary Tonga and Samoa, the Sabbath of Sunday is still regarded as a day of absolute rest. It is a serious breach of community values to do anything except rest, worship, and dine together on Sunday. Food is prepared the day before, and only the laying down of the *umu* can be seen to on the day, by the men, before attendance at church. Before Sunday, the wood for the fire must be cut and the pit dug, ready to receive the food.

By the middle of the 19th century, all attempts at the missionary-brokered (but at times militant) establishment of Christianized chiefdoms in the islands had failed. Subsequent collaborations between church authorities, local leaders, and imperial powers in Europe became increasingly ineffectual as the power base shifted so that larger scale commercial entities gained control. The rapid consolidation and takeover of the commercial trade system followed so that, thenceforward, economics would dictate the character of political leadership. The planters and, in turn, the new colonial authorities, would take over from where the church left off, but largely at the behest of globally powerful consortiums.

COLONIALISM AND AGRIBUSINESS: FIJI

Fiji is an example of a relatively large land mass by Pacific standards being drawn into the British Empire and its colonial system, to which many Pacific Island groups were subjected to during the later 19th and early 20th centuries. Fiji consists of a total land area of just over 7,000 square miles made up of almost 850 islands and islands, of which 106 are occupied today. The island group is dominated by the two main islands of Viti Levu and Vanua Levu, which account for 4,010 and 2,137 square miles, respectively. Fiji is situated about 1,000 miles north of New Zealand. It became the center of British colonial interests in the Pacific between 1874 and 1970. Fiji was where the governor of the colony, also High Commissioner for the Western Pacific, resided until independence was granted to the island group in 1970. Under British rule, the sugar industry was developed but, faced with the refusal of the indigenous Fijians to man the plantations, the government turned to another of its colonies, India, from which indentured laborers were brought in to work. Indenture meant poor living conditions, little pay and long hours. Up to 1916, some 60, 000 Indians, supplemented by Solomon Islanders, came to work in the cane fields and factories of Fiji. This forced migration was a familiar story in much of the Pacific. Colonial powers were quick to consolidate a labor base to help with resource extraction. Japanese and Vietnamese worked in New Caledonia in the early 20th century; indentured Chinese were brought to work in Australia in 1848. Indentured laborers worked in all the primary island industries, producing sugar, copra, coconut oil, and pineapple (Hawaii). The practice was finally banned in 1920. Colonialism inaugurated a period of bureaucratic control over islanders. Slavery, blackbirding, and the indenture system were outlawed, but other ways were found to control the labor market, with big business playing a major role.

The Australian Colonial Sugar Refining Company (CSR) rapidly transformed Fiji into a sugar economy and, in 1913, Fiji surpassed the West Indies as the largest sugar producer in the British Empire. The Indian industry workers received only 2 percent of the export proceeds, while the predominantly white planters got 36 percent, and CSR received 62 percent. By comparison, in Australia, CSR received 30 percent of proceeds. Moreover, CSR profits were not reinvested in Fiji, but remained in the hands of a wealthy few.[25]

Fijian food culture strongly reflects the broader colonial history of the Pacific, which routinely brought peoples together that were considered only as workers without a thought for their ultimate welfare, happiness, or well-being. Indian and Fijian populations, while tolerant of each other today, represent distinctly different cultures that were given different rights on racial grounds from the start, something that obviously suited the colonial authorities. Racial integration between Fijians and Indians was actively discouraged by the British, who later conferred ownership of 80 percent of the land of Fiji to indigenous Fijians, extending only rights of leasehold (99 years) to Indians; this system remains in place today. As a long-term consequence of this history, ongoing resentment on the part of Fijian-Indians has largely been based on their diminished political rights; furthermore, some Fijians still regard Fijian-Indians as outsiders.

A gastronomic consequence of the Indian presence is a vibrant and successful food culture. Indian-Fijians have evolved their own culinary-cultural identity, in part as an expression of solidarity and ethnicity. Their food and cuisine is characteristically Indian, full of spice and color. Indian farmers also grow many food crops: wheat, rice, sugar, lentils, mangos, pineapples, bananas, chilies (a great favorite), eggplant, okra, snake beans, radish, bitter gourd, pumpkin, ginger, melon, and numerous green leafy vegetables including *bele* (*Hibiscus manihot*) and *churaya* (*Amaranthus viridis*), both spinach-like in flavor. These foods form the basis of Fijian Indian cuisine. Whereas mixtures and hybrid forms of food are a commonplace in the Pacific, the cultural identity and ethnic pride of Indian-Fijians is expressed and maintained through their distinctive cuisine, one of the finest in the whole region. An unintended and no doubt unforeseen outcome of colonialism has been this strengthening of ethnic identity through food culture. Colonialism has inadvertently played a crucial role in the social and gastronomic history of Fiji. Despite the spate of political coups in recent decades (1987, 2000, and 2007), which have attested to ongoing ethnic tensions, Indian-Fijian food culture continues to thrive.

By comparison, the decline of the control by the kings of Hawaii (Kamehameha I, II, and III, the latter dying in 1854) reflected the rise of power of ordinary Hawaiians. The power of the monarchy effectively became weaker and weaker until, finally, in 1893, Queen Liliuokalani, the only crowned queen of Hawaii, was forced to leave the throne by the United States. But in terms of food culture, ordinary people—like the Indians of Fiji—would have less influence on Hawaii than America, which would annex the islands in 1900. It later became an American territory and a strategic naval base in the Pacific region. After the attack on Pearl Harbor in 1941, Hawaii was in a state of martial law until the end World War II. In 1959, Hawaii was made the 50th American state. Food culture often changes as a function of broader geopolitical currents and not simply as the result of culinary or gastronomic trends or traditions. Today, Hawaii's food culture is eclectic, but little of its indigenous foodways remain.

WORLD WAR II

World War II contributed to an overall rise in the influence of the United States in the Pacific region, a consolidation of the commercial interests and power bases located in Australia, New Zealand, and France, increased economic activity, and the introduction of new technology and communication systems. All of these things had major implications for food culture. The incorporation of island economies into the world cash economy transformed the island way of life. Following on from the United States and allied forces' presence in the region, increases in the importation of Western-style foods ensued in this period. Today, Hawaii, Guam, and American Samoa illustrate the profound degree to which the diet has also been Americanized, a process that began in the war years but was consolidated because of the continued presence of large military bases in Guam and Samoa; in the case of Hawaii, this transition was further facilitated as a result of the island group becoming the 50th state of the United States of America.

The war changed the way islanders ate and the way they viewed the West; it also changed the way Australians and New Zealanders ate. Australia significantly stepped up its industrial processing and packaging of canned and dehydrated foods, especially for the war effort, which resulted in the availability of similar products in the consumer market in the 1950s.

Several thousand tons of dehydrated egg were manufactured for the armed forces, for example, and later this technology would be used to create domestic products like packaged cake mixes, custard powder, and other premixed items.[26] Similarly, numerous canned foods, dehydrated instant foods, and, increasingly, frozen goods, fuelled the market for consumer foods. Canned and dried foods were especially suited for importation into the island communities.

Other factors also added to this transformation in terms of broad shifts in community life and organization. Following the war, the cash economy, urbanization, and imported goods irrevocably changed the way islanders ate and thought about food. The decline of communal living occurred over many years as the social cohesion of village life was steadily eroded. The values of cheapness, ease of preparation, and immediate gratification were adopted from the Western world, to the extent that islanders began to forget their traditional food-related skills like cultivating and preservation. The introduction of fridges, freezers, and eventually microwave ovens would make the transition complete. While the old ways persisted, the technological infrastructure was in place to revolutionize cooking and eating on the islands.

During and after World War II, Western nations were able to consolidate interests in the Pacific and made inroads into the diet of islanders with the introduction of greater and greater supplies of Western-style foods. France's control of New Caledonia, which it secured in 1853, also meant the total domination of French cuisine. Native Kanak people still cook native foods in traditional ways at times, but mainstream food culture in New Caledonia is overwhelmingly French, as it is in French Polynesia. There is certainly something odd about Pacific islands that import the majority of their food supply from a far-off European country to the extent that, for all intents and purposes, the food culture appears to be French. The French Government chooses to forego food and wine imports from much closer sources (like NZ or Australia), or from developing production on the islands themselves, partly, it seems, because it supports a large number of French citizens who choose to work in the islands for a period and then return to France.

The immediate postwar period naturally brought more stability to the area, more investment in developing its resource potential, more people and goods traveling into and out of the region, and incremental changes to food culture. Indicative of a new focus on the region as a whole, and also in recognition of island people's shared needs in the face of change, the South Pacific Commission, now called the Secretariat of the Pacific Community (SPC), was formed in 1947. Based in Nouméa, New Caledonia, the SPC also has a branch in Fiji, and carries out research all over the Pacific. Started by a group of countries with economic and political interests in the region (Australia, France, The Netherlands, New Zealand, the United Kingdom, and the United States), the SPC acts as an intergovernmental organization whose member states include American Samoa, the Cook Islands, the Federated States of Micronesia, Fiji, French Polynesia, Guam, Kiribati, the Marshall Islands, Nauru, New Caledonia, Niue, the Northern Mariana Islands, Palau, Papua New Guinea, the Pitcairn Islands, Samoa, the Solomon Islands, Tokelau, Tonga, Tuvalu, Vanuatu, and Wallis and Futuna. These have all been territories of the founding group members, but have now mostly become independent. New Caledonia, Wallis and Futuna, and French Polynesia remain French territories. According to its mission statement, the SPC aims to improve, through information and advice, the capability of Pacific Island people "to enable them to make informed decisions about their future development and well-being." The SPC has put a lot of effort and research into various health-related programs, including many aimed at nutrition and diet. Campaigns using lectures, workshops, public, and school education programs, leaflets, posters, videos, and television programs have targeted health, declining standards of nutrition, disease prevention, the benefits of island foods for island people, cookery skills, exercise, and values like moderation. These programs seem to have had only limited success, but efforts continue to educate and inform island people about their food choices and the role of food in terms of the benefits and threats it presents to physical health and well-being.[27]

The major source of change in the postwar period came not from island communities themselves but from outside, which explains why an organization like the SPC was instituted and became involved in regional development. Given the interest of the foreign-owned businesses and governments economically active in the area, helping islanders to cope with change remains a priority. Postwar investment in island infrastructure and public utilities, especially communications, paved the way for greater trade and economic ties with the world's economies.[28] Media also further opened up the image of the tropical South Seas to the Western traveler's imagination.

REGIONAL ECONOMIC DECLINE

The money generated by exporting food products has not always flowed back into the local economy of island communities and, over time, even the profits made have largely failed to offset the rising price of imported goods, including increasing amounts of food. This is because processing and production have mostly been managed by foreign interests. Products, resources, and sectors like tourism have all largely been controlled economically from abroad. Since contact, this has always been the case. Exploitation of island resources has been ongoing and, in the 20th century, spread to the environment as a whole when tourism began to affect the region. But earlier in the same century, island economies became increasingly subject to economic schemes that in the longer term created a degree of uncertainty for island people.

A repetitive economic cycle has afflicted the primary production sector of island nations over the years. It begins with some potential being realized. Sandalwood and sea cucumber, followed by whaling, copra, sugar, and pineapple, all earned vast profits for large companies who helped invest in infrastructure and labor recruitment in the islands. Whaling reveals how this boom and bust approach affected island life. A source of valuable industrial oil (rather than food), whales were a lucrative product until exploitation and the discovery of new fuels challenged the commercial viability of whale oil. Prices for whale oil subsequently slumped, and the island infrastructure set up to service whaling declined with them.

Encouraged by New Zealand, a few resident Rarotongans began to produce cotton when it became scarce as the result of the American Civil War, but the market soon fell away once the Civil War ended, and just as quickly cotton production was no longer viable in the islands. Cotton production lasted somewhat longer in Fiji. Even the massive investment in pineapple plantations in Hawaii could not stop competition and the eventual decline of that industry in the 1990s. As for the sugar industry in Fiji, although new contracts have recently been signed for millions of U.S. dollars worth of Fijian sugar for the European Union, the industry is also stagnating. Coffee was grown in the Cook Islands during in the mid-1800s, and sales provided the London Missionary Society with church contributions in the early 20th century.[29] But the long-term viability of coffee growing in an era of globalization is minimal. Although recently there has been renewed interest in producing boutique-style organic coffee (on Aitutaki in the Cook Islands), which is also produced elsewhere (PNG, in particular), the export earnings are comparatively small.

The story of the Cook Islands' production of citrus fruit well illustrates how the shifting balance of global trade affects the island economies. Rarotonga's longest running export venture was that of citrus fruits, including tangerines, mandarins, and grapefruit, but particularly oranges and, later, canned juice. Tomatoes, bananas, pineapples, coffee, vanilla, copra, and arrowroot were all viable crops for the Cooks' export market at one stage.

Rarotonga appeared to have a rosy future in exporting such products. By the 1960s, the small island was earning about 4600,000 U.S. dollars a year from the export of clothing and jewelry, while the citrus juice canning factory, built in 1961, was making about 770,000 U.S. dollars annually after several years from the export of 640,000 gallons of juice.[30] "Raro," as the juice was called, was a very popular product in New Zealand, but most of the profits from this industry, as was typical of other food export efforts in the region, did not flow back to the local economy in question. Steadily, the orange growers' profits dwindled, until eventually they literally pulled up their groves of trees. Today, oranges still grow in Rarotonga, but juice is imported, as is most other food and drink. This consequence of globalization has been marked in the Pacific since the time of James Cook. As soon as the economies of these small islands were connected to those of world powers, change became inevitable. In this case, the export rather than the import of foods was based on an unsustainable production and delivery system. Isolated and lacking their own means of bulk transportation, exporting and importing products was both costly and subject to changes in foreign as much as in local demand.

Overseas stakeholders hungry for profits, however, were not the sole cause of decline in many islands' primary food production. Competition within the global economy drove prices down, making it harder for the isolated islands to compete. In today's climate of higher fuel costs, and with a premium set on quality products in the world market, the opportunities are there; however, careful quality control needs to be implemented. This is not always possible when little local investment is available and, unless there is a big profit to be made, foreign business concerns are not interested. Bananas grow well in the islands but, today, New Zealand gets its bananas from Ecuador, while Australia has a protectionist policy for its Queensland banana producers. Furthermore, orange juice imported into Australia from China and elsewhere has led to Australians just dumping their crops on the ground, because the prices offered for the produce are too low to cover the cost of processing. As a result, some growers have been pulling up their trees, just as they did years ago on Rarotonga. This is perhaps free market economics at its worst. Copra and coconut products have been more cheaply produced in Asia than in the Pacific for some years, and perhaps this is just a sign that primary industry will never again be the main source of revenue for island states. Copra, traditionally one of the most lucrative industries of the islands, is well in decline. Sugar, one of Fiji's largest export crops, is in decline following successive waves of crop damage from storms in the 1980s, which severely hampered production and, consequently, forced many from the land. Mounting political instability in the country confirms the need to radically rethink the forecast for economic prosperity and growth, but always lurking as overall indicators are the seemingly random fluctuations of the global economy. Other factors can also mitigate against economic growth and prosperity. Riots that occurred in Tonga in 2006 still affect business confidence and growth, and a decline in the GDP of 3.5 percent in 2007 only recovered by 0.8 percent in 2008. External payments to Tonga, amounting to 45 percent of the GDP, presently sustain its economy.

Some profitable export crops have appeared to be relatively immune to economic downturns or global market fluctuations. The most notable example is pineapple. Just mention pineapple, especially in America, and the immediate association will be with Hawaii, which, during the first half of the 20th century, became almost synonymous with the introduced spiny-leaved South American bromeliad that grew so well in the rich volcanic soil of the islands. Production in Hawaii began after the entrepreneur, later dubbed "the pineapple king," James Drummond Dole (1877–1958), arrived around the turn of the century and launched a canning business after successfully growing pineapples on his 60-acre farm on the island of Oahu. Aided by the mechanization of peeling, coring, and canning operations that coincided with the development of Dole's enterprise, by 1922 he had expanded his business to over 200,000 acres of pineapple plantation on the island of Lanai; by 1925, mechanized processing was peeling, slicing, and canning up to 100 pineapples every minute. During the first half of the 20th century, the Lanai plantation produced over 75 percent of the world's pineapples, and understandably became known as Pineapple Island. Drummond's success, however, was also the result of his business acumen, since he realized the potential of advertising to sell his canned product early on, launching the first nationwide consumer advertising campaign in the United States. He became famous and wealthy as canned pineapple became ever more popular and sales soared. As a result, it is not the traditional foods of the islands, but the labels of canned and processed tins of pineapple and coconut products, depicting alluring tropical vistas, that have become enduring emblems of Pacific food.

Hawaii's world supremacy in pineapple production waned after World War II and, by the 1970s, so had the taste for Hawaiian food like barbecued ham steak with pineapple, which by then had become a culinary cliché. Americans, however, have retained their love of pineapple, which has found its way into many dishes and cuisines. The invented "Chinese" concoction known as sweet and sour took advantage of the popularity and sweetness of pineapple to add that special touch to pork or fish. The essential compatibility of pineapple with so many dishes was part of the fruit's long-running success, along with its sweetness and versatility in terms of its variant products: crushed, sliced, chunks, or juice. Pineapple made Pacific cuisine, becoming a symbol of island life, at least in the eyes of the Western world. Cocktails, snacks, barbecues, and desserts could easily incorporate the fruit, and numerous recipes in cookbooks of dubious authenticity use the descriptor "Hawaiian" to indicate nothing more than the inclusion of pineapple as an ingredient. Under the influence of Dole, the fruit became a lasting icon of the Pacific Islands.

Perhaps pineapple's success is due not only to its delicious taste, but also its exotic look. The frilly topknot of leaves suggests a palm, while the fruit itself represents sweet relief from summer thirst and heat. This natural-seeming affinity with island life also made the fruit's association with Hawaii easily exploitable in the advertising and on the can labels, which often featured sunsets, palm trees, and brown-skinned natives, even though the product itself had virtually nothing to do with Hawaii's food traditions .

While the production of some island-grown food products like sugar still remains significant in terms of exports (in Fiji, for example), the pineapple industry in Hawaii was the longest running success story and the only product apart from coconut cream (most of which does not come from the islands today) that became associated with the Pacific in the cuisine of the West. The pineapple industry was the last to decline. In 2008, industry leaders decided to step down pineapple production in Hawaii as it and most other Pacific Island nations adapted to the forces of globalization. Pineapple production for canning is no longer as economically viable in Hawaii, although harvests of fresh pineapples are still made. Thailand is now the world's largest producer, while other Pacific Rim countries like Indonesia and Malaysia also produce for the export market.

Other examples suggest that there are still new opportunities for local product development waiting to be picked up on. Who would have thought that the islands could become a net exporter of fresh water in the last few years? The boom in global bottled water sales has made it so. Foreign ownership of "a taste of paradise" now takes the form of water in plastic bottles. The brand name, Fiji water, is linked to a product sourced from an apparently pristine aquifer in the Yaqara Valley of northern Viti Levu, is sold all over Fiji and elsewhere in the islands, but, more significantly, has been a stellar international success, with growing markets in the United States, Europe, and Australia. American-owned, the Fiji water brand is marketed with labels bearing the slogan "The Taste of Paradise" and, with a production rate of over 13 million gallons a year, is presently one of Fiji's biggest export earners alongside sugar, clothing, gold, and tourism. The advertising image underlines purity, a notion long associated in the imagination of the West with the islands, which are viewed as pristine paradises away from it all. Indeed, this has become the standard mantra for selling not only Fiji (water), but also the Pacific in general.[31] Contradicting this idea is the fact that, in an economic sense, the islands are very much connected with the rest of the world, and suffer from the same environmental problems, for example, as elsewhere. "Paradise" has been a convenient term used to maintain the commercially attractive image of the island idyll, as the labels on millions of cans of pineapple or coconut cream reaffirm.

TOURISM

Primary industry decline shows no sign of abating, while one industry now towers above the rest: tourism. Tourism has actually provided the template for a future plan for regional growth and wealth creation. Food culture plays an important part in this plan. Almost as if it were a replacement for all the now largely unprofitable primary industries, tourism has come to the economic rescue of many island nations. While resources like fish and other seafood provide valuable revenue (tuna is a major fish export out of the Pacific, to Japan, for example), monitoring the vast oceans against poaching is difficult, and local ownership of fishing fleets is not mandatory (although in NZ, Maori have successfully reclaimed the rights to coastal fishing). It is tourism that has most successfully created opportunities and jobs across the wider community, and shaped the direction of how the islands market and promote their image, how islanders see themselves, and how they identify with their home and culture as part of a 21st-century world culture. Tourism is more a commercial sector than an industry, and touches the lives of many people not directly involved in tourism activities. Restauration and food provision, food production, environmentalism (ecotourism), communications, transportation, retail, heritage, and history are all tourism-related, and can bring many people together in the direct provision of tourism products or services, or in other areas.

Boutique businesses and entrepreneurs involved in services like food and drink provision, gastronomic and ecotourism, indigenous arts (including cookery with native and local ingredients), and herbal lore also have a direct involvement in the micromarketing of particular tourism activities. These have extended the traditional island holiday pursuits like swimming, diving, fishing, and relaxing to include awareness of indigenous foodways, environmental care, and protection through education about local species and habitat. Travelers and tourists who, in the past, may not have wished to engage with or learn much about local traditions, are now demanding more from their holiday experiences. A diverse range of local enterprises are consequently becoming viable as adjuncts to the travel and tourism sector. Hotel and resort facilities are capitalizing on the new customer demand for home-grown, fresh, or organic foods by encouraging local producers to grow specialty products. Other developments reflect wider community care perspectives that extend beyond tourism's ambit but that have followed its lead to some extent. Initiatives like the "Foundation for Rural Integrated Enterprises 'N' Development" encourage community involvement in different commercial activities, including food production. Under the label, *Friends Fiji Style*, a range of pickles and chutneys are made in Lautoka by local people who volunteer, train on the job, and are paid for their labor. Part of a wider effort to relieve poverty, the foundation has affiliations with nongovernmental organizations, commissions, aid agencies, and commercial enterprises. Other programs aimed at kick-starting local enterprise are more directly associated with tourism, either by way of providing products like authentic foods (such as local fish or shellfish varieties) or new forms of what is called experience tourism. Experience tourism takes full advantage of the fact the contemporary tourist often wants more than the package of sightseeing and relaxation. Tourists are taking more of an interest in what they are eating, for example, which means not only sampling local foods in restaurants, but also visiting farms and markets, taking cooking lessons, or attending heritage venues. If they are interested in sustainability, ecotourism, or organic gardening, there is a good chance they will be looking for products that have this pedigree. They will want to talk to local people about local foods, learning about how they are traditionally prepared, grown, cared for, and harvested; this is even more the case if there is a health advantage. Many "exotic" fruits and vegetables are becoming popular on the strength of their nutraceutical potential, and several island varieties meet these criteria (see Noni juice). Contemporary tourism involves communication as much as merchandise, and so tourism in the islands is providing a way for islanders to reengage with their on cultural past and identity. Even though much of the newer image of island food cultures as local, environmentally friendly, and health promoting is being communicated through marketing, packaging, and advertising, the older clichéd representation of Pacific Island food as one of beach parties, cocktails, and tropical fruits is finally giving way to a richer expression. Globalization, so often criticized for being a force of standardization, has actually provided island food culture with a new means of representing itself to a more diverse potential clientele, one that so far has benefited island communities, their identities and economies. Albeit as a means to sell products, products themselves are no longer simply regarded as commodities produced for consumption. Culture is a product that is seen as having diverse applications, adding value to products and services. Thus, traditional islander culture has been given an opportunity to reconnect with its authentic cultural history, and to serve it in this authentic form to tourists and consumers alike.

Importantly, tourism has also added much-needed revenue to island coffers, but to some extent it is still a mixed blessing. Considering that before the arrival of "white men," islanders managed fairly well by themselves and had certainly achieved a remarkable stability in their isolated island environments, contact heralded the end of isolation and self-sufficiency. Caught up in a more powerful economy based on money, in many ways island culture as islanders then knew it disappeared almost overnight. From not needing anything from the outside, islanders would eventually need everything to be brought in. The traders, planters, missionaries, colonists and those involved in commerce all lived in the islands and, to some extent, changed the food culture because they brought their tastes with them. The tourists also bring their taste, which only lately, and mainly with regard to elite tourism, has shifted from the clichéd version of island food to something more authentic. The irony is that it is tourists who bring the most valuable commodity of all, money, something more or less unknown before contact, but now indispensable to islanders.

In the Cook Islands, all land is owned by the islander families themselves, but control (through leasehold) still makes for exploitation and diminished return. Ocean-side properties with magnificent views no doubt appeal to the foreign visitor wishing to get away from it all, but this kind of business is also subject to global economic forces. A pertinent reminder of the problems that global economics has brought to island locales stands on the road south of Rarotonga's heavily-touristed Muri Beach. On the site of what was once the largest orange grove on the island is a half-built condominium complex spreading over several acres, a project stalled over a decade ago because of land development red tape and funding problems. The derelict buildings' well-weathered shells stand as an eerie testament to big plans gone awry. Once drawn into global flows of capital, in this case via realty investment, entrepreneurial island ventures are vulnerable to failure. Deals hinge, often crucially, on foreign investment; this also means that development is under foreign control and susceptible to changes in the global investment climate. Where the oranges that were once Rarotonga's pride grew as living proof of a viable economy now stands the Sheraton, without a tourist in sight.

For most Pacific countries today, their local food culture tells the same story of decline, whether measured in terms of health, wealth, or levels of local production. Reliance on imported staples like rice, flour, and noodles has undermined wealth because local, family grown vegetable staples like taro, breadfruit, and cassava have been marginalized in the diet by the convenient and easy-to-prepare packet foods. A reliance on imported foods and the shift from vegetable-based foods supplemented by fresh meats and fish to high-fat, processed meat products (like Spam or tinned corned beef, confectionery, snack foods, and fat-rich items like chocolate and ice cream) has contributed to rising obesity, heart disease, and Type 2 diabetes rates, particularly in countries like Tonga and Samoa, where a fuller figure is traditionally admired (see chapter 8).

As global food and fuel prices rose in 2008, a process that was completely out of islanders' control, the cost of living in island communities was adversely affected in a number of ways, particularly for the poor. The poorest 10 percent of Fiji's population spend 50–65 percent of their income on food, whereas the wealthiest 10 percent spend less than 20 percent on food. There have been recent calls, put out by the SPC, for people to grow more of their own traditional foods. Population pressures, with an increase of 4.5 million expected in the region in the next 20 years, make such changes in people's attitude to food provision even more necessary.[32] Whether the calls will be heeded is another question. The dietary changes taking place have been increasing steady for well over half a century. To some extent, time and money rule the lives of islanders in the same way as they do the lives of people the world over.

CHANGING DEMOGRAPHICS

Pacific populations have had different rates of decline and growth. In the precontact past, lack of resources to support ever-growing numbers of islanders was routinely dealt with using a variety of measures: contraception, abortion, infanticide, and emigration all played a role in keeping numbers sustainable. Today, the natural increase in population of the islands is offset by a constant pattern of migration to countries both in and outside the region.

Micronesia, Polynesia (excluding NZ), and Melanesia combined have a relatively stable population at about 9.5 million (including PNG's 6.3 million people); this is growing at a rate of around 1.5 percent each year. Melanesia's population is expected to grow by nearly 50 percent, to just over 12.5 million, by 2030, while Polynesia and Micronesia, combined, will grow by about 300,000, to 1.5 million. Thus, the total population of the region is expected to reach 14 million by 2030.[33] Adding New Zealand (4 million) and Australia (21 million) gives a total of 39 million. From a combined population of an estimated 1.5 million people in Polynesia, Micronesia, and Melanesia (excluding PNG) in the late 1700s, the overall population of the region has markedly declined, but over the course of the 20th century in particular it has grown steadily overall, although this population is now made up of a mixture of many ethnic groups.

Demographic change has been a feature of the Pacific region that has influenced food culture to a great degree. Ever since the most widely traveled of the migrating peoples, the Polynesians, spread through the whole eastern region of Oceania, foods, technologies, and practices have also moved, becoming adapted to specific local conditions in the process. But the continuous flow of people over the last two centuries in particular has contributed to a complex mix of cultures in various Pacific countries. Today, expatriate islanders have established large communities in the United States and New Zealand, the inevitable result of both the islands' inability to support ever-expanding populations and of opportunities abroad, particularly work that brings vital income that can be used to help family members back home. The Cook Islands present a typical example. In 1961, the population of the Cook Islands was 18, 378, while in 2007 it was only 13,000. This has been primarily due to emigration to New Zealand. Similarly 56,000 Samoans, 76,000 Guamanians (from the tiny Micronesian island of Guam, site of a major regional U.S. military base), 27,000 Tongans, and 151,000 Hawaiians of native descent, now live in the United States. Auckland, New Zealand, is considered the biggest Polynesian city in the world, and New Zealand as a whole supports 265, 974 people of Pacific ethnicity, mostly from Samoa, the Cook Islands, Niue, and the Tokelau Islands.[34] About 1500 people live on Niue today, whereas 18,000 Niueans or people of Niuean descent live in Australasia or elsewhere. This all makes for an interesting mix of food cultures, and is one of the only ways in which Pacific food culture as such has been successfully exported. Yet, the effects of this are marginal, given that islander foods and cooking tend only to be reproduced in the context of expat communities, and not in the wider multicultural community of the adopted country. But visits home to the islands frequently involve the transportation of large buckets of fried chicken (KFC), for example, that are so much relished in the Pacific region.

Visits to friends and relatives living in the islands also account for a large part of total human traffic to the islands. Fifty-six percent of all those visiting American Samoa, for example, are in this category, compared to only 14 percent visiting as tourists. But such figures vary greatly. In the

Cook Islands, which does not have the business infrastructure of American Samoa (one that supports large numbers of employees), tourism accounts for 85 percent of all visits to the islands and, in 2008, drove the GDP growth of 3.5 percent.[35]

And what of the Pacific Islands' food culture today? What are the trends that typify island cuisine at the start of the 21st century, beyond the fact that so much everyday food is supermarket fare, processed, canned, dried, or frozen? There are parallels with both New Zealand and Australia, since both multiculturalism and localism have been influential additions to more traditional forms of cookery in the islands. Food trends tend to take effect quickly in Westernized nations, as globalization very quickly turns ideas into fashions due to the immense capacity of existing infrastructure, including internet media, finance, and transportation. Growing diversity of choice, more imported foods in the form of chain or fast-food eateries and ethnic restaurants now dominate the scene. Rarotonga has its popular Italian restaurants as well as the traditional weekend or market day *umu* food. More than ever before, Islanders eat imported, processed, and refined foods bought from supermarkets. They grow less for themselves. The odd fish, caught by a friend, uncle, or relative, might occasionally find its way into the diet, but the diet of the average islander is probably not as good as it once was because there are more of the wrong sorts and less of the right kinds of food available.

It is difficult to predict what food culture in the Pacific Islands will look like in 10, 20, or 50 years. What it will look like depends on how islander communities manage their environment and ecology. Unlike much larger countries, these resources cannot sustain degradation for long. If economics dictate the future path, then the picture may be bleak. More imported food of low quality, more health problems, more land lost to commerce and housing, less gardening and self-sufficiency. No one can blame islanders for wanting to increase their wealth and aspire to a lifestyle like some Westerners have, but if they are to achieve a higher standard of living and a better way of life they will need to strike a balance between the past and the present. Tourism, the most important industry in the islands today, will continue to shape trade and wealth in the Pacific region. If managed properly, taking advantage in particular of the latest trends in food-related tourism, a greater attention to ecology, environment, sustainability, and organic farming could put food culture at the centre of life again. A return to a past where sustainable fishing and agriculture, organic produce, good cooking, and happy and contented people existing apart from the world at large—the traditional island way of life—is not possible, or any longer desirable. Yet, taking advantage of a developing market for good quality, healthful food, ecotourism and the marketability of environmentalism and health could potentially bring Pacific Island food culture full circle, enabling islanders to enjoy the best of both worlds, ancient and modern. There are major problems to overcome if any plateau of sustainability is to be reached, but if islanders can reinvest in traditional foodways and farming techniques (that now seem to serve directly the needs of 21st century tourism), then part of their heritage will live on in a way that is real, practical, and profitable. Reconnecting the past and the present is what islander foodways have always done, and still do. It will make a huge difference if food culture gains more than a merely symbolic efficacy (such as is the case at the *umu* or family gathering), thereby reconnecting islanders to the island environment and the ongoing need to adapt to its changing demands. Connecting land, sea, and people with practices of sustainable agriculture and aquaculture that supply delicious products to a hungry market will also educate, sustain, and satisfy in deeper ways, rooted to traditional island food culture in its fullest sense.

AUSTRALIA AND NEW ZEALAND

The diet of hunter-gatherer Australian Aborigines, who never practiced systematic or organized agriculture, was governed by what was available; crops, including taro (which grows in the tropical north of Australia), never figured as staples and have not been associated with the traditional Aboriginal diet. Regional variation is the hallmark of Aboriginal foodways, reflecting the vastly different climatic and environmental conditions of a huge land mass. Like their islander counterparts, Aborigines made use of everything that potentially could feed and sustain them. The knowledge that they accumulated over what might have been 60,000 years can only be guessed at because of all that must have been lost since the marginalization of Aboriginal culture over the last 230 years.

Initially, contact with Europeans brought the same devastation as in the islands, although there was less trading and more killing of native peoples by fire power. Aborigines were forced out of the towns and eventually the cities, and forced to live in areas allocated to them or to regions where European settlers had no interest in going. In the broad, arid, inhospitable central region of Australia, and in other remoter areas, some remaining Aboriginal communities still eke out their existence employing traditional skills of hunting and gathering, supplemented by the addition of supermarket foods when they can get them. But their world, although unknown to most Australians, has not been untouched or unaffected by Western influence. Having proved on average far less desirable as locales

for settlement or for resource extraction than the green verge of prime agricultural around the edge of the continent, Aboriginal lands may be relatively free of Westerners, but the influences are still there. Like in some of
the isolated islands, the impact of the West on greater central Australia
has been felt with less force, although mining and atomic testing are two
notable exceptions, both of which have caused extreme disruption and
death.

Australasia was discovered by Europeans in the 17th century (notably by the Dutchman, Abel Tasman). The country was inhabited by native Australians, Aborigines, who had been there for perhaps as long as
60,000 years in advance of Europeans. The settlement by Westerners of
both Australia and New Zealand did not take place until the late 18th
and early 19th centuries; those who settled were largely from the United
Kingdom (a third of them Scottish, in the case of NZ). The bulk of migration to New Zealand occurred in 1837–1850. In the case of Australia,
the first major influx of Westerners came in the form of convicts in the
late 1700s, transported from Britain to serve jail sentences in Tasmania
and at the country's first settlement in Sydney, NSW. The convict ships
initially carried criminals (although the guilt of many of these people is
questionable, and certain that transportation, as it was called, was a convenient means of removing undesirables from overpopulated and squalid
cities in the UK). The convicts transported on the first of three initial
fleets, which carried some 3,000 persons in total (approx. 500 died during
the voyages), were serving sentences ranging from a few years, to life, im-
prisonment, and constituted a mix of largely unskilled people with varying experience and backgrounds, although they almost certainly had in
common the experience of hard manual work for little pay. This would
stand many of them in good stead for a similarly hard life in the fledgling colony and in the challenging climate and environment of Australia.
Many were from rural backgrounds. Some would have been arrested, con-
victed, and transported for nothing more that striking for adequate wages
in the country regions of England, or for petty crimes of theft, like a loaf
of bread. Whatever the reason, of those registered among the over 1,000
convicts arriving at Botany Bay on board the First Fleet in 1788 were
but a few butchers and a single farmer. Many also were from the cities,
like London, which had swelled in size in the age of early industrialization, absorbing many displaced rural workers into its factories and slums.
Thus, these new, inadvertent colonists were already disadvantaged with
regard to food culture, as the means by which they had produced and
cooked their own food before being uprooted had been denied them in
the cramped, impoverished conditions of slum life in the city. Paying for

or stealing food had become the new way to feed oneself and one's family. These people, and the culture to which they belonged, undoubtedly had an effect on the development of Australian food culture that remains to this day, because the disconnection between production and consumption was established prior to settlement of the colony. Coming from the mother country, Great Britain, to the Australian colonies, the entrepreneurial "squatters" who immigrated and helped to develop livestock farming, in particular, reproduced the new British industrial production model in this new land, without much regard for the possibilities and limitations that Australia presented in terms of food culture.

Many found Australia to be a quite alien place, peopled by a hostile "primitive race" and abounding in strange flora and fauna that must have appeared too odd to eat. It seems that the colonists lived mostly on a basic diet of bread, salted meat, and tea, with lashings of rum (from the West Indies, but which was later made from the waste cane of the sugar industry in Queensland). The convicts received rations based on those specified for the British Navy: 7 pounds of bread or flour (or about 4 loaves by today's standards), 4 pounds of salt pork or 7 pounds of salt beef, 3 pints of dried peas (legumes), 6 ounces of butter and a 1/2 pound of rice or 1 pound of flour in lieu. Women received two-thirds of this ration and children a half. This bland and barely adequate diet was part of the foundation for the future foodways of the country. In this early period, an almost total dependence on importation, much like that which has now ensued in the Pacific Islands region, meant that it was not the quality or diversity of food rations that was a problem, but the adequacy of supply. The colonies relied on shipments of supplies from England, and there grew an ever-pressing need to find reliable local sources of food. The first attempts to breed animals, like beef cattle (which were brought on board the first fleet), for food failed and a generally hostile response to the diet of Aborigines made matters worse. Seeds brought from England also failed to produce, although fertile land was available.

While a general distaste for local foods can be identified, there was naturally a lot of ignorance as well. People simply did not know what was edible or otherwise among the local plants and animals. Reluctant, suspicious, or unable to learn from Aboriginal people about their self-sustaining foodways, the early settlers were also prejudiced by their predominantly working class taste, a taste that reflected the newly urban industrial environment from which many of them had come. The cultural clash between these essentially modern individuals from halfway around the world, strangers in a strange land, and the indigenous, community-centered people, the Aborigines, who had inhabited the continent for at least 40,000 years, must have been brutal, and appears pitiable, but was probably unavoidable.

Aboriginal Australians, although of Austronesian ancestry, are an exception to the Pacific pattern, in that they largely remained hunter-gatherers in their land of Australia, with its wealth of edible flora and fauna, and of such size as to obviate any competition for food between different tribes. In addition, the environmental pressure to grow plants or husband animals was not felt in the same way as it was in the islands. Once isolated by rising sea levels (6000 BCE), the Aboriginal cultures had little reason to attempt migration elsewhere (to other islands), and adopted a mostly nomadic way of life based on the seasonal search for food. They diversified and extended their food gathering and hunting practices within various, contrasting environments within Australia. The Aboriginal cultures are unique cultures, attuned to typically Australian conditions; from the cool-climate island state of Tasmania, situated south of the southeastern state of Victoria, to the massive "red" desert regions of Australia's interior, to the tropical Northern Territory and the island communities still further north, in the Torres Strait, which separates Australia from Indonesia and Papua New Guinea.

Of course, none of this was known in the early days of colonization, and little notice was taken of Aboriginal foodways. But local foods consumed by Aborigines were also in time eaten by colonists who, probably through necessity, needed to find a source of food that was *freely* available. Most of the locally available foods consumed by the new arrivals were shoreline vegetables like Australian samphire (*Sarcocornia quinqueflora*), New Zealand spinach (*Tetragonia tetragonioides*, also called warrigal greens in Australia), sea celery (*Apium prostratum*), grey saltbush (*Atriplex cinerea*), native wood sorrel (*Oxalis* species), and numerous fruits including native appleberries, cherries, and various types of fig.[36] The starchy stems of bracken (*Pteridium esculentum*) would have been a standby, but were largely overlooked. Other plants that were incorporated into the diet included currant bush (*Leptomeria acida*), which commonly grew on the sandstone ridges around Sydney, which was partly attractive because of its antiscorbutic qualities (scurvy is caused by a deficiency of vitamin C). Currant bush was one of several plants believed to cure scurvy, among them native sarsaparilla (*Smilax glycophylla*), from which the English made a bittersweet tea, but was probably of no use against the disease.

Such foods only formed a supplement to the daily ration. Today, the food value and eating qualities of many of these plants remain largely unknown to the general Australian public, which only eats them as an occasional indulgence undertaken out of curiosity. Australia's food culture would develop in step with its Anglo-Saxon heritage, influenced to a much lesser extent by the continental cookery of Europe, until after the mid-20th century, when immigration once again changed the foodscape of Australia.

There were many opportunities in the new lands to duplicate the kind of farming that British farmers enjoyed, particularly in New Zealand, where the temperate climate and the development of huge tracts of grazing pasture assured success. In Australia, with its much fiercer summer heat, cattle and sheep farming was also a success (although it is challenged today by severe drought); by the close of the 19th century, both countries became major exporters of primary food products, including meat, butter, and cheese, to the UK market. These foods had also become the mainstay of the local diet by this time.

Australia's gastronomic heritage, shaped by the working class tastes of 19th century Britain, was also preordained: food production had already become mechanized in Britain by that time; therefore, Australia would be a country with its sights set on the industrial-scale production and processing of food. Without the peasant ethos, economy, or tradition of food production that undergirds so many of the world's great cuisines, the food culture of Australia was on the road to large-scale farming from the very beginning.[37] The provision of food was a problem to be solved by the most powerful in the land rather than being a product to be home- or community-grown. Australia was planted with wheat, rye, barley, and oats, and with pastures for meat and dairy producing animals, as farmers strove to turn a continent with an entirely different ecology from Northern Europe into something worthy of the old country. In part, they were successful. Certainly, almost all of the vegetables and fruits that thrived in Europe also thrived in Australasia. Indeed, the warmer southern summers favored excellent fruiting for stone fruits, Queensland and the Northern Territory could sustain all the tropical varieties, and the colder winters favored apples, pears, and all the common winter vegetables. Grapes also fared very well and, today New Zealand and Australia boast hundreds of award-winning, world-class wine producers. Sauvignon blanc from Blenheim in New Zealand and South Australian shiraz, in particular, have achieved international acclaim.

Indigenous foodways in Australasia fared far less well. Maori and Aboriginal food systems and knowledge were marginalized, abandoned, or forgotten, although when needed, indigenous foods were recommended. The starchy-centered sago palm, the fruit of the pandanus, the buds of varieties of wild banana, bamboo, and other plants with edible shoots were emergency standbys, just as during World War II, servicemen fighting in New Guinea and the surrounding islands were issued with booklets describing wild edible plants that could be eaten when rations ran out. The diversity of plants listed gives an indication of the richness of New Guinea's edible flora: taro, yams, cassava, sugar cane, palm lily, sago palm, breadfruit, coconut, native spinach, and varieties of beans, watercress, ferns, wild raspberries, and passion fruit, water vines, nipa palm, paw paw (papaya), mangosteen, and mango, among them.[38] Not far to the southwest, in Australia's far northwestern region of Dampierland, a differently diverse range of wild bush foods (indigenous flora and fauna) are still gathered by native peoples, including the Karajarri and Bardi. Among these are kurrajong nuts (*Brachychiton diversifolius*), bush onion (*Cyperus bulbosus*), which grows in the mudflats, *magabala,* a long, green, vine-growing fruit that is sweet and juicy, and bloodwood apple galls, called *dardaws,* produced by a small fly (*Fergusonina nicholsoni*), the edible larvae of which feed on the young stem's sap and form the gall as protective armor. The larvae are eaten by native peoples when the *dardaw* is broken open. The *dardaws* form on host trees, typically eucalyptus (*Eucalyptus globulus*). Commercial interests, where involved, have characteristically recognized the market value, but not the gastronomic, cultural, or ecological value of promoting local foods. This may not be the case if considering the impact that bush foods could have in the growing area of nutraceuticals, also called functional foods because they contain significant quantities of substances that are known to be beneficial to human health. Feeding the commercial and public demand for foods-as-drugs is another option for the biodiverse Pacific, but care will have to be taken to prevent exploitation. The *kakadu* plum (*Terminalia ferdinandiana*), for example, has the highest known amounts of vitamin C per volume of any plant in the world; at 5 percent of its weight, this represents 50 times more than the vitamin C content of oranges. But, in 2005, the Australian Government House of Representatives' Standing Committee on Aboriginal and Torres Strait Islander Affairs heard that the American-based Amway company had exported *kakadu* plum plants to South America for reproductive purposes, having flouted the rights to intellectual property of indigenous Australians, the erstwhile caretakers and harvesters of the fruit. Like in earlier times, not much of the profit from any larger-scale enterprise involving native food is necessarily going to flow back to indigenous people.

By contrast, commercial links with some Pacific islands were established early on, if not always with the knowledge or consent of the islanders. In the days before mineral deposits of phosphates were exploited to produce fertilizers, American and European interests were involved in the lucrative trade in guano, for example, the name given to the sizable, phosphate-rich deposits made from the accumulated droppings of sea birds. Large deposits of guano were found in Peru, a country bordering the Eastern Pacific, giving it easy access to the Pacific Islands in that region. Peru was consequently involved in the blackbirding of the Pacific Islands for its guano production operation in the mid-1800s. This exploitation of island labor was typical of what was to come, region-wide, in the Pacific. When it was discovered that Nauru Island was a rich source of natural phosphate, Australia was very keen to get this supply of fertilizer to boost soil productivity for the growth of its cash crops, including wheat. Australia's porous, sandy soil needed such products to raise growth rates. This represented another form of exploitation. Although Nauruans were eventually remunerated for years of phosphate extraction (making it one of the wealthiest income per capita states in the world), the destruction of much of their island, their culture, and their community was the ultimate cost of this commerce.

Australia and New Zealand developed their own agricultural production systems that, in time, provided adequately for a growing population. The same basic varieties of everyday foodstuffs (grains, vegetables, fruits, meats, and fish) are readily available in both Australia and New Zealand, and mainstream tastes still converge insofar as the traditional fare of both countries derives from the Anglo-Saxon cookery of the 18th and 19th centuries. The other component of public taste was elite connoisseurship, which tended to take French haute cuisine as its model. The acknowledged 19th century supremacy of French cookery had a lasting impact on the popular understanding of food style and culinary quality in the colonies, although this is no longer the case. While French cookery is still highly regarded internationally, as in Australasia, as a percentage of the restaurant market, the number of French restaurants has steadily declined over recent decades. Still regarded as elite in the 1960s and '70s, subsequently, French cuisine no longer reigned supreme, while French-style bistros, brasseries, and cafés became more popular, reflecting a shift to more informal dining.

In Australia (but not to the same extent in NZ), the influx of Greek and Italian refugees following World War II, along with refugees and emigrants from other European countries, brought their European foodways with them. It has been noted that the home-style "Italian Australian" food of emigrant families in Australia today still looks like Italian food in Italy during the prewar years. Such is the process of assimilation and adaptation as it applies to food culture. Migrants fleeing persecution, war, or both often arrived in the antipodes with little more than a few basic belongings. Most families also possessed amateur, domestic skills, cookery among them. Even when they had no personal history of cooking, discovering that Italian food was an attractive and exotic alternative for jaded Australian and New Zealand diners, migrants from the continent were quick to capitalize on their heritage. Pizza and pasta restaurants became instant successes. Especially in the larger Australasian cities, Italian and Greek food flourished, particularly in the form of cafe and alfresco dining restaurants, which very much suited the warm, Mediterranean-style climate of parts of Australia. For some migrants, cooking the foods they once enjoyed at home was also a direct way to hold onto the lives they had previously led by reliving them in the present, in the kitchen and around the dinner table with family and friends. No differently, expatriate islanders share the foods of their cultural heritage to express their belonging to the group.

Australia's current gastronomic distinctiveness has come about following separate waves of immigrant peoples who have arrived and settled in the last 60 years or so. First, it was the Italian, Greek, and Eastern European refugees and émigrés. Then came Vietnamese, Cambodians, Thais, and Malaysians who, like the Indian and Chinese communities before them, established ethnic restaurant traditions in their adopted country. Australia's gastronomic diversity is greater than of New Zealand, which has not sustained the same amount of immigration over the years. More recently, New Zealand has been taking many more migrants from Asian countries in particular but, traditionally, New Zealand's migration pattern was different. Many more Pacific Islanders than Asians or Europeans made their home in New Zealand. Although there are Yugoslavian, Latvian, and other ethnic groups represented, it is really only the more recent migration of Asian peoples that has made multiculturalism in foodways part of the New Zealand experience. Australians have had a lot longer to recognize and appreciate the enriching value of the range of cuisines, which have influenced eating habits and contributed to what has been called Modern Australian cuisine. This phrase recognizes that the food that dominates in nonethnic restaurants is a fusion-style cuisine that reflects Australia as a unique place. As it developed, it also reflected the changing tastes of Australians as diners, who were becoming more adventurous. Mod Oz, as it is sometimes called, marked the point at which Australian chefs and the dining public looked to themselves for new food styles, but also to the region of which they were a part.

The Mod Oz style was one essentially dictated by the use of good quality ingredients, simple preparation, and exciting flavor combinations. Seafood, basic cooking techniques like barbecuing or char-grilling, salads, and less fat and cream, were traits of the new cuisine. It was also influenced by ethnic (particularly Asian) cuisines and styles, which had grown greatly in popularity. This was not only because Australians liked Thai and Vietnamese cookery, but also because many of the ingredients used in these cuisines were freshly available in Australia. The tropical Northern Territory and Queensland produced all the ingredients needed to make authentic Asian cuisine: chilies, coriander, lemongrass, snake beans, pandanus leaf, Vietnamese mint, Kaffir limes, ginger, and galangal.

Some of the best chefs Australia has produced can also be given credit for this change in Australian cuisine. In the mid-1970s, Australian-born chef Phillip Searle, and Malaysian-born Australian chef Cheong Liew, both independently pioneered fusion-style cuisines, later dubbed "East meets West" as the trend caught on internationally, but particularly in New World, Western countries (the United States, Britain, Australasia, Canada, South Africa). For the first time, an innovative way of approaching food and cooking was developing that challenged the culinary orthodoxy of professional hotel cookery that dominated up to that point. Chefs like Searle and Liew asserted their creative right to rethink what the fundamentals of a modern Australian cuisine might require, given the country's geographical, cultural, and historical circumstances. Experimentation was the result, as foods and techniques were reappraised without culinary prejudice. Such a deliberate approach to cooking established a gastronomic oeuvre based on a full range of techniques and ingredients, tastes and aesthetics, appropriate to the changing tastes of the dining public. This, significantly, moved beyond the stifling hegemony of French haute cuisine. Australia's proximity to Asia, its source of produce in the tropical "top end" and Queensland, and its population's diverse ethnic makeup, buoyed this movement, which would become a sort of culinary reformation. Asian and Indian ingredients, in Searle's case, like saffron, ginger, lemongrass, anise, curry leaves, black cumin, Shao-hsing wine, and coriander, and techniques like stir-frying, steaming, and twice-cooking (Chinese), suddenly added new, sophisticated gustatory dimensions to a whole repertoire of dishes. In fairness to French flair, Searle owed something to the refined aesthetics of nouvelle cuisine, an internationally influential food fashion that also emerged in the 1970s, but each creation was quintessentially his own. Searle paved the way for the Mod Oz movement in fusion cuisine, not to mention inspiring a number of copyists.

New Zealand's cuisine tends to be influenced by what happens on the international stage, which makes sense in a nation of only four million people whose heritage has been dominated by Anglo-Saxon cookery. Ethnic restaurants have multiplied in recent years, but were underrepresented compared to Australia. This was not only the result of different immigration policies, but also because New Zealand lacks big, cosmopolitan cities like Melbourne and Sydney, where the tastes of urban diners predispose the food culture to culinary change. Nonetheless, New Zealand is now developing a similar type of fusion cuisine to that of Australia, given that its chefs and restaurateurs are championing local, quality produce, which is often organic, biodynamic, or wild. Indigenous uses of native plants, known by Maori for their culinary uses and eating qualities, have also been giving high-end New Zealand restaurant cuisine a trendy local character, while Maori restaurants are virtually nonexistent. Neither are there Aboriginal restaurants in Australia. The cookery of indigenous peoples does not tend to be found attractive by the mainstream population. The same is true in the islands. Only very few restaurants exist that specialize in authentic Fijian cuisine, although certain dishes in the repertoire are certainly available in restaurants that serve a variety of styles, or a blend on Fijian and Western.

Regionalism is not well developed in New Zealand, even compared with Australia, although it is on the rise, particularly as New Zealand's distinctive wine regions become well known. A few decades ago, much of the stony farmland in the region of Martinborough would not sell easily at any price. Today, viticulture has driven up land prices as the local grape of choice, pinot noir, wins accolades from the world's wine critics. Already world-famous, the sauvignon blanc of Marlborough (northern South Island) reveals a similar story. The brand *Cloudy Bay* has become the benchmark of this distinctive style, which New Zealand vintners have managed to tailor impressively to a global market.

Consumers are also increasingly interested in the distinctive flavors and qualities of regional foods, having of late identified the importance of the provenance of a product (*terroir*). The *terroir* of foods and wine is foregrounded at the growing numbers of farmers markets that have sprung up all over Australasia in recent years. This trend has also inspired chefs who, in accessing the products on offer in the farmers' markets, tap into the best the country has to offer, capitalize on current consumer demand for quality and difference, and satisfy their own desire to use the best ingredients in their culinary creations. Having begun as colonies with a relatively narrow Anglo-Saxon food tradition, New Zealand and Australia have emerged as free-thinking and now regionally aware gastronomic nations. The success of and demand for Australasia's inventive chefs and innovative, cutting-edge food style, is also reflected by the global accolades and awards received by numerous food magazines, such as New Zealand's *Cuisine*, and the Australian-produced *Gourmet Traveller* and *Vogue Entertaining*.

NOTES

1. K. R. Howe, *Vaka Moana, Voyages of the Ancestors: The Discovery and Settlement of the Pacific* (Honolulu: University of Hawaii Press, 2007), 21.

2. Kenneth F. Kiple and Kriemhild Coneè Ornelas, eds., *The Cambridge World History of Food* (Cambridge: Cambridge University Press, 2000): 1351–1366.

3. Eric A. Powell, "Kon Tiki Fried Chicken?" *Archaeology* (June 4, 2007), http://www.archaeology.org/online/features/chicken/ (accessed July 4, 2008).

4. Patrick Vinton Kirch and Jean-Louis Rallu, eds., *The Growth and Collapse of Pacific Island Societies: Archaeological and Demographic Perspectives* (Honolulu: University of Hawaii Press, 2007).

5. Goran Burenhult, *New World and Pacific Civilisations: Cultures of America, Asia, and the Pacific* (St Lucia: University of Queensland Press), 153.

6. Douglas L. Oliver, *Oceania: The Native Cultures of Australia and the Pacific Islands. Vol 2* (Honolulu: University of Hawaii Press, 1989).

7. Randolph R. Thaman, "Deterioration of Traditional Food Systems, Increasing Malnutrition and Food Dependency in the Pacific Islands," *Journal of Food and Nutrition* 39, no. 3 (1982).

8. Carol Kaesuk Yoon, "Alien Species Threaten Hawaii's Environment," *New York Times*, December 29, 1992.

9. K. R. Howe, *Where the Waves Fall: A New South Sea Islands History from First Settlement to Colonial Rule* (Sydney: George Allen & Unwin, 1984), 53.

10. John Morrison, Paul Geraghty, and Linda Crowl, eds., *Fauna, Flora, Food and Medicine, Science of Pacific Island Peoples* (Suva: University of the South Pacific, 1994).

11. Oliver, 270.

12. For a digital copy of Cook's journals, link through Internet Archive: http://www.archive.org/stream/threevoyagesofca04cook/threevoyagesofca-04cook_djvu.txt (accessed August 9, 2007).

13. Greg Dening, *Islands and Beaches: Discourse on a Silent Land, Marquesas, 1774–1880* (Carlton, Victoria: Melbourne University Press, 1980).

14. H. E. Maude, *Of Islands and Men: Studies in Pacific History* (Melbourne: Oxford University Press, 1968), 236–37.

15. Howe, *Where the Waves Fall*, 49.

16. I. C. Campbell, *Worlds Apart: A History of the Pacific Islands* (Christchurch, NZ: Canterbury University Press, 2003), 74.

17. Felipe Fernández-Armesto, *Near a Thousand Tables: A History of Food.* (New York: Free Press, 2002), 183–84.

18. H. E. Maude, *Of Islands and Men*.

19. H. E. Maude, *Slavers in Paradise* (Canberra: Australian National University Press, 1981), 191.

20. Campbell, *Worlds Apart*, 188.

21. Pamela Goyan Kittler and Kathryn P. Sucher, *Food and Culture*, 5th ed. (Belmont, CA: Thompson Wadsworth, 2008), 390.

22. Howe, *Where the Waves Fall*, 96.

23. Graham Harris, "Nga Riwai Maori: The Perpetuation of Relict Potato Cultivars within Maori Communities in New Zealand," in *Vegeculture in Eastern Asia and Oceania* (JCAS Symposium Series No 16), ed. Shuji Yoshida and Peter J. Mathews, (Osaka: Japan Centre for Asian Studies, 2002).

24. Brij V. Lal and Kate Fortune, eds., *The Pacific Islands: An Encyclopedia* (Honolulu: University of Hawaii Press, 2000), 202–4.

25. Bruce Knapman, "Capitalism's Economic Impact in Colonial Fiji 1874–1939: Development or Underdevelopment," *Journal of Pacific History* 20 no. 2 (1985).

26. D. P. Mellor, "The Role of Science and Industry," in *Australia in the War of 1939–1945* (Canberra: Australian War Memorial, 1958).

27. The Secretariat of the Pacific Community, http://www.spc.int/corp/index.php?option=com_frontpage&Itemid=1

28. Moshe Rapaport, ed., *The Pacific Islands: Environment & Society* (Honolulu: Bess Press, 1999), 405.

29. Earnest Beaglehole, *Social Change in the South Pacific: Rarotonga and Aitutaki* (Aberdeen, UK: George Allen & Unwin, 1957), 92.

30. A. H. McLintock, *An Encyclopaedia of New Zealand* (Wellington, NZ: R. E. Owen, Government Printer, 1966), 179, http://www.teara.govt.nz/1966/I/IslandTerritories/CookIslands/en.

31. See John Connell, " 'The Taste of Paradise': Selling Fiji and Fiji Water," *Asia Pacific Viewpoint* 47, no. 3 (2006): 348.

32. "Food Crisis An Opportunity for the Pacific: SPC." Statement issued by the SPC at the World Food Summit 08, held in Rome, Italy. Reproduced in *Pacific Magazine*, June 5, 2008.

33. Based on Secretariat of the Pacific Community statistics (for American Samoa, the Cook Islands, Fiji, French Polynesia, Guam, Kiribati, the Marshall Islands, the Federated States of Micronesia, Nauru, New Caledonia, Niue, the Northern Mariana Islands, Palau, Samoa, the Solomon Islands, Tonga, and Tuvalu). See http://www.spc.int/sdp/index.php for more information.

34. 2006 New Zealand census statistics.

35. Chris Cooper and Colin Michael Hall, eds., *Oceania: A Tourism Handbook*, (*Aspects of Tourism*, 17) (Buffalo, NY: Channel View Publications, 2005), 83, 177.

36. See Tim Low, "Foods of the First Fleet: Convict Food Plants of Old Sydney Town." *Australian Natural History* 22, no. 7 (1988).

37. See Michael Symons, *One Continuous Picnic: A Gastronomic History of Australia*, rev. ed. (Melbourne: Melbourne University Press, 2007), 21–22.

38. General Staff issued under the authority of the Commander of Land Forces S. W. P. A., *Friendly Fruits and Vegetables*. Melbourne: Arbuckle Waddle, 1943).

2

Major Foods and Ingredients

Among Polynesian Pacific Islanders, food is referred to as *kai* or its equivalent, a term of Austronesian origin with cognates in 31 Polynesian languages. Traditionally, *kai* is not *kai* unless it includes staple starchy foods like taro, yam, or breadfruit. *Kai* stands in opposition to *kina*, or food eaten with another as relish. *Kakana dina* is the equivalent Fijian term for "real food" and, like elsewhere in the Pacific region, also refers today to root crops like sweet potato and cassava (relative latecomers to the islands). Cassava (*Manihot esculentai*), also called manioc and *tavioka*, originated in Central America, and was brought to western Micronesia in the 16th century by the Spanish, who also brought the sweet potato, another native of the Americas that is now a staple of the islands. Coconut, bananas, and plantain, of which there are many different varieties, are also regarded as *kakana dina*.[1] In the past, these foods were the mainstay of the diet. Today, there has been a move away from the traditional foods. While the old symbolism associated with the traditional diet remains strong, many new foods have been incorporated, marginalizing to a varying extent the *kakana dina* foods, if not their symbolic function. Typical of the sorts of foods that have made significant inroads into the staple diet are carbohydrates like rice and wheat flour products. This shift from locally produced root crops to imported starches is perhaps the most striking change in the major ingredients of island cooking. What is also different today is that a far greater total number of food types contribute to the diet of islanders. The influence of the West, once again, has been crucial to this changing consumption pattern, which has steadily eroded the traditional diet. Imported sugar, meat, and fat (oils and dairy food) are more a part of the daily intake. Economic exploitation of the region has been partly responsible for these changes to diet, as well as changes to lifestyle, urbanization, and increased disposable income among islanders. A greater choice of foods and ingredients available through retail outlets is sustained by the greater flow of capital. Ingredients used in cooking at home have also changed. More convenience foods and easy-to-prepare products have replaced the staple island foods to a large extent. Processed foods have replaced fresh products. Traditional islander foodways are no longer a feature of everyday life and the everyday diet, particularly in urban areas where it is now more likely that foods such as bread, cereal, polished white rice, dairy products, fried foods, and confectionery will be found. In rural areas and in poorer social groups, traditional foods are still grown and consumed on a daily basis, but the diet is also supplemented by flour (and flour-based products), sugar, tea, and, to some extent, dairy products (canned, UHT, or powdered milk) and various condiments.

Over the years, the foods that once were regarded as condiments, such as meat, fish, and seafood, have become a greater part of island diets. This reflects the influence of global culture and of individualization, in particular. Younger generations of island people are relating more to a world culture as represented in the media, and perhaps less to their traditional ways of life. Food culture is always at the heart of cultural life in general because it involves daily social communication and, thus, the reinforcement of culture-specific values, attitudes, and desires. The Pacific Island cultures are no different in this respect, and are constantly adapting by incorporating new foods, styles of cookery, ingredients, and modes of consumption. Large amounts of traditional foods are still consumed, although taro and yam are regarded almost as luxury products as their price has been rising in comparison with substitute foods like bread and rice.

THE STARCHY STAPLES

Taro

Taro (*Colocasia esculenta*) is known throughout the Pacific. In Tahiti it is *fafa*, in Fiji, *dalo*, in Hawaii, luau, and in the Cook Islands, taro. Taro was the most widely distributed starchy food of the ancient world, and is thought to have been the first cultivated food crop to be introduced to the islands. A member of the *Araceae* family, to which the common calla lily belongs, taro is grown primarily for its root, the main food source of the plant, which is technically a corm (the swollen base of a stem), and takes four to six months to mature in fertile soil. Taro was brought to the islands from China, where it was already eaten as a staple food. Taro thrives in the tropics, in wet or swampy areas, and is easy to propagate from a cutting. In time, both the taro corm and leaves became particularly significant as a food source, partly because the plant could be cultivated in a variety of places, including virtually soilless atolls.[2]

Taro has been a staple food of Pacific peoples for centuries. From Easter Island to Hawaii, New Zealand, PNG, and the Mariana and Caroline Islands, although New Zealand Maori rejected the taro for sweet potato (kumara) because taro prefers a warmer climate. There are four main types of taro. *Colocasia* is known as the "true taro," also called swamp taro, where it grows to a height of about four feet, and is regarded as the best-tasting of the taro varieties. *Alocasia*, or giant taro, is a hardy plant that can grow in drier conditions than *Colocasia*. Its corms rise above the ground. *Cryptosperma* taro is grown on atolls, which have poorer soils than most islands, and is sometimes called giant swamp taro. It is a good source of zinc. *Xanthosoma* taro is grown in Melanesia and was introduced to the islands only about 120 years ago from tropical Central America.

Taro for sale.

The leaves and corms of taro must first be cooked, typically with coconut milk or cream, the combination of which forms one of the distinctive flavors of Pacific cuisine. Because of the presence of calcium oxalate crystals, which can cause discomfort if eaten, taro must be well-cooked. This destroys the sharp crystal formations that cause intense irritation in the mouth and throat. For the same reason, the hard top of the stem to which the broad leaf is connected is also removed before cooking. Taro corms, which are typically pale in color, elongated, evenly round, and rough-skinned, are first peeled, then steamed or baked in slices. Because the leaves are soft and broad, these can also be usefully employed to wrap other foods before they are cooked and eaten. This has become a signature technique of Pacific cuisine.

The taro corm is a starchy food with a bland, although slightly perfumed, taste and a texture like a very waxy potato. It is the perfect type of food to be accompanied by tastier items, seasoning, or sauce. Indeed, its own leaves have a spinach-like flavor, and, when cooked with fresh coconut milk, taro leaves form a tasty accompaniment dish that Rarotongans call *rou rou*. The popular *rourou meredane* includes onion, garlic, and ginger as flavorings for the taro leaves and coconut. Corned beef or braised beef brisket, sliced onion, and coconut cream are traditionally wrapped in leaves; this is thought of as a staple food in its own right. In Fiji, this dish is known as *palusami*, or *rukau*, the Polynesian Maori name for essentially the same dish. It is not uncommon to see *rukau* being eaten as the first meal of the day, especially when open-air markets cater to consumers who no longer depend on home-cooked meals.

Taro remains an important part of island life because it is still much esteemed as a high-status food at feasts, taking pride of place along with yams. The higher consumption of many introduced foods, as well as the increasing replacement of taro with the more easily grown cassava, together with imported rice and potatoes, has actually served to increase the status of taro, which has become more expensive than cassava and so more of a treat. In the old days, cost was not the question, since growing taro was simply a necessity. To grow abundant taro signified prosperity for the whole community. Today, offering taro still carries the traditional message of abundance and hospitality, but now with an added sense of financial sacrifice on the part of the host. Although most islanders buy rather than growing, gathering, or catching their food, taro included, it has retained its prestige as a special food.

Taro (corm and leaves) is a nutritious vegetable, containing protein, iron, calcium, and niacin in useful amounts, and micronutrients like vitamin B1. It is typical of a complex carbohydrate in that it can form a sound nutritious base for a diet. Taro does not keep particularly well once harvested, and this partly explains why the technique of fermenting the corm, as a paste, was developed (see chapter 3). In Hawaii, this is known as poi.

Although its use has been affected by the incursion made by cassava, rice, and noodles (cheap and convenient alternatives), taro is still grown widely and also exported. The size of the New Zealand taro market is estimated to be around 8,000 tons annually. Fiji began exporting taro to New Zealand in 1950, and Samoa followed in 1957. Continuity of supply varied from these sources, but Fiji now exports 80 percent of what the New Zealand market needs. The previous domination of taro export to New Zealand by Samoa reflected the size of the Samoan expatriate population in New Zealand. Today, these expatriate Samoans number about 190,000, with 90 percent of them living in Auckland, the country's largest city. There is a second but significantly smaller population in Wellington, New Zealand's capital. The islander population of New Zealand is expected to double in the next 30 years.

Grated taro pudding (Tuvalu)

Four servings
2 medium-sized taro

Banana leaves

1 c. coconut cream

Toddy syrup (optional)

Peel the taro, grate it and wrap in softened banana leaves; bake or steam for one hour. When cooked, cut into squares and mix with coconut cream (toddy can be added for sweetness). Serve.[3]

Yams and Sweet Potatoes

Known to have been the main food crop of the Kanak people of New Caledonia before white settlement, yams are another important starchy staple that was historically significant in the island diet. The greater yam (*Dioscorea alata*), the wild yam (*Dioscorea nummularia*), and the sweet (or lesser) yam (*Dioscorea esculenta*) are three common cultivars of this dryland root crop that above ground forms a climbing vine.[4] The giant yam grows to an enormous size. Twenty pound-plus yams, over 10 feet long, are not uncommon. Yams can be successfully stored in the ground or in a dry, cool, dark, and well-ventilated place, an added advantage in tropical

conditions. Special storage huts were traditionally built for this root vegetable in various Pacific cultures whereas today yams are regularly seen in
Pacific Island market stalls and are a staple in Fiji, where they are called
uvi, also *ufi,* or *uhi.* A favorite in the region, yams are particularly popular
in the Western Pacific, where it thrives on the high islands of Micronesia
(Pohnpei, Yap, and Kosrae). Trellised yam gardens also grow in the dry
savannah area surrounding Port Moresby in PNG (Papua New Guinea).
Yam is traditionally cooked in the *umu,* but can also be boiled until soft.
Compared to some other root crops, it is quite sweet, somewhat like sweet
potato.

Sweet potatoes (*Ipomoea batatas*) are another of the starchy root crops
(commonly called "yams" in parts of the United States) and are native
of South America. They were carried into the Pacific by Portuguese and
Spanish ships returning to Europe from the new world in the 15th and
16th centuries. Sweet potato is called *kau kau, kumala,* and kumara in
the Pacific region. It can be stored, tolerates drier (nontropical) conditions than does the taro, and therefore became a staple of New Zealand's
Maori, who called it kumara. Sweet potato is the main staple of the PNG
highlanders, and is highly nutritious, easily grown, matures quickly, and
crops well. Unlike other staple crops, it tolerates altitude. When cooked
(baked, steamed, or boiled), it tastes flavorsome and sweet, and has a
creamy texture. Sweet potatoes vary in color from a pale whitish to a dark
purple skin, and from pale cream to deep yellow flesh. Sweet potatoes can
be harvested after three to seven months. A popular food in Australasia as
well, sweet potatoes are versatile and are favored by chefs for their sweet
flavor, creamy texture, and bright color. They can be mashed or sliced
lengthways in layers; once cooked, they can also be used to line a mould,
which can then be filled with a savory mixture, covered with more sweet
potato slices, baked, and turned out. The sweet potato also lends itself to
that ubiquitous restaurant staple, French fries. More so than the other
root crops of the Pacific, the sweet potato has made an impression on the
West's cuisine, and also been included in variations of traditional culinary
themes in the islands. In Tonga, *hoho,* an adaptation of the dish *palusami,*
is made using pumpkin and sweet potato, tinned meat, and coconut, and
wrapped and baked in taro leaves.

Cassava

Of the newer ingredients introduced into the Pacific, cassava, or manioc
(*Manihot esculenta*), is the most recent in terms of its widespread use and
consumption. A tropical plant, the root of which is another important

Fijian Indian farmer with young cassava.

source of dietary starch (carbohydrate), cassava contains 25–31 percent starch, a little protein (0.5–1%), and some fat. It is also a major source of calories in the tropical Pacific, and is the most widely grown root crop in Fiji. Cassava's dried flour is made into balls known as tapioca (sometimes erroneously referred to as sago), used primarily as a thickener. The Fijians call cassava *tavioka*. It ranks with wheat, rice, and maize as a primary world food source of energy, and tolerates both poor soil and low rainfall. It can be harvested after six to nine months, and is very easy to grow. The young leaves are very nutritious and, once cooked, can also be eaten. The main disadvantage of cassava is that it does not store well, showing signs of deterioration after a few days. The roots can be stored longer in damp sawdust or clean sand. In this way, cassava will last three to four weeks. It has little fiber and a dry and starchy, although not unpleasant, consistency when cooked. Like other root vegetables, cassava takes up flavor and liquid easily, and works well in stews and curries. It is a good source of vitamin C, but is low in protein.

Cassava's popularity is due to a combination of factors: its easy propagation and minimum tending, quick growth, simple harvest and preparation, versatile character, and pleasant texture and taste. As a consequence, cassava is a cheap food, and curried cassava with fish or chicken is a common choice for a quick meal. Cassava cooks in a little more time than required for rice or noodles.

Non-root Vegetables

Of the non-root vegetable crops producing a staple starch, sago is a major crop and source of carbohydrate for the lowland peoples of New Guinea and the Moluccas (to the west of New Guinea). Sago (*Metroxylon sagu*) is extracted from the sago palm's trunk, the pith of which is washed to drive out the starch; when dry, it is nearly pure carbohydrate. A tree of about 12 years of age is ready for sago extraction, and some palms can yield over 600 pounds of sago, much of which can be stored for later use. Westerners know sago in the form of small white granules that, when cooked, go clear and form a pleasant dessert, typically sweetened and flavored (with lemon). In PNG, sago it often used to make a form of pancake that is normally eaten with fish or meat. It is an important food, particularly since it often grows in swampy areas that do not easily sustain other edible vegetation. Sago is also an important feed for livestock.

Of Asian origin, but found in Hawaii and other parts of Polynesia, Polynesian arrowroot (*Tacca leontopetaloides*) is known as *pia*. It is a thickening starch like sago. and is used as such in desserts made with fruit or vegetables (papaya, pumpkin, banana), called *po'e* in Tahiti, and *poke* in the Cook Islands. *Pia* is sometimes called arrowroot or tapioca because its starch resembles that of both these plants. Traditionally, *pia* was also mixed with coconut milk or cream and steamed, boiled, or baked into the dessert pudding called *haupia*.

Breadfruit is another non-root vegetable starchy staple, a substantial fruit that comes from a large tree. Two main types of breadfruit (*Artocarpus*), seedless and seeded, are grown in Oceania. Hybrids formed in Western Micronesia, with the variant strain, *Artocarpus mariannensis*, and these spread as far as Samoa. Spreading from the east, as is the case with much Pacific flora, breadfruit has been grown widely, and its starchy pulp is cooked and eaten as far north as Hawaii, as far east as the Cook Islands and the Tuamotu archipelago, and as far south as New Caledonia. Fresh breadfruit are covered in a sticky white sap, which is reduced by leaving the fruit in the sun for an hour or after harvesting. Seeds and cores are removed before cooking. Like other starchy crops, breadfruit can be baked, steamed, boiled, pounded, or grated depending on the dish being prepared. Breadfruit leaves are also used to wrap foods for cooking. Breadfruit pulp adds

Plantain and banana at Noumea market.

texture to cakes, and can be flavored with herbs or cooked with meats, soaking up the flavor like other starches. Roasted whole or in halves, it can also be cooked in an open fire or in the *umu*. It can also be made into fries. The common traditional treatment is to grate ripe breadfruit, mix it with coconut cream, wrap it in leaves, and cook it in the *umu*. A problem that arose in relation to breadfruit was its abundance in season. Oversupply was dealt with by fermenting the excess, which also preserved it over time. The sour doughy paste that results from the process has many names throughout the Pacific region: masi, *ma, mahi, madrai, mahr, namandi, furo,* and *bwiru* among them. Still made in Micronesia (Pohnpei), the practice of making masi paste is dying out elsewhere in the Pacific.[5]

Plantain (*Musa paradisiaca*), which looks somewhat like and is closely related to the banana, is normally smaller and straighter than the bananas seen commonly in North American supermarkets. Known as a food since ancient times, plantain is enjoyed from India to South America, and is a primary source of starch throughout Oceania. Although it resembles a stumpy banana, plantain, or *vudi* (Fiji), is firmer and generally requires cooking before eating. It is considered another staple crop of the Pacific.

Propagation requires a wetter climate. Fruit is available all year round, but most fruit are harvested between December and March.[6] Plantain are baked in their skins in an *umu*; they are also peeled and boiled in salted water, mashed and baked in cakes. Sometimes, they are also fermented. They can be used to make Western-style chips, dried and made into flour, or made into a drink. *Maoli*, a sausage-shaped plantain with rounded tips and 6–8 inches in length, is the main variety of plantain found in Oceania from the western Pacific and 4,000 miles east to the Marquesas.

NON-STARCH STAPLES

Coconut

In terms of food, cultural, and economic value, combined, coconut (*Cocos nucifer*) is probably the most important of the island crops. Introduced to the Pacific Islands from Asia, the coconut is cultivated widely across the Pacific region (except Easter Island), including atolls, where it often provides the only cash crop and contributes as a primary source of food. Coconut palms can grow up to more than 100 ft tall. A thick husk surrounds the coconut, which is filled with a firm white flesh and, when young, a sweet watery liquid. Coconuts, their flesh and juice, have a multitude of culinary uses in Pacific Island cookery. Coconut milk is almost the universal cooking liquid, commonly mixed with the starchy staple foods like taro or breadfruit that are baked in the *umu*. Foods are also simmered in coconut milk, and placed in a container in the glowing embers of a fire. The kernel (endosperm) of the mature nut is used raw, cooked, and fermented in a variety of ways, as a staple food, a relish, and a dessert on festive occasions. Mature kernels can be hung in the rafters as an emergency food for up to 10 years. The soft flesh of the immature nut is an important weaning food for infants, while its juice is a nutritious local beverage and, in some regions, like Kiribati, it is considered sacred. Sap from the flower spathe is used to make unfermented and fermented toddy and syrup, which are nutritionally significant foods in Micronesia and on many atolls. Coconut water is consumed as a daily drink. When the coconut drops from the tree, it can be left for 2–3 months, in which time it will shoot, sending up a green leafy stem and a root formation. At this stage, it can be replanted, but if split open reveals a sweet, porous white foam that is a delicacy called *uto* in the Cook Islands.

Coconuts have multiple culinary and gastronomic uses depending on the age and ripeness of the fruit. In the Tokelau Islands, there are at least 14 different ways of utilizing the coconut, from the jellylike flesh of the

young nut to the crisp meat of the older coconut, from the light quench-
ing juice of the young nut to its dense cream when mature. The sweet sap
(coconut honey) of the tree is also used as a sweetener and to make *kaleve
vi*, an intoxicating drink similar to toddy. In Tokelau, one dish, *vaihu
tamoko*, is made only from coconut, but from different coconut preparations and from nuts at different stages of development. It is a good example
of Polynesian cooking because, while it is a complex, processed product,
it is not actually cooked. It consists of four parts of the grated, tender eye
of the young green coconut, which contains a jellylike flesh that is also
added. Half this amount of the custard-like meat of a slightly more mature
coconut is grated and added. This is then moistened with the sweet milk
of the young coconut and, if not sweet enough, some reduced sap is added.
The whole is stirred and eaten immediately.[7]

The enormous versatility of coconut is common across the region where
"the tree of life" grows in such abundance. Once other ingredients are
incorporated with it, coconut, in its many forms, enters cuisine as the
culinary mainstay of Pacific foodways. *Kokoda* is a famous Fijian example
of marinated raw fish (or clams) that is so representative of island cultures and their use of coconut as a marinating liquid. *Kaikoso* (*Anadara
antiquata*), a type of cockle that lives in mud flat areas, is prepared in this
way, by simple marination in coconut milk and sometimes citrus juice; it
is still much loved by Fijian villagers, but is also typical in many island
communities.

Coconut milk or cream, obtained by grating and then squeezing the
nut's flesh, also lends itself to a variety of cooked dishes. Meats, fish, vegetables, and fruits can all be prepared in this way. Some are cooked, while
others are simply marinated in what is a simple sauce that adds richness
and flavor, creaminess and acid sharpness: perfect flavor counterparts.
Various stages of maturity produce different textures and consistencies in
the milk and flesh, which gradually becomes more brittle, and its moisture
content more fat-rich. Western recipes for dishes using coconut cream
will normally specify the canned product (since fresh coconuts are hard
to come by, there can be little variation in the outcome). In the islands,
however, many variations in flavor, consistency, and richness exist, and
great knowledge and understanding of how best to utilize the coconut
products in a dish were once widely held. These days, canned products
are also used by islanders and the older ways are fast becoming another
forgotten aspect of island life.

A species of screw pine, of which over 20 common varieties exist in
Oceania, pandanus (*Pandanus tectorius*) is as important as the coconut
in some island groups, such as in Tokelau, and especially on atolls where

Selling fruit from the back of a truck in Rarotonga.

almost all parts of the pandanus are used for something. As food, it is
mainly the fruit that is consumed, although the starchy core of its aerial
roots can be eaten in times of hardship. Spread very widely throughout the
Pacific, pandanus fruit was recommended to Australian servicemen and
women on active duty in the Southeast Asian region during the World
War II because, at that time, it was most frequently found in coastal areas
that gave easy access to military personnel. Trees bear fruit, the segments
of which are known as *fala* in Tokelauan, and which are made up of hundreds of small ovoid containers, each surrounding a seed suspended in
an oily, wine-like juice. *Fala*, or *penu* (the name given to the fruit's pulp
when removed) is eaten as a snack by all ages in the Tokelau Islands. The
seeds can be sucked and also eaten (but usually only as an emergency
food). The crushed or sliced pulp is used to make a variety of dishes: *fala
tukituki*, a cooked puree; *lolo fala*, a cooked pudding made with starch and
coconut cream; and *fala fakapita*, which is made by wrapping the fruit in
leaves, cooking, and then sun-drying, which preserves it. The stalks and
fruit receptacles are fed to pigs. Pandanus is also a valuable source of fiber
for making sails, and its wood is used for making homes. The leaves are

Woman selling cockles, in piles, at Suva market.

used medicinally, as well as for weaving mats, stuffing pillows, and serving as cigarette papers.[8]

Pandanus fruit is a good source of micronutrients. A campaign in Micronesia, where pandanus is an important crop, is presently being run to encourage islanders to eat its fruit to help protect against vitamin A deficiency, night blindness, diabetes, heart disease, and certain cancers. Pandanus fruits are also now known to contain valuable amounts of beta-carotene, which is thought to be the most important of the provitamin A carotenoids; the deeper the orange color, the more nutritious the fruit.

The shiny green leaves of the ti plant (*Cordyline fruticosa*; *auti* in Tahiti, *ki* in Hawaii) are used throughout Oceania to wrap foods for cooking. Its tuber is rich in carbohydrates and was traditionally prized by Polynesians who baked it, like other root vegetables, in a pit oven (*umu*). The result was a sweet, candy-like confection. Europeans also fermented beer from the root and later distilled a liquor from the root called *'okolehau*. Several varieties of ti plant, known as Cabbage Tree (the native variety is *Cordyline australias*), were also a traditional food of the Maori, who prized the flesh of the trunk, steaming it whole in the hangi (*umu*).

Other important regionally produced foods include fruits (Polynesian terms are given): pineapple (*ara*), mango (*vi*), guava (*tuava*) paw paw (*nita*), spondias (*vi kavakava*, or Tahitian apple), banana (*meika*), and noni fruit, the juice from which is bottled and sold as a health product. Vegetables include beans (*pi*); green leaves (*kai raurau*), including various Fijian varieties of Indian origin like *bele* (*Hibiscus manihot*), which is also grown in Samoa but does not do well on atolls; tomatoes: various gourds: eggplant: and *duruka* (*Saccharum edule*), a seasonal food related to sugarcane. The tender stems are blanched; they are much-loved in Fiji. Some foods have associations that mean they are not liked. Mango, for example, is not liked by Aitutaki Islanders (in the Cook Islands) because it is deemed pig food. This belief is shared by other islanders. Some traditional European tubers, particularly the potato, have also been grown in the islands from as early as the 1950s. Potatoes are grown in PNG, Fiji, Tonga (where they are popular among islanders), and Vanuatu.

Meat

Pigs were introduced into Oceania (PNG) roughly 5,000 years ago, and spread from there as far as Hawaii, the Marquesas and Tuamotu Islands, and Tonga. "Pigs are our hearts" is a traditional Melanesian saying that reflects that people's love of pork, as well as pigs' value within society as a mark of wealth and prestige. In western New Guinea, the Kapauku people express a similar sentiment when they declare that relatives, pigs, shell money, and sweet potatoes are all they care about in their life. Of great value as a food, pigs are also synonymous with wealth, particularly in communities that still operate according to their traditions of husbandry and food provision, clan organization, and dowry payments. Naturally, the consumption of such a highly valued animal is a socially symbolic act full of potential in such communities. Pigs are therefore an important part of ritual celebrations as food, and sharing pig meat reinforces social bonds and relationships. Owning or offering pigs or pork can also serve to maintain political power. In different communities, on the other hand, the pig may only be summarily recognized as symbolic of culture, family ties, and a way of life. As islander communities continue to adapt to cultural influences from elsewhere, the practice raising, keeping, slaughtering, and consuming the pig has waned as the money economy has allowed islanders to become consumers rather than producers. Having lost some of its literal importance in the economy of the household, the symbolic centrality of the pig, like that of the starchy staples, remains strong.

Leafy greens at a Fiji supermarket.

Chickens, brought from Asia into Polynesia, are also now thought to have been introduced into South America by way of Polynesia, attesting to a long history of use in the Pacific region. Locals in many communities today prefer the plumper, tender imported chickens to the stringy examples that can be seen in most rural areas in the islands. In modern day Rarotonga, locals mostly buy cheap, low-grade chicken pieces from the supermarket, imported from major U.S. or New Zealand suppliers like Tyson and Tegel. Chicken is a popular and versatile meat, used as elsewhere in numerous dishes, like curries, barbecue, and stir-fries, all common styles in the Pacific Islands, Australia, and New Zealand, as in other parts of the world. Eggs are also imported and are consumed in far greater numbers compared to locally produced eggs. Battery-style production exists, but in some cases, like on Rarotonga, it has been a recent development. In Fiji, the Crest Company kills 26,000–27,000 chickens a day, and sets smallholders up with breeding pens, chickens, and feed. When the chickens are ready for slaughter, they are sold back to Crest at a profit for the producer. Crest does not buy chickens from those who are not in this system; it effectively has a monopoly on the commercial production of chicken in Fiji.

In Tonga, imported meat in the form of lamb flaps from New Zealand, a very fatty low-grade cut from the belly of the animal, have proved very popular since they were introduced, especially when curried in the traditional way. Currying has become a part of the cuisine in Tonga and Samoa. This type of hybridizing is an example of transculturalism, whereby a dish is created using lamb, a food unknown to the islands before colonization, and curry powder or paste, a product of Indian origin that came into the Pacific region during colonization.[9] Both foods come together to produce a new Polynesian dish. Thus, curried flaps are traditional in Tonga even though they derive from elsewhere. The people of Tonga have made them their own. Recently, lamb flaps have been banned due to the increasing high incidence of obesity and, consequently, of heart disease and diabetes (Type II) in that country. The health issue is complex, since it is not only taste or habit that dictates a preference for frequent consumption of these high-fat imported foods. Healthier low-fat protein foods like fish can now cost between 15 percent and 50 percent more than mutton flaps and imported chicken, the latter also being more convenient to purchase.

Changes of diet related to meat consumption have been striking over recent years. In 1999, the average regional daily per capita calorie intake in the form of meat was a little under a third of the total. Traditionally, something in the order of a tenth of the intake would have been from meat. Fiji, a country of some 950,000 people (with over 400,000 tourists visiting annually), presently imports around 12,125 tons of meat and meat products a year. While representing only about an ounce per day per head of population, this figure is significantly boosted, in particular, by the substantial amount of chicken that Fiji also produces for domestic consumption. In contrast, atoll island groups live exclusively in village-based communities rather than in towns or larger urban areas, and generally face a different set of constraints. The Republic of Kiribati (consisting of 33 atolls that include the Line Islands and the Phoenix Islands) is home to 85,000 people, less than a tenth of Fiji's population, who depend more on aid and imports than their regional neighbors (like the more self-sufficient Fiji). Imports come mainly from the United States, Europe, and Japan, whereas Fiji imports substantial quantities of meat, vegetables, rice and flour (130,000 tons per year) from Australasia. The Republic annually imports over 4,400 tons of sugar (that's over 4 oz. of sugar a day for everyone), 3,850 tons of wheat flour, 1,650 each of meat products and polished rice, 440 tons of nonalcoholic beverages, and 33 of tea. The widespread daily consumption by islanders of bread and sweetened tea, to which the statistics for Kiribati attest, is somewhat typical of the region-wide, long-term shift from home-grown staples to imported convenience products.

While sweet tea and bread, either with or without butter or margarine, must now be considered as a regional staple, other regional differences in consumption, make it difficult to generalize overall about changes to diet among Pacific Islanders. In the Federated States of Micronesia (FSM) 120,000 people annually consume 5,511 tons of chicken meat and over 7,100 tons of rice, 1,600 tons of beef and pork products, over 2,200 tons of nonalcoholic beverages, 4,400 of wheat flour and 2,700 of refined sugar, but tourism plays a lesser role in consumption than it does in Fiji. The 100,000 people who inhabit the Royal Kingdom of Tonga consume over 5,500 tons (or roughly 5 oz per day) of imported chicken, lamb, and mutton, but significantly lower levels of beef and veal than in the FSM. Tongans supplement their calorie intake with excellent supplies of seafood, and they also love home-grown suckling pig, in particular, which is enjoyed at the numerous celebratory feasts held throughout the year. Lifestyle must therefore be taken into account, as it can reflect total daily calorie intake of products like meat. Ice cream, pastry, soft drink, confectionery, dairy products, and breakfast cereal also appear to be very popular choices in Tonga, but again the statistics differ from country to country.[10]

Fish and Seafood

Various forms of seafood supplement the diet of Pacific and Oceanic peoples. Seaweeds, mollusks like paua (*Haliotis iris*), pipi (*Paphies australe*), *tuatua* (*Amphidesma subtriangulatum*), toheroa, mussel, oyster (Maori: *tio para*), limpet, giant clam, conch, periwinkle or "cats eye"; sea urchins (*kina*), crabs, crayfish, turtle, various reef and deep water fish, and eel are among an extensive range of choices. Fishing and fish have formed a part of the mythology and technology of island peoples for centuries. Islanders have invented hundreds if not thousands of techniques and devices for catching or procuring the bounty of the ocean. In the Tuamotu Islands, fishermen still dive with traditional funnel-shaped nets to snare fish, which can be flown fresh to Tahitian restaurants the same day, while elsewhere the modern-day fishing boat does the same job in the waters round islands supporting their own restaurant culture. Tuna (the most numerous being skipjack tuna, *Katsuwonus pelamis*; but also yellowfin tuna, *Thunnus albacares*; bigeye tuna, *Thunnus obesus*; and albacore tuna, *Thunnus alalunga*), *wahou* (*Acanthocybium solandri*), dolphinfish, snapper, and a variety of smaller reef fish supplement local and tourist diets alike. Fresh fish is a major food in the island restaurant and resort catering sector. Sea-food salads, grilled fish steaks, and Tahitian raw fish salad are all standard dishes in the islands that make the most of the fresh produce available. Ten to fifteen percent of fish caught off the Hawaiian Islands is consumed locally, and Hawaiians are among the most discriminating seafood con-sumers in the United States. Varieties of fish like swordfish, caught in the waters around the Hawaiian Islands, are also exported to mainland U.S. destinations, where they are highly sought after by restaurateurs and consumers alike. Hawaii also exports high-grade tuna to Japan, as do the Cook Islands and other Pacific island nations. Nine thousand tons of bigeye tuna were fished from the Pacific by the United States in 2007, with a large amount destined for retail as fresh fish (for cooking or sushi). Fifty-six thousand tons of skipjack tuna is also taken, much of which was once destined for canning, but now has increased value as a fresh product, partly because of the international influence of Japanese cuisine (sushi). Fresh marinated raw fish remains an island treat for visitors and locals.

U.S. territories in the Pacific, including Guam, do not have the same scale of market for fish as Hawaii, which exports a substantial tonnage to the massive $70 billion a year U.S. consumer market for seafood. Tuna fisheries extends over much of the Pacific, and an international treaty in operation presently extends fishing rights to the United States in zones around Australia, FSM, Palau, PNG, the Marshall Islands, Fiji, Tonga, Kiribati, Samoa, the Solomon Islands, Vanuatu, Nauru, New Zealand, Niue, the Cook Islands and Tuvalu.

An excellent source of protein for islanders, fish was also tradition-ally dried fish; the drying process concentrates its protein content. Both canned fish and shellfish also have a high component of protein, com-parable to meat and eggs. Canned fish (often sourced from outside the Pacific) has assumed the role of a staple in modern island life.

IMPORTED STAPLES

Wheat flour (and products made from it, like bread and biscuits), other grains, rice, noodles (the name islanders give to pasta as well as Asian noodles), and sugar are the main imported sources of carbohydrate, and account for a growing proportion of average calorie intake in the Pacific islands. The uptake of bread as a staple has been ongoing. For instance, in the Kingdom of Tonga, the first bakery opened during the 1970s, and bread was available in the capital city, Nuku'Alofa. Demand was slight, and only a single sack of imported flour was used per day. Over the last three decades, demand has grown exponentially. Bread symbolized mod-ern, Western food, a point underlined by advertising campaigns. Better roads across the island of Tongatapu has also made access to the capital much easier, further facilitating the buying of bread. Villagers have also entered the cash economy in order to buy bread; as a result, many young people come into the town looking for work. Thus, bread is a factor in the changing economy of the islands, and not merely a new addition to the diet. Eating bread rather than traditional foods (which carry with them traditional roles and obligations in village life) also means the erosion of traditional social life. Imported flour tends to be of lower quality, to match the modest spending power of local people, so there are nutritional issues as well, making bread typical of the new foods that represent broad social change and are contributing to declining standards of nutrition.

Bread is also imported, supplementing locally baked products, including muffins and other cafe-style baked goods. Cabin biscuits (also called water crackers) are normally large (2-1/2 square inches), square-shaped, unleavened baked biscuits made from flour, salt, and water. They are a perennial favorite among young and old. Without containing any fat, which can spoil in the tropical heat by quickly going rancid, cabin biscuits are often stored for periods in tins without being affected. Premixed baking products are also available, and many islanders are now dependent on such food imports.

Other Imports

Supermarkets in the islands resemble their counterparts elsewhere, differing only in terms of there being a more limited choice. Fresh vegetables, including brown onions, carrots, cabbages, and lettuce, are imported from New Zealand and Australia, and increasingly, China, whereas tomato, eggplant, pumpkin (squash), zucchini, capsicums, and shallot onions, are often locally produced. Biscuits, crisps, snacks, candy, condiments, oils, spices, and confectionery are mostly imported, along with dairy products like butter and cheese, although in some communities (Rarotonga) these are not so popular among islanders. Canned and packaged products like coconut cream and UHT (ultra-heat treated) longlife milk, however, are substituted for fresh ingredients. Local brewing takes place in the islands (Fiji, Samoa, and Rarotonga produce local beers) but bars, as elsewhere, need to cater to the tourist market and tend to carry a range dominated by imported products.

Condiments

Curry powder (a mix of coriander, cumin, turmeric, chili, fenugreek, fennel, cinnamon, allspice, nutmeg, cloves, pepper, and ginger) came

Eggplant at Suva market.

with Indian migrants to the Pacific, while Chinese and Japanese influ-ences can account for the initial introduction of soy. The Japanese had a considerable presence in Micronesia up to and including World War II, and Okinawans sent to work in Hawaii added their taste for shoyu (which is still the name used for soy in Hawaii) to the ethnic mix of cuisines that would come to represent foodways there. Of course, the Chinese used soy extensively in their restaurant cuisine. Both curry powder and soy can be found in any supermarket in Oceania.

Chili is another ubiquitous condiment found in Oceania's kitchens, in-cluding popular forms like Tabasco sauce. Hawaiians make chili pepper water by steeping a puree of peppers in boiling water. Salt, garlic, and vinegar are optional additions. Fijians are also fond of chili and use it to season coconut milk and cream added to baked dishes of fish or meat. Fresh chili seems to be favored over dried.

Spices and condiments have added a certain something to island fare for more than 50 years. In *The Pacific Hostess Cookbook*, published in 1956, the "great hostess" Lamora S. Gary includes her Hawaiian barbecue sauce, which contains ketchup, soy sauce, Worcestershire sauce, Tabasco sauce, mustard, and sugar.[11] Kikkoman, which soy sauce also became known as in Hawaii, became a basic ingredient of the hybrid cuisine that developed there. The Hawaiian Islands' hybrid cuisine made up of ingredients from far and near oddly excluded pineapple, which although grown there in great quantity and marketed to the world with such force that the South American fruit achieved its false reputation as a Pacific food, in Hawaii it only gained a marginal place in local cuisine.

Processed Canned Fish and Meats

Corned beef (sold in a variety of sizes, including gallon-size tins) and various types of canned luncheon meat (Spam) have long been loved by Polynesians, in particular, often being preferred to the more traditional fresh cuts of meat that would have been used in days gone by. The most prevalent hybrid dish in the Pacific is probably *palusami*, baked taro leaf parcels containing corned beef, onion, and coconut cream. But other canned, preserved, pickled, corned, and frozen products (or sometimes a combination of these processes in a single product) have also made inroads into the islander diet. The diversification of such products and the market penetration they can achieve through being relatively cheap and long-lasting have further offset the consumption of fresh meats and fish. Fresh meat such as chicken, beef, pork, and lamb are also imported (the restaurant trade can afford a higher premium on fresh food imports), but the bulk is frozen, coming in a variety of processed products like chicken frankfurters, beef burger patties, and pies. Similarly, frozen fish products range from ready-to-cook fish fingers to crab meat and oysters. Fresh fish is usually available from local suppliers but at a relatively high price.

AUSTRALASIA: MAINSTREAM, ABORIGINAL, AND MAORI FOODS

Food consumption patterns in Australia and New Zealand have changed markedly in recent decades, with many trends still in evidence today that began post-World War II, gathering momentum in the 1950s. As in other parts of the Western world, refrigerator-freezers, canning, dehydration, and ready-made meals all changed the way people ate. More processed foods and, into the 1970s, fast food, made an impact. But so did cars, televisions, and other modern appliances. Television became a focus at mealtimes, while the foods advertised on television also started to change eating habits. In addition, special audience-friendly foods like dips, snacks, and bite-sized foods became popular with new generations of viewers. Such foods were created and marketed (on TV) by large food companies. The kinds of foods eaten were adapted to suit changing lifestyles and situations. Television viewing suited certain foods, as did sitting in the back of the car, or eating away from home, late at night, or at work. More flexibility in terms of where food could be consumed also allowed for greater variety, another of the key changes to affect the Australasian diet. Choices can be deceptive. Supermarkets now stock thousands of product lines, but many of them are very similar in terms of eating quality and price. Dozens of oils, for example, are available, but the differences between them are slight. This is a phenomenon that applies to many everyday products like bread and cheese. In Australia and New Zealand, the public's taste for cheese is fairly unremarkable, diverging little from three standard varieties of cheddar: mild, medium, and sharp (known locally as "tasty"). Other products, like mozzarella, are different more in shape or packaging than taste; while it borrows the Italian nomenclature, it barely resembles its continental counterpart. Some of the variety of piquant, aged, or blue cheeses enjoyed in European countries are imported, while the vast majority of Australian (and NZ) cheese are fairly bland by comparison. In recent years, laws prohibiting the manufacture of cheeses made from unpasteurized milk have eased, and gourmets were jubilant when this also coincided with a ban of several years being lifted on the importation of the famous French sheep's milk blue cheese, Roquefort. Ewe's milk cheese is made in Australasia, as are goat's milk cheeses, which have a larger market.

In recent years various other artisan products have appeared, or reappeared; bread in particular. Many old bakeries around Australia have reemerged as producers of sourdough style breads that use natural ferments, local whole wheat flours (including stone ground), and that typically are baked in a traditional wood-fired oven. Something of a renaissance of bakeries and handcrafted bread-making has taken place.

In the postwar period, major foods, those consumed as part of a main daily meal, remained based on the meat and three vegetables model, with meat taking pride of place. Beef and lamb were traditionally preferred in Australasia. But from the early 1950s, growth in the number of chickens produced led to the dominance of the consumer meat market. Chicken has become the most popular meat eaten on a regular basis. The establishment and growth of the battery chicken farm system has been called the greatest success story of a primary industry in Australia.[12] New Zealand also experienced a shift in consumption of a similar kind. The changeover to chicken is indicative of broader changes at work, including the industrialization of the food industry, but also public attitudes to foods (chicken is perceived by many as being a healthier choice than red meat today). In 1950, Australia was producing about 3 million broiler chickens (for roasting, frying, or grilling). Production increased five-fold in the 1950s, seven-fold in the 1960s, and further doubled in the 1970s. By 1996, almost 330 million chickens were being slaughtered per year.[13] Today, close to 500 million birds are processed. About 4 percent of these are free-range, of which about half are certified organic. The success of chicken as an alternative also has to do with its versatility as an ingredient, and is therefore indicative of broader trends in the food industry in both Australia and New Zealand. Chicken can be sold in pieces, or whole, and is called for as a basis for dishes in almost all cuisines of the world. It is an ingredient used variously in stir-fries, stews, curries, roasts, salads, and terrines. Chicken cooks quickly, and easily, is lean (leaner without the skin), can be eaten cold or hot, and, being tender, is suitable for children through to elderly people. But another aspect of chicken's success relates to the products that are now on offer, which, with the addition of chicken, can become a meal in minutes. Bottled or canned stir-through sauces require minimal cooking time. Chicken remains popular on the basis of its convenience. More and more adjunct products are being marketed that take advantage of chicken's versatility and of the consumer's desire for ease as well as difference. A combination of factors including low production costs, affluence, a greater range of choices, a consumer better-educated about foods and cuisines, the desire for difference, and, to some extent, an awareness about the health implications of food consumption, have reinforced the success of the chicken industry.

The proliferation of a wider range of food products, and particularly, of ready-cooked or quickly prepared meals, reflects the time constraints of contemporary consumers, who now shop more often and with more of a propensity to try different foods and ingredients. The weekly shop of yesteryear has given way to shopping for food as more of a lifestyle option, which implies adventurousness and the willingness to try new flavors. This trend also reflects the longer-term influence of ethnic cuisines, beginning with the postwar influx of migrants; migrants continue to affect public taste, and their contribution has been noticeable. But other factors play a role here as well. Globalization has made many more ingredients available. Increased global travel has further boosted Australasians' desire for new foods and the culinary styles of other cultures. The globalization of information (magazines, television, and Internet) has also affected consumer taste.

Fish and seafood has become increasingly popular, whereas historically neither Australians nor New Zealanders could be called fish eaters by choice. Meat was always the first option, reflecting in part the cultural myth that red meat was the most potent or "masculine" food, as well as the fact that production of beef and lamb was a primary industry. Rising seafood prices have pushed fish into the luxury food bracket for many, although, with the advent of fish farming in the last 30 years, salmon has become a particularly popular choice (and more popular at Christmas than the traditional turkey).

Potatoes were once considered a necessity at mealtimes, but now pasta, couscous, lentils, chickpeas, noodles, rice, bread, or polenta can grace the Australian or New Zealand table. From the late 1960s, ethnic influences saw a diversity of more exotic spices, herbs, and foods of all kinds entering the home kitchen. Gourmet products for the home cook, like duck or other game fowl, are on the wane today as consumers, particularly in a younger demographic, want challenging and new foods but do not necessarily want hands-on products that require skills and knowledge to cook. Making food in a flash has become the culinary ethos, presumably in part because of the influence of television celebrity chef shows. The fact that cookery takes time is often elided in these fast-paced programs.

Major traditional foods of the Aboriginal people included kangaroo and other large game, but also hundreds of other available foods: from *bunya* nuts to witchetty grubs and Murray River cod, the range of foods in the Aborigine's inventory of foods was once immense, the result of a knowledge developed over millennia through the application of foodways adapted to a continent quite different from any other. Today, however, to speak of Aboriginal food culture means describing two cultures: One survives in part as it once did, a few remote communities living at least in part as hunter-gatherers. The other is a partly assimilated culture of Aboriginal people who have taken on a Western lifestyle for better or worse. The damaging influence of Western foods and diets (including, significantly, alcoholic beverages) has made incursions virtually everywhere. More generally, for those Aborigines who have most contact with mainstream Australia, their choice of foods follows the pattern established in the Pacific Islands. The cheapest and not always the best quality foods are the ones consumed. Aborigines tend to be of lower socioeconomic status and this affects not only direct income, but education, informed food choices, and, ultimately, health. Alcohol-related abuse and the continuing decline of food-related Aboriginal health is a problem for many Aboriginal people today, as it is for the governments and agencies that try to help. The real difficulty is, once again, a cultural one. Aboriginal people would have healthier diets if their well-being was enhanced in other ways. Mostly marginalized by white society, and taken up with the struggle to find some stability in life, Aborigines do not necessarily pay particular attention to food and diet.

   The case is somewhat different with the Maori, who recognized opportunities in the culture of the pakeha (New Zealanders of European de-
cent) and assimilated better to the way of life and economy of the West
than did their indigenous neighbors in Australia. Already fiercely competitive among themselves prior to the arrival of Europeans, Maori were
well-versed in the arts of war, unlike Aboriginal people in Australia. With
so much land to cover in search of food, the latter did not develop the
warring style or competitiveness of Maori, who occupied a much smaller
country. Weaponry and fighting were largely developed in New Zealand
because of tribal rivalries that ensued over valuable food-producing land.[14]
Kumara was the most important Maori staple crop, having replaced the
taro that their ancestors enjoyed in the islands. But Maori also adapted to
the Western diet and became bread, lamb, and beef eaters, as well as drinkers of milk and beer. For the Aboriginal Australians, such adaptation was
only partially successful. Marginalized by the encroaching culture of the
Westerners to which they had difficulty adapting, they also incrementally
lost access to the treasure trove of fruits, berries, nuts, seafood, meat, insect
pupae, and all the tasty edible things that the huge continent of Australia
had provided them for millennia. Western-style farming and the raising of
stock forced Aboriginals from their traditional lands, and into towns and
eventually cities, where their dietary choices were often the result of dire
need (see chapter 8). Few Aboriginal foods have ever crossed the cultural
divide. Even kangaroo meat, an export product for human consumption
that is sent to many countries, is less popular in Australia.
   In New Zealand, the crossover of Maori foods into popular diet has been
equally marginal. With the exception of kumara, which is much loved
by most Kiwis, most other Maori foods (and methods of cookery) have
not been appreciated. The distaste for Maori foods has been popularly
expressed, with reference to a favorite food of traditional Maori. Commonly known in New Zealand as sow thistle, puha (*Sonchus oleraceus*;
Maori: *puha rauriki* and *puha porirua*, both smooth-leafed, and *Sonchus
asper*; Maori *puha tio tio*, the less favored prickly variety) once grew wild
in many parts of New Zealand, but now seems to be dying off, in part
due to more vigorous plants taking over habitat. Puha has been regarded
by mainstream New Zealand society as perhaps the quintessential Maori
food. There was also the popular ditty, "Puha and Pakeha," a commercially successful song in New Zealand recorded by Rod Derrett (c. 1965),
the lyrics of which make less than politically correct references to cannibalism (widely practiced by Maori and other Pacific Islanders before and
after European contact). Puha was also regarded as a weed by European
settlers and their descendants, and never adopted as a food. This only

added to its cultural effectiveness as an icon of Maori, in the sense that it served to reinforce the boundary between the apparently civilized newcomers and hostile natives.

Not many pakeha (white) New Zealanders would have ever tried puha, but today, like other local foods, it is attracting renewed gastronomic interest. Typically, puha is cooked simply, or used in a simple dish. Maori like it braised with pork bones (smoked hocks or ribs), for example, but a traditional dish that has some similarity to the island dish *palusami* consists of corned beef, puha, onion, vinegar, potatoes, and *kouka* (cabbage tree) hearts, cooked in the style of a braise. (Puha can have a bitter taste on account of the milky sap contained in its thick hollow stems, but washing it helps remove this. Any flowers and the thicker stems are first removed before being cooked.)[15]

Overall, the major food types included in the diet of indigenous and other Australasians have diversified according to global economics, technologies, and cultural influences. While older traditions in indigenous culture—in both Australia and New Zealand—are being explored and to some extent rekindled, and with regard to indigenous foods, rediscovered and commercialized, this has mainly been for the benefit of commercial interests, rather than having any noticeable effect on local consumers' diets. Part of a global trend is the diversification of food products: turning indigenous fruits, nuts, and berries, which can be harvested and processed relatively easily, into sought after boutique products for the gourmet and export markets. The diet of Aborigines and Maori have been mostly unaffected by the recent interest in "bush food." More choices and ingredients are available, but the exercise of choice does depend on income and this is where differences can be identified. Aboriginal, Maori, and islander populations of Australasia tend to belong to a lower socioeconomic group, and therefore their food choices are often disadvantaged.

At the same time, food culture in the form of advice and recipes (magazines and other media), as well as ingredients, is proliferating. Non-food publications like lifestyle, home, and even car culture magazines, now feature food pages, while small grocery sections have also become a normal part of gas station services. Information about food, the marketing of food culture as lifestyle, and an increasing amount of food products and eating-related services (restaurants, but also many add-on food and drink dispensing franchises or operations associated with other businesses) are all raising the profile of food and eating as a part of life. Whether this overexposure will change food consumption habits for the better is questionable, while much of the information available is very upbeat about enjoying one's food and consuming a greater range of foods and drinks.

NOTES

1. Nancy Pollock, "Food Classification in Three Pacific Societies: Fiji, Hawaii and Tahiti," *Ethnology* 25, no. 2 (1986): 108.

2. Morrison, John, Paul Geraghty and Linda Crowl, eds., *Land Use and Agriculture*. Science of Pacific Island Peoples (Suva: University of the South Pacific, 1994), 19.

3. Adapted from *Taro*, South Pacific Foods Leaflet, no. 1, rev. 1992.

4. See *Yam*, South Pacific Foods Leaflet, no. 14, 1990.

5. See Diane Ragone, "Breadfruit Storage and Preparation in the Pacific Islands," in *Vegeculture in Eastern Asia and Oceania*, ed. Shuji Yoshida and Peter J. Mathews (Osaka: Japan Center for Area Studies, 2002), 217–232.

6. Susan Parkinson, *Cooking the South Pacific Way: A Professional Guide to Fiji Produce* (Suva: Tourism Council of the South Pacific, 1989).

7. Gwen Skinner, *The Cuisine of the South Pacific* (London: Hodder and Stoughton, 1983), 60.

8. W. Arthur Whistler, "Ethnobotany of Tokelau: The Plants, their Tokelau Names, and their Uses," *Economic Botany* 42, no. 2 (1988): 158–59.

9. Nancy Pollock, " 'Good Food' in Pacific Societies: Transculturation and Selection" (paper presented at the History, Health and Hybridity symposium, Dunedin, NZ, 2005).

10. Estimates based on FAO statistics, http://www.fao.org/es/ess/toptrade/ trade.asp?disp=countrybysharetop (accessed December, 12, 2008).

11. Lamora Sauvinet Gary, *The Pacific Hostess Cookbook* (New York: Coward-McCann, 1956).

12. Jane Dixon, *The Changing Chicken: Chooks, Cooks and Culinary Culture*. (Sydney: University of New South Wales Press, 2002), 82.

13. Dixon, 83.

14. Se, Jared M. Diamond, *Guns, Germs, and Steel: The Fates of Human Societies* (New York: W. W. Norton, 2005).

15. Gwen Skinner, *Simply Living: A Gatherer's Guide to New Zealand's Fields, Forests and Shores* (Wellington, NZ: Reed, 1981).

3

Cooking

Pacific Island cooking is unique in many ways. The ingredients themselves and combinations of foods found in Pacific Island cuisine are both
distinctive to the region, but it is the cooking techniques and technologies employed for cooking (and preserving) that are truly distinctive.
Cooking and processing technologies appear in a number of variant
forms that reflect local adaptations to the particular conditions of the
island environment and ecology, different localized tastes, and variability
in the supply of certain foods. Underground cooking, raw preparation,
fermenting, drying, and smoking foods are the principal culinary methods employed. Although some of these practices are found in other parts
of the world, Pacific Islanders developed techniques (like fermentation)
that were specific to their region. Over time, of course, other methods
of cooking and processing have been adopted, mostly from Western cultures. Modern fuels—in the early days, paraffin and kerosene, then later
electricity, fuel oil and natural gas—together with Western-style stoves,
refrigerators, and, finally, microwave ovens, have also had a great impact
on both domestic and commercial cookery in the islands. Appliances like
toasters, food processors, blenders, and mixers have also made a difference, particularly in the larger towns and cities. In country areas, fire is
still used as a daily means of cooking, and electricity, where it is available, is supplied by virtue of a mobile generator. Older methods of cooking also survive in remote areas, the countryside, and on outlying islands
and atolls, but in the more urban areas, traditional cookery (like using

the underground oven) mostly occurs out of custom, while new styles of cooking proliferate as they have in other parts of the world.

DECLINE OF POT CULTURE

Although today and since the time of early contact, pots have been sought after and used by islanders for the purposes of everyday cooking, traditional island cookery evolved in such a way as to render pots inessential.[1] Pots were certainly taken into the Pacific during the migrations, but always remained more popular in Melanesia than in Micronesia and Polynesia, where their use eventually died out. Various clay cookery and storage vessels have been found (famously, those made by the Lapita people, who date from around 3000 BCE), although none of the fragments found so far prove conclusively that pots were used for cooking. The nature of any pot cooking that may have taken place remains undetermined, but, as the diet of islanders developed on the basis of the staple consumption of root crops and breadfruit, it was the *umu* (underground oven) that assumed a central role as the most favored form of culinary technology. There are several probable reasons for the decline of pot culture that also serve to explain the popularity of the *umu*. Pots need to be made from clay and fired; clearly, this was not an option on many of the coral islands, in particular. The farther away from the Western Pacific, the more difficult it would have been to secure a consistent supply of pots from mainland Asian or East Oceanic sources. Thus, pots were difficult or impossible to make and procure in many island environments. The *umu*, however, was eminently suited to island conditions. It only required coconut or banana leaves for containers, could literally cook for hundreds at a time, and required minimal fuel (per head), the supply of which, while certainly finite on smaller islands and atolls, could still be managed fairly economically because, once heated by hot rocks, the *umu* cooked for as long as the food remained buried; that is, long after the fire had died out. The *umu* also provided long, slow cooking that, in terms of taste, suited the staple foods of taro, sweet potato, yam, and breadfruit. A further advantage of this method was that the toxicity of uncooked taro and yams was dispelled by *umu* cooking. Additionally, unlike conventional pot cooking, the *umu* did not require freshwater (although seawater was used to moisten and season foods), which, given the drier climate of many islands, made it a better adapted cooking technology than the fire and pot. Finally, the *umu* triumphed because, in all probability, it produced specific flavors and textures that proved to be most desirable. Unlike pot boiling, which leaches flavor (and nutrients) out into the liquid in which the foods are cooked, *umu* foods have concentrated flavors, emerging perfectly soft but without any reduction of natural taste.

While the argument from the point of view of taste cannot be easily substantiated from any anthropological standpoint, there is ample evidence that even though Pacific Island food is often thought to be bland by Westerners, flavor and texture were very important in traditional islander cuisine, which encompasses a huge variety of tastes, cookery techniques, and methods. The basic format of central starch supplemented by various condiments (including meat, fish, and green vegetables) is thought to have been a translocated gastronomic format originating in ancient China. Whereas the Chinese favored the liberal use of spices in some of its regional cuisines, in the Pacific, the lack of spice was made up for with the concentration of natural flavors with a seasoning of salt, as well as dried, or fermented foods.

There are some other likely reasons as to why the *umu* dominated over pots that further explain its popularity. Rice, a staple of the early migrants, was brought into the Pacific and would normally have been cooked in a pot. Indeed, rice was grown in Micronesia, and presumably cooked in pots, at least until the time of Magellan (today, rice is still grown on some islands, principally Fiji). On the whole, however, rice culture failed to emerge as regionally dominant because its production was not well-suited to island environments (climate, ecology, and soil). The success of other starchy staples—breadfruit, yam, and taro—only added to the collapse of both rice and pot cultures. And, seemingly sealing the fate of rice in the Pacific was the fact that it became overcooked in the *umu*. Thus, to some extent, perhaps it was another taste preference that determined the course of culinary history in the Pacific.

There are several other possible minor causes that contributed to the demise of pot culture. Principle among these is that using pots for storage, normally an advantage, was not taken up by islanders because there was a need to hide food from enemies during hostilities between island neighbors. Easily transportable (but also breakable) pots were hard to conceal or secure, particularly when the built environment of the islands was relatively insubstantial. The storage of food was achieved by other means, notably underground, a requirement of the fermentation process used to preserve taro, breadfruit, and plantain for more than a month at a time. In preparing foods for fermentation and for the *umu*, strong wooden vessels were adopted for the pounding of the various pastes, a purpose also unsuitable for ceramic pots. Therefore, for a number of interrelated reasons, pots became largely impractical in the island context. In Polynesia, the inhabitants of Samoa and Tonga were among the last to give up pottery making, sometime in the Christian era.[2]

Some of these causes must be put in context because, over a long period of time, not all technical advantages will necessarily be realized or instrumentalized; as Pacific food culture developed, so did the taste, and not merely the technology, of islanders. Taste has arguably played a big role in shaping the types of technology used in the islands, rather than technology necessarily shaping taste. Thus, while sensible reasons can be given for the demise of pot culture on the basis of social (security) and technological (manufacture) advantage, as cooking continued to be developed in the islands, choices were likely also made on the basis of taste preferences.

FIRE: THE FIRST COOKING TECHNOLOGY

Although *umu* culture assumed dominance as the major culinary technology, indispensable to the production of grand feasts, it was entirely reliant on the technology of fire. Foods to be cooked in the everyday context required the fire, which became both an important tool and symbol. As with most, if not all, customary food-related activities of Pacific Island cultures, importance was placed not only on the practical, but also on the symbolic meanings associated with the preparation and use of fire. These were often, as with many island practices, expressed in terms of social relationships. Eating food cooked over a fire fuelled by wood collected by a villager's maternal uncle was tabu among some Fijians, for example.[3] Many such rules applied, and could relate as much to familial relationships as to the community. In village life, fire was generally thought to drive away evil spirits or predators.

Using coconut husks, dry leaves, and wood (sometimes hard wood), fires were made in Fiji inside the thatched village huts. This had practical advantages because the smoke from the fire helped to harden and preserve the thatched roof of the hut, and also kept mosquitoes away. Similar huts, with conical roofs to allow for the escape of smoke, were built by the Kanaka people of New Caledonia. Fires were in part kept alight to show that the household was being well cared for. Thus, it is embarrassing to be told (in Fiji) that *sa moce e matadravu na koli* (the dog is sleeping in the fireplace), because this image suggests that one is being neglectful of family and of others in general.[4]

Again, in Fiji, domestic fires for use by a family were traditionally started by friction using two pieces of wood, as they were in other Pacific island villages. Once started, the fire could be kept going for a considerable time, and frequently overnight. Fires and hot coals were employed for smaller, everyday meals, as well as for heating the stones needed for cooking food in the *umu* or in wooden boiling vessels. The flames themselves can cook, as in roasting, but the embers are equally important, depending on the culinary effect required. Various root or starchy crops can be baked directly in the embers, or wrapped in leaves or, in modern times, aluminum foil. Hot embers are a way of slow cooking in a more gentle heat. Whole fish or pieces of meat can also be cooked in this way, although smaller fish can be broiled using a sharpened stick. Improvisation and making do are always a feature of cookery in cultures where the economy of cooking matters. Limited fuel and technology does not allow for waste. Rather, many adaptations are made to make use of the simple methods available; the fire presents perhaps the most versatile option of all. Even when the fire has died, foods can still be baked, for example, in the hot ashes.

The decline in the use of fire in modern times reflects the impact of urbanization and, with it, the adoption of successive alternative fuels: paraffin, kerosene, gas, and electric cooking stoves. In the urban areas, fire may have been, as elsewhere, relegated to the barbecue, but traditional fire cookery remains a necessity in village life across the Pacific region.

RAW FOOD

Cooking is commonly taken to mean the transformation of foods by heating, which is the conventional Western understanding; but in its broadest, anthropological, sense "cooking" means to transform or change food in some way before consuming it. In the Pacific, therefore, the term must extend to the preparation of many uncooked foods, which form an important part of the traditional diet. Most traditional island foods were locally grown or procured and, in the tropical heat, to consume such foods before spoilage occurred was naturally an imperative. Once fish are killed, plants uprooted, or leaves plucked, humidity and heat soon degrade the quality of both raw and cooked foods. This partly explains why food was traditionally eaten on the spot, wherever it was found, or, if immediately available, whenever needed. Thus, to some extent, tropical constraints dictated that food delicacies be eaten raw, that is, absolutely fresh. Long-term adaptation to the environment also tends to elicit the best health outcomes from dietary intake and, certainly, eating fresh food had this advantage in many cases. Fruits, leaves, buds, fish, and other seafood are all enjoyed raw or lightly marinated in island cultures today. This type of snack is often consumed on its own, and never constitutes a meal. Work-

ers in the plantations would often have this type of snack as well. One of
the perennial favorites of Pacific cuisine remains *poisson cru*, or raw fish
salad, a now Westernized version of a simple island dish. This combination of raw fish, citrus juice, and coconut can be enjoyed in many different
variations. This type of preparation should be considered cooking, since
the citrus juice and coconut act on the fish, changing its chemistry in a
way similar to the action of heat. Such raw food is a theme in Pacific cuisine, and many varieties of seafood are prepared in this way.

UMU: EARTH OVENS

Apart from fire and raw food marination, the most common device used
for cooking in the Pacific is the *umu*. Used mainly for feasts and community meals, the *umu* is also used in villages and family life, but making
even one *umu* a day (never more) is not always practical. Fire and other
means of cooking provide for the day-to-day requirements, since the *umu*
needs a lot more effort. In Tonga, the word for *umu* is *ngaua*, which means
"an oven of food." Translated into English, *ngaua* literally means "work."

Various names exist for this generic form of earth oven, or to use the
ancient Proto-Polynesian term, *qumu*. Over the centuries, derivations of
this name and other terms for the earth oven have been coined: *imu* (Hawaii), *mumu* (PNG), *'umu* (Samoa), *lovo* (Fiji), *motu* (Solomon Islands),
koua (Rotuman, a small dependency of Fiji), hangi (NZ Maori), *ahima'a*
or *hima'a* (Tahiti), and *bougna* (New Caledonia). All of these terms describe pit-style ovens used mostly for cooking for larger numbers: whole
villages and communities, but today, also families and extended families
on special occasions. Many examples of earth ovens have been uncovered
by archaeologists, which are generally round in shape and form a basin
in the earth. Evidence of ancient fire-affected rocks and remains of food
(bones, etc.) are also often found. *Umu* can be up to two yards in diam-
eter, but would normally be 4–5 feet across. In the past, a cookhouse,
where cooking preparations were carried out, would also have sheltered
the *umu* in wet weather. Cookhouses consisted of an open-sided struc-
ture with a coconut-leaf thatched roof. In Vanuatu, as elsewhere in the
islands today, root crops, meat, or a *lap-lap* (a type of pudding made from
pounded vegetables—typically cassava, yam, or taro—coconut milk, and
meat, fish, or sometimes the "flying fox" bat, which is then wrapped in
banana leaves and baked) are still cooked in such ovens. But local variations exist. In Tonga, for example, small pigs are roasted over the open
fire (*tunu*) to crisp their skin, rather than being put into the pit as would
be the case with the Maori hangi.

Basket of *umu* food ready for cooking.

In their various, but generically similar forms, *umu* are still regularly made from Hawaii in the north to New Zealand in the south, and from the Society Islands (French Polynesia) to Papua New Guinea. The Maori hangi tends to be deeper than other versions elsewhere; atoll *umu* must rely on coconut husks and any dry tinder available for firing, whereas in PNG there are supplies of good timber. Australian Aborigines also employ underground cooking techniques. In many areas of coastal Australia, historical sites have been excavated where middens containing remains of cooked pipi, cockles, mussels, crabs, abalone, various fish, freshwater crayfish (yabbies), snakes, and lizards have been found. Deeper underground ovens were also used to cook kangaroo or emu. Typically, kangaroo's nostrils are left exposed above the ground, and steam rising from them acts as a gauge of doneness.

The whole community is often involved in *umu* preparation; provisioning food for the *umu*; digging the pit; collecting fuel and suitable stones; gathering leaves with which to wrap the foods; preparing the dishes themselves; and assembling and laying down the *umu*. Hard woods, coconut

Umu meat prepared.

Umu ready to cover (note whole fish plaited in coconut leaves).

Umu banana leaf cover.

husks, and any dry tinder are used for firing an *umu*, which essentially requires that a large hole be dug in the ground in which a fire is laid using timber or other fuel, and which burns with an intense heat. Large stones (preferably hard river stones or volcanic rock) are placed directly in the fire to heat through. Sometimes two pits are dug, one for the fire, the other for the food, followed by the hot stones. While the holes are being dug and the fire laid, the preparations of various foods are being completed, which means either wrapping in banana leaves or securing within woven coconut baskets (larger fish can be encased in this way). As with most Pacific cultures, variations exist. Native flax is used by Maori in New Zealand. The food, once prepared, is brought to the *umu*, where the fire has been exhausted and the pit cleared of ash. The foods are carefully packed into the *umu*, sandwiched, where needed, between more layers of leaves to protect the food from too much smoke, heat, and any contact with the soil. Quantities of soil are put back into the pit, covering the hole completely and sealing in the food parcels. The pit oven is then often covered with more leaves, or today with wet sacks, a tarpaulin, or canvas. After what is normally a few hours, the earth is carefully removed

Burlap sacks cover *umu*.

Umu complete and left to cook.

and the wrapped food is served from its protective sheath of leaves. Meats are considerably more tender when cooked in this manner, with the maximum retention of juices. The slow cooking time and relatively low cooking temperature also benefit the starchy foods: taro, yam, breadfruit, sweet potato, and cassava.

Umu can cater to thousands, as records show. Hundreds of pigs and thousands of kumara (sweet potato) were cooked on occasion in New Zealand Maori hangi and Hawaiian *imu*, another regional variation on the earth oven.[5] Eating, in this context, remains connected to producing and working. Enjoyment of the feast is partly determined by the effort made in its preparation. The cultural meaning of the earth oven and of the terms that designate it suggest more than just an oven. *Umu* are clearly *events*.

Not only regional, but also local variations of the *umu* illustrate how adaptable and versatile this mode of cooking has proved to be. The traditional earth oven of Papua New Guinea, commonly called *mumu*, can take several forms (and names). A *mumu* is made using black river stones and hard wood, of which there is abundant supply and which is preferred for

Umu cooked and sacks off, with just the banana leaves to take off.

Preparing to serve *umu*.

heating purposes. The *mumu* is more popular in the mountainous country where pottery is limited, but locally there are several different kinds:

Rabaul: Where the stones are heated in the pit, banana leaves are conditioned over the heating stones and then used to wrap foods that have been prepared with coconut cream. The wrapped foods are covered by more hot stones; this layer is then covered by banana leaves and jute bags. No soil or sand is used. The temperature can reach 480 degrees Fahrenheit.

Alotau: This is sometimes called dry *mumu*, since no coconut cream is used in the preparation. In this baking process, essentially similar to *Rabaul*, additional heat is maintained on the top layer of stones by the addition of a layer of soil that is designed to compensate for the heat conducting properties normally provided by the coconut cream.

Goroka: Banana leaves are put on top of the stones and the foods are wrapped in separate portions. Earth is also used to complete the covering. Then, water is poured in through a special opening, creating steam inside the *mumu*. Shorter cooking times typify this kind of cooking, and while more earth is needed on top to maintain heat, the temperature does not exceed 212 degrees Fahrenheit.

Mt Hagen: This is mainly used in the Western Highland Province, where a deep conical shape pit is dug and lined with banana leaves before the hot rocks are put in. Food is put in and then hot stones are placed directly on the food. No coconut cream or water is added, and the whole pit is covered over with leaves and the mumu left to bake.

A range of taste differences is implied by these variations in technique and materials.[6] In general, *umu* food has a rich, sometimes smoky flavor, and items taste of themselves insofar as they are not seasoned or mixed with other ingredients before cooking. For Polynesians, the primary use of the earth oven was to cook the starchy root crops and breadfruit, but meats could also be conveniently cooked over long periods without risk of burning or of not being cooked through, as might have been case with grilling. Wrapping the foods with various kinds of leaves also imparted flavors; alternatively, by placing sliced taro next to meat in the *umu*, flavors would also be absorbed.[7]

Regional differences do result in particular preferences, and Polynesians from the Eastern Pacific are not generally fond of the *bougna*, a Frenchified term for a particular type of *umu* found in New Caledonia, but which refers more precisely to the way the foods are prepared for cooking. A mixture of taro, yam, sweet potato, banana, chicken, fish, crab or lobster, and coconut cream is first wrapped in banana leaves and tied with palm fronds, thus forming a large parcel, which is then baked either on hot coals or in a shallow *umu*. Mixing the foods together like this in the style of the native Kanac people (of Melanesian descent) blends the flavors too much according to the taste of their Polynesian neighbors, who prefer wrapping each ingredient separately or at least keeping them apart in their own coconut basket or banana leaf packet.

Modern-day Western equivalents of communal cooking events like the *umu* exist in the form of the clam bake, the barbecue, and Thanksgiving, although the social significance and importance of the *umu*'s role in traditional island food culture has been and remains of crucial social importance, as it provides for cohesion among diasporic Pacific Islander communities throughout the wider region. For migrant Polynesians living in New Zealand, for example, whether from Tonga, Samoa, Tokelau, or the Cook Islands, regular community *umu* form part of each culture's community activities, bridging the gap between place and identity.

DRYING

Several forms of food preservation are used to avoid the kind of spoilage that so easily occurs with ripe fruits (or vegetables), among them sundrying and drying or smoking over a fire or in an earth oven. In Micronesia, *nambo* is the word for dried starchy foods that islanders traditionally processed in order to preserve them over time. *Nambo* has a biscuit-like crispness. Breadfruit, taro, and *oki* (Tahitian chestnut, *Inocarpus fagiferus*) were traditional favorites, but today breadfruit *nambo* is the most common. Making *nambo* is typically a community affair directed by women, and extended families can dry large quantities of breadfruit when in season (twice a year). The fruit is harvested when ripe but firm, and is roasted the next day using an open fire. Up to 100 breadfruit can be are roasted at one time. The skin blackens while, at the same time, the flesh softens within. The fruit can be eaten at this stage, but if it is to be dried, it is peeled and the flesh cut into chunks an inch or so square. Drying is then carried out using an earth oven lined with coral rock, which is thought to enhance the flavor of the *nambo*. The *nambo* is placed to oven dry on racks for a period of about 12 hours. When cooled, *nambo* has a crunchy texture and is stored in leaf-lined baskets, typically above cooking fires. *Nambo* keeps for up to a year and can be redried if needed. A popular snack, it is eaten alone or with nut varieties like *ngali* (*Canarium* species), *alite* (*Terminalia catalpa*) and *cut* (*Barringtonia* species). It is also cooked with coconut milk and eaten with green leafy vegetables.

FERMENTATION

Breadfruit and taro (and to a lesser extent, plantain) were traditionally fermented in underground pits. Breadfruit were cooked, peeled, quartered, and wrapped in *Heliconia* leaves, placed in pits lined with more leaves (of coconut, banana, or breadfruit) and left for a little over a month. In Samoa, this process was known as *lua'i masi* (the actual name for the *masi* pits), *ma* in the Marquesas, *ma'i* in The Cook Islands, and *maratan* in Ponape, although the practice is no longer common anywhere in the Pacific. Much revered, fermented foods became a delicacy associated with feasts and special occasions. In Hawaii, in particular, poi was the name given to a purplish fermented taro paste that was traditionally held in the highest esteem among the chiefs and community at large. Poi is still made, but there has been no regional commercial development of fermentation as a production technique, and the practice is dying out.

Fermentation has been an important traditional form of culinary preparation in the islands for almost as long as the islanders have been there themselves. It was certainly being practiced at the time of first contact with Spanish explorers.[8] Developed as a technique for processing and preserving foods, fermentation of foods in underground caches served a number of purposes, not least of which was to utilize an oversupply of fruit or other crops. Fermentation also makes foods resistant to the microbial spoilage that is commonplace in the tropics. The fermentation (mara) of foods like breadfruit (*madrai ni viti*, "bread of Fiji") also improved the nutritional benefit by enhancing B vitamin levels in particular; over time, the inherent healthiness of the food would have also been recognized and valued. The other advantage of the technique was twofold. Pit fermentation effectively preserved food before the onset of drought and famine and, at the same time, hid it, preventing it from being stolen, consumed, or destroyed by hostile enemies during an attack.

Like most fermentation of food, the making of *madrai* (breadfruit) involves bacteria that, by consuming the starch (essentially sugar), produce by-products, including lactic acid. This process is technically known as acid fermentation. Lactic acid, found in milk, is an important chemical component in the process, and accounts for the fact that *madrai* is often compared by Westerners to a strong, smelly cheese. Other by-products, specifically carbolic and acetic acid, as well as carbon dioxide, add to what is in fact a heterofermentation, as more than one chemical agent is present. It is important to seal the breadfruit parcels well because the carbon dioxide produced under these circumstances helps to exclude oxygen, a gas that will cause agents like butyric acid to build up, giving the *madrai* an unpleasant smell. Fresh breadfruit, which is over 60 percent starch, has an almost neutral pH of 6.7. After a week, the fermentation has a pH of 5; after two weeks, this drops to and remains at 4 (more acidic). Once fermented, the breadfruit, which by this stage has been reduced to a pulp, is pounded into a paste, and this is formed into patties. These are again wrapped with *Heliconia* leaves that have been lined with *pe'epe'e* (Polynesian word for thick coconut cream), and these parcels are baked in an *umu* for two hours. The result is a bread-like pudding with a pungent smell that some say is reminiscent of limburger cheese.[9] The taste for fermented food developed over time, and islanders came to relish the sour, pungent flavor of the fermented paste. Fermented foods could also be added to other freshly cooked foods to give a different dimension or accent of taste.

TECHNIQUES

Wrapping

No earth oven would normally be prepared without the intention of baking staple root vegetables like breadfruit and taro. Before baking in the earth oven, it is standard practice to wrap foods for the *umu* cooking. Which type, or types, of leaves, whether banana, coconut pandanus, or ti, are used for wrapping foods for cooking, depends on location. Banana leaves, when available, double as serving plates. Leaves (banana leaves are large and flat and so provide good coverage and insulation) and coconut fronds are also used to cover the layers of foods once they have been prepared and laid in the *umu*. The leaves protect the food from drying out and also, if desired, keep each type of food separate. In the Cook Islands, coconut palm leaves are stripped from their stem and woven into baskets, which are then filled with vegetables like pumpkin and cabbage, as well as the more traditional foods. Coconut leaves, which are firm, strong, and pliable, can also be plaited around a whole fish, an effective way to protect the fish and keep its form intact. In Tuvalu, in the old days, coconut fronds were also be lit and placed over medium-sized fish resting on a bed of coral pebbles. When cooked, the fish would be washed off in sea water before being eaten.[10]

Parcels of layered taro leaves with a central filling are wrapped in banana leaves and tied before baking, as are poi (pounded taro and coconut puddings), which, in the Hawaiian Islands, also get baked in the underground oven. The wrapped puddings form a solid shape that sets during cooking. Wrapping foods is a vital part of Polynesian and islander cookery in general. Without it, foods would not be protected from the earth that the *umu* is filled with, or from the full force of the steam and smoke that penetrates the foods cooked underground in this way.

Today, wrapping has taken on a modern twist in that the contemporary cook uses aluminum foil instead of banana leaves. The *umu* is also an improvised occasion in today's context, and foil, wire baskets, and metal boxes often replace the customary materials used. Anyone using fire sticks to start the fire would only do so if no other means were available, but matches and lighters are so commonplace as to relegate the older skill to a bygone era. Wrapping vegetables or fish in foil for baking in the embers of a fire or on the barbecue is the logical replacement for leaves, and is standard when using a conventional oven in an urban context.

More broadly conceived, wraps are a generic form that finds representation in many cuisines. The Italians have calzone, the Mexicans have tacos, and the Indians have roti. The latter are a popular favorite in Fiji today, where the influence of Indian cuisine has been profound. Standard fare on most modestly priced Indian restaurant menus are a variety of dishes served with roti, which are segmented using one's fingers and conveniently form a wrap for the other foods. Some skill is required before becoming dexterous in this art of eating with one's hands, but the pleasure of eating foods in this way, shared by island peoples, adds another sensuous dimension to the experience of Pacific cuisine.

Wrapped foods have morphed into many contemporary forms, which also reflects the casualization of dining and public eating. Perhaps this is yet another ironic twist in the history of the islands because, since the

Improvised domestic hearth in rural Fiji.

early missionaries dissuaded native peoples from eating with their hands and promoted the use of knives and forks, the West's codes of conduct have eased to the point where touching one's food and sharing from the same dish or course of dishes now has become perfectly acceptable. As a result, a lot of snacks and other easily consumed foods have proliferated, including innovations like roti wraps, for example.[11] Other contemporary forms of wrapped foods include sushi, which has been a big success in the Pacific region, utilizing, as it does, raw fish. Sushi also makes sense in the islands, because the trend of casual eating (at the beach or on the deck) obviates the need for plates, knives, and forks. Eating with the hands creates an atmosphere of authenticity that is often encouraged at food-related events, and which makes these wrapped foods fit right in.

Stirring

A sharpened stick (koso) was traditionally thrust into the ground and used to husk coconuts. Today, a sharp machete is used to deftly split the nut in two. Tongs are used to handle the hot stones; these are made of a coconut mid-rib or pandanus root. A wide range of wooden bowls are used for liquids (including coconut milk and oil), but also for pounding starchy

foods. Half coconut shells are used for drinking, as ladles, and as containers for some forms of cooked puddings. Woven baskets, strainers, mincers,
stirrers, spreaders, and splitters, all made from wood, fiber, or other natural
material, are also used. The coconut grater is particularly important, and
consists of a head made from metal; before contact with the West, however, this was made from coral, shell, pearl shell, or stone, lashed to a base
of wood. Foods were served on mats (*laulau*), and wooden bowls (*kumete*)
were also used, together with cuplike containers called *ipu*.

Today, in the islands, all the normal techniques for mixing and stirring are the stock-in-trade of household cooks and professional chefs
alike. Food processors and blenders have taken the work out of traditional
methods using simple wooden implements.

Pounding

Many of the root vegetables cooked and eaten by Pacific Islanders are
pounded before being steamed in the form of cakes or pudding. One of
the reasons given for the demise of pottery containers was that sturdier
wooden versions were better-suited to the heavy pounding of cooked taro
and breadfruit, required to make poi and *masi*. Thus, pounding requires
special implements, traditionally made of wood and resembling the standard form of the pestle and mortar. Some of these can be quite large to
accommodate quantities of breadfruit or taro. Pounded pastes of taro or
breadfruit are mixed with coconut cream or milk and cooked again in the
umu. The result gives a unique texture and flavor, and is sometimes called
Polynesian pudding. Today, a masher or a food processor can do the same
job, although with every technique comes a slightly different result.

Other Tools and Preparation Methods

Aside from the *umu*, stone boiling in wooden or shell pots was another
traditional method of cooking. Heated stones were submerged in the wa-
ter-filled vessels, which would quickly bring the water inside to a boil. A
variety of foods could be cooked in this way. Variations on this theme
included the use of coconut shell containers (known as *kao* in Tuvalu),
filled with chunks of fish and seawater, and placed in the fire. When the
fish was cooked, the shell would be broken open and the fish eaten with
fresh, mature coconut meat.[12] In New Zealand, in addition to the available cooking technology of fire, naturally boiling water and steam (boiling pools, blow holes, and steam jets) in many thermally active regions of

the country provided a primary means of cooking; these could all be used for cooking baskets of food.

Other methods in the islands included using sections of bamboo for steaming, baking, and occasionally for boiling. These were stuffed with foods and cooked in the embers. Open fire roasting using skewers was also practiced, and was useful for cooking smaller fish, for example, after first wrapping foods in (breadfruit) leaves. *Faka-fana e tau kai he umu* means to reheat food in the *umu* (Niue Polynesian), and this technique was widely used. Various utensils, pounders, graters, coconut splitters, fire tongs (made from coconut frond), cups, bowls, and platters were traditionally fashioned from wood, various plant fibers, shell, and stone.

COOKING INGREDIENTS

Techniques and technologies have changed substantially over time, and new foods and ingredients have been incorporated that reflect changing tastes. Other factors influencing the rate of change have been the need to economize, shorten cooking times, and make preparation easier and more convenient. One food that represents this shift in attitude is cassava, which is widely consumed in the islands today, and has assumed the role of daily staple even though, in terms of status, it is less highly prized than the taro, yam, and sweet potato. The secret of cassava's success is the fact that it is relatively easy to grow, is ready to harvest after only three months, and is cheap to buy. It is also easy to prepare and cook, and has a very agreeable taste and texture that lends itself to curries and casseroles. It has a slightly coarser texture than taro, yam, or sweet potato, but like them is versatile and filling. While it can be used as one does taro or yam, many different ways of preparing and cooking cassava are now practiced. Cassava can be pureed and turned into dumplings, form the basis of soups, stews, curries, or be baked in cakes once it has been turned into flour. Grated, baked, and sprinkled with sugar it is called *valavalava* in Fiji, or if plain, *falawa*. Also, *bila*, a sort of bread made using cassava, is popular. This involves soaking the cassava root in water for several days before baking in long strips. Fiji has taken to this root crop in no uncertain terms, and it can be seen countrywide at the market and growing in gardens, fields, and household yards. Cassava has effectively replaced the more expensive taro and yam in many dishes, and breadfruit in the traditional pudding called *qalu*, which is now based on a cassava dough made from the mashed, cooked root mixed with a syrup reduction of sugar and coconut cream that has been constantly stirred during its preparation.

The success of cassava exemplifies the sorts of changes that have over-taken island foodways because it represents the triumph of economy over quality, speed over anything that requires more time, and convenience by and large over taste. Cassava is a versatile and enjoyable food, but it also threatens the gastronomic status of other foods, which, because of their higher cost and the effort required to produce them (taro needs tending), have lost popularity. This has a flow-on effect in that the skills needed for the propagation of other plant food crops and the use of these other crop foods in the preparation of dishes is also neglected, then for-gotten, resulting in an end to the significance and cultural meaning of a food. Such things can affect well-being but exactly how and how much is difficult to access. The shift from communalism to individualism brings both benefits and problems. Pacific foodways have gradually shaken off traditional patterns and adopted a wider range of products in the pro-cess. Foods are available without much effort. The downside to this is that self-sufficiency and the practice of traditional styles of cooking at home are now almost things of the past, except for smaller rural villages and outlying islands. Given the susceptibility of the islands to the peaks and troughs of global economics, how local people might cope now that there is a dependence on imports is uncertain. Rising costs of imported foods and fuels show little sign of abating at present, and this puts a lot of pressure on household budgets. The potential for a sensible economics of cooking at home has been compromised to a large extent by the desire for premade and processed foods, which are not always that cheap in terms of nutritional value. Working against the uptake of home cooking is that these alternative imported foods are also perceived as being high-status Western products. It is most often the worst of the West's food prod-ucts (in terms of nutrition and known health consequences) that end up being consumed by islander populations. The demand for low cost draws in the low-grade products, although, in some cases, the prices are not low at all. A 20-piece pack of KFC (including mash, coleslaw, fries, and Pepsi) was advertised for $69.95 (US$40.00) in Fiji in 2008, which, as a proportion of average weekly earnings (managerial staff could expect to earn US$200.00 per week) is significant for one meal (advertised to feed 10–12). Home cookery makes sense economically, but has competition, nonetheless. Products like "Traditional Roast Beef," on sale in Fijian su-permarkets, comes already cooked, preserved, and frozen, ready to heat in the bag, and presumes to elide any difference between homemade and commercially produced. Making matters worse for any future return to the home kitchen is the seemingly inexplicable fact that, as the global financial downturn bites in 2008–09, sales in fast food have actually risen significantly. McDonald's reported an over five percent rise in sales across the United States. This is also probably the case in the Pacific islands, because it is the perception that, in hard times, a treat (like fast food) makes life seem okay, that drives this demand, rather than any real concern for the relative cost of food.

COOKBOOKS

In the West, methods, techniques, and recipes presented in cookery books were originally passed down through generations as an oral tradition. In the islands, too, the young traditionally learned from those who came before them, not only how to cook, but also how to grow, preserve, and care for food. Recipes as such were particularly numerous among Micronesian and Polynesian islanders, and less so among Melanesians, despite a diversity of terrestrial and aerial fauna and flora in the latter region. More pot cooking and comparatively less *umu* cooking was practiced in Melanesia, but Polynesians and Micronesians had more cookery skills and specializations having adopted South America grinding stones and other culinary skills. Overall, this regional difference in knowledge (including recipes) may have had more to do with social obligation and the gendered division of labor than with any environmental factors. Many different sets of rules applied in different island societies, designating who did the cooking. Culinary and gastronomic knowledge developed and accumulated on a foundation of experience, experimentation, observation, and oral tradition, but according to social rules that may or may not have had an effect on how that knowledge was passed on and whether it benefited a broader gastronomic culture or not.

Knowledge of plants, how to process them, and what culinary processes they needed to undergo (for safe and palatable consumption) must initially have proceeded from trial and sometimes fatal error. The only edible part of the *tutu* berry, for example, is the juice. Maori people had a fairly complicated and rigorous technique for removing everything else before the juice was consumed; a process that one can only imagine had proved necessary due to prior fatalities or illness. This kind of knowledge, in the form of a recipe in this case, was typical of the lore that became embedded in food-related practices passed on by demonstration and word of mouth.

Pacific Islanders, of course, possessed language, but not in a written form, and so recipes existed as an oral lore passed down from generation to generation. Naturally, cookbooks were completely unknown in the islands before Europeans arrived. Visitors inevitably brought them to the Pacific, but few among the natives could read or use them. Furthermore, these visitors would not have been able to obtain or reproduce the foods or dishes described in the recipes. The first cookbooks in the islands that made any difference belonged to the missionaries, who had a clear vision for totally changing the cooking and eating practices of the islanders as part of the social program of reform. Early pioneering colonists would also have needed cookbooks because, if they did not possess the skills of cookery, there might not be anyone to call on to help out in the kitchen.

A concise way for knowledge to be transported, the recipe form also serves as an effective means of preserving the home country's food culture and, thus, its social ideology as well. After all, cookbooks represent a form of social regulation, and 19th-century Anglo-Saxon cookery books and guides to household management, in particular, were extremely comprehensive attempts at the total rationalization of the running (and staffing) of the home. They must have had little relevance for colonists or natives in the islands, except insofar as they emphasized the "upstairs-downstairs" mentality of masters and servants. Not surprisingly, islanders were soon to be trained as cooks, and became servants to wealthier colonists and businessmen.

Recipes based on European staples like flour, fat, sugar, and eggs (cakes for example) posed problems, but these items could all be imported, and eggs were available locally. Some blending of island ingredients was possible, so that arrowroot starch could supplement wheat flour, for example, but more often than not it was the islanders who gained a taste for Western-style foods and not the reverse. Educating the natives using cookbooks supplemented a broader program, since in the late 19th and early 20th centuries, dietetic science and nutritional science were already emerging fields that were significantly influencing cookery practice (in the form of cookbooks). The basic diet of carbohydrate, protein, and fat was understood, and conveyed in the cookbooks, as was vitamin theory and rudimentary laws of nutrition.

Above all, however, cookbooks conveyed middle-class European or American taste. Mrs. Thomas Lascelles Iremonger, resident in the Gilbert and Ellice Islands in the early 20th century, wrote one of the early island cookbooks (c. 1910), titled *Our Daily Bread*. It was written with the intent of providing information to natives and colonists alike. Mrs. Iremonger noted that she wrote the book after three months in the region, having known little about cookery beforehand. Her book includes a recipe for roast pig that specifies the use of an oven, and the suckling pig called for is also well cooked (meats are often preferred underdone by Western standards in some parts of the Pacific). The book includes frequent reference to nontraditional, imported foods like potato, rice, milk, butter, sugar, jam, and wheat flour, and there is an introductory note on the baking of bread. While some of the recipes indicate home-grown foods like taro, this is often given as an alternative to potato or rice.[13]

Gold Pudding

2 eggs

3 oz. butter

3 oz. flour

1-1/2 oz. sugar

2 Tbs. honey or jam

1/2 tsp. baking powder

Beat the butter with a fork, add the other ingredients, and mix for 15 minutes. Butter a basin, put the mixture into it, and boil for two hours. Eat with Sweet Sauce for Puddings.

Sweet Sauce for Puddings

1 Tbs. jam

1 Tbs. sugar

1/4 pint water

lime juice

Put this mixture by the fire to boil while the pudding is cooking. When it is ready, pour over the sauce, and add a little lime juice.

Over time, cookbooks gradually incorporated island foods and techniques; two clear traditions emerged in the cookery literature. First, there were books that were designed to educate and provide information for island people; for those who would be required to cook for them; and for others, including colonists and migrants to the islands. The recipes provided in these books and pamphlets tend to give basic instruction for nutritious dishes using a mixture of local and imported products. At best, they establish culinary and gastronomic standards while remaining sensitive to the needs of islanders and non-islanders, who represent different culinary heritages. The books of Susan Parkinson, for example, a New Zealand-born nutritionist and author who has lived in Fiji since the early 1950s, is indicative of this style.[14] The emphasis is on simple, fresh produce prepared in a way that upholds the traditional emphasis of island cuisine: the use of coconut milk, in particular, and the incorporation of island ingredients like taro leaves in traditional preparations like *palusami*.

Techniques like wrapping food in leaves is also adapted to a wider range of ingredients than the traditional cuisine. Health is also a theme strongly emphasized in Parkinson's books. Whereas the habitual islander choice of filling might be based on canned corned meat, Parkinson's suggests a seafood variation. Parkinson is concerned with the changing eating habits of islanders as they adopt Western foods, and how healthy eating can be maintained through the provision of good advice. Her later books include photographs that typically depict simple but attractive dishes and raw ingredients, as an adjunct to detailed recipe instructions.

Other examples in this group are cookbooks that cover history and culture. Among the best of these are Time-Life Books' *Pacific and Southeast Asian Cooking*, written in the early 1970s, and Gwen Skinner's *The Cuisine of the South Pacific*. More recently, Jennifer Brennan's *Tradewinds and Coconuts* provides comprehensive coverage of the main dishes and techniques. All of these examples sensitively evoke the place, people, culture, and food, region by region, while attempting to provide recipes that can be managed by the Western cook.[15] Other important works that concentrate on particular island cultures (and that include numerous recipes) include R. J. May's *Kaikai Aniani: A Guide to Bush Foods, Markets and Culinary Arts of Paua New Guinea* and Rachel Laudan's study of Hawaiian foodways, *The Food of Paradise*.[16] As might be expected, French cookery has certainly had an impact on Pacific cuisine, and this has recently been expressed in an interesting and effective way in a cookbook on the food of New Caledonia (Nouvelle-Calédonie). Based largely on the French techniques and sense of style, the incorporation of Asian ingredients like ginger, soy, fish sauce, lime leaves, and coriander add an exotic influence, one that reflects a sophisticated multicultural expression of Pacific food. The recipes are illustrated with photographs that showcase culinary and cultural style and that express the best of each cultural influence.[17] Reflecting tourism's influence in the region, trendy adaptations of Pacific food have also been represented in two cookbooks recently published in Fiji, *Unforgettable: A Coconut Cookbook* and *Under the Mango Tree . . . The People, the Palate, the Pleasures*, both books being produced in association with the Nadi Bay Resort Hotel in Fiji. Both also represent the lively use of local products, which are incorporated wherever possible in a variety of recipes.[18] There are other recipe books of a more generic kind that cover such subjects as tropical fruits, the best of the latter being *Tropical Fruit Recipes: Rare and Exotic Fruits*, published by the Rare Fruit Council International (1991).

The other generic type of Pacific cookbook has been designed to appeal to the cook who is inspired by an imaginary paradise isle, or is merely attracted by a colorfully presented culinary theme. There are plenty of these books, most of which are not much more than compilations full of clichéd illustrations and, typically, recipes for tropical fruit drinks and cocktails, appetizers (the food of choice for cocktail-sipping party-goers), barbecue foods (including numerous marinades with or without pineapple or paw paw juice, both known for their meat-tenderizing properties), dishes that as if by necessity rather than taste include coconut cream, and an assortment of salads. None of these bears any realistic relation to the real food of the Pacific, except if that is taken to be the food of tourists, who flock to the islands and soak up the casual dining atmosphere that this cuisine represents.

These books are clearly for those who prefer their Pacific island culture in a processed and predigested form. The image of the tropical paradise has been a supremely successful marketing hook for numberless food writers wishing to create island favorites. The culture of the island beach party that has inspired many such books and magazine features has been a long-standing tradition that goes back to before World War II (when Pearl Harbor, Hawaii, was a naval base) and continues to influence the interpretation of Pacific cuisine today as one comprised of cocktail party-cum-barbecue fare accompanied by exotic fruit and alcohol-based drinks. Cookbooks that reflect this leisure culture have also been around since the 1930s. Trader Vic's, one of the original Pacific-themed venues serving food and drink, produced its *Pacific Cookbook* in 1968, and the company continues to publish today with an emphasis on cocktails and snacks.

AUSTRALIA AND NEW ZEALAND

In terms of technology and industry, cooking in Australia and New Zealand historically followed the trends of other modern industrialized nations, including the adoption of innovative home kitchen appliances: modern gas and electric stoves, refrigerators, microwaves, juicers, blenders, and food processors. A strong tradition of domestic cookery inherited from Great Britain also dominated in the 19th and up until the middle of the 20th century. Australian cookbooks were few and far between up until that point, with notable exceptions being some of the earliest examples, including the first Australian cookbook, Edward Abbot's *The English and Australian Cookery Book: Cookery for the Many, as well as for the "Upper Ten Thousand"* (penned anonymously "by an Australian aristologist") and published in London in 1864. This book showed some sensitivity to the Australian scene, including recipes for kangaroo, wombat, and emu, but most cookbooks routinely deferred to

English and also French cookery (books) as the only real setters of culinary and gastronomic standards worth emulating.[19] Even in the immediate postwar period, during which immigrants from war-torn Europe arrived in the thousands, books like *Australian Cookery of Today Illustrated* (c. 1950) were for all intents and purposes British (with deference to French culinary method and terminology), and while the introduction to this book declares that it has been written with the particular problems of the Australian housewife in mind, these apparently relate more to the lack of home help than the need to produce an innovative cuisine suited to Australia's unique environment and climate.[20] Something called Continental cooking also crept in, signaling renewed interest in gastronomic pleasures. Things were about to change on a number of levels, however, as steadily growing affluence and the dawn of the baby boom generation meant that women were back in the home and kitchen as mothers and cooks. The era of supermarkets, cars, freezers, open-plan living, industrially processed food, and hostess dinner parties generated a new popular taste, reflected in more adventurous choices and experimentation in cookery. Cookery was touted by food manufacturers as fun as well as a duty. By the 1960s, haute cuisine cookery set the standard for the professional and home-based amateur connoisseur, driven to an extent by class aspirations. The standard here was still firmly French, but that would change in the 1970s as the effects of migration were felt more widely in gastronomic culture. Ethnic cookery became the new trend as Italian, Greek, then Thai, and numerous other Asian cuisines vied for the public palate in cookbooks and restaurant cuisine.

Thus, cooking at home was increasingly challenged on two fronts in the broader postwar period: by public dining culture, with more and more people eating out more often, and by increasing amounts of convenience foods that required minimal or no cooking skills. A new generation of women was also rejecting the values of their parents and any preordained role of wife, mother, cook, and hostess. More recently, trends suggest that younger and younger people and many more men than before are being inspired to cook, at home and as a profession. Chefs, many more of whom are now women, also attain celebrity status in their own right, adding to the kudos for cookery. As contemporary media further raise awareness, inspire, and attract those who have an interest in food, food culture diversifies its knowledge base. While cookery and food-related programs on television have had an impact here, the availability of more and more products, including specialty items, and the desire for new experiences has also driven demand, along with growing sophistication in marketing, packaging, and customization.

Gastronomically speaking, Australia and New Zealand have grown up in the last 30 years, largely due to the influx of migrant groups, commercialization and improved media, transportation and food manufacturing technologies. Today, Australasia has a multicultural populace and a multicultural cuisine. Particular Australian traditions of cookery have remained strong, including the barbecue, which is ideally suited to the Australian climate and lifestyle, but the broader trend in both countries has been one of diversification and growing sophistication in both cooking and eating cultures.[21]

Australia has had the larger share of Asian immigrants than New Zealand. The Chinese were the first, but today, Thai and Vietnamese cuisines are considered as "Australian" as Foster's lager or meat pie, at least in the larger urban areas. To a lesser extent, this is also true of New Zealand, but there the political and social conservatism has been a stronger influence on the development of multiculturalism. Today, however, ethnic, cosmopolitan, and global trends can be seen to have had a lasting effect on food culture in New Zealand, one which is certain to continue. The colonial past, which is still expressed through mainstream tastes like that for roast lamb and mint sauce (still a national favorite) now compete alongside multicultural influences, including Asian cooking techniques like stir-frying and particular flavors and ingredients like chili, coriander (cilantro), ginger, and lemongrass (Thailand), Vietnamese mint, sweet soy, fish sauce and *blachan* from Indonesia, bok choy, *choy sum*, and Chinese broccoli (China), and star anise and curry spice mixtures (*laksa*) from Malaysia and Singapore. Particularly in rural areas, where there are comparatively fewer migrants, simpler, plainer fare is still standard in both countries, although supermarkets and fast food outlets provide a broader range of food choices, including ethnic variations in product styles.

Regarding the professional kitchen, Australian and New Zealand chefs are esteemed internationally as innovative and inspiring; their overall style is typified by an openness to experiment and a cross-cultural infusion of tastes and techniques, above all reflecting a willingness to incorporate new ingredients and cooking methods. Increasingly, interest in local and regional produce has also been productive in the restaurant sector, with high-profile professional chefs now championing products that are either organic or biodynamic, as well as alternative provisioning like farmers markets, and who wear freshness as a badge of honor. The "clean green" image of Australia and New Zealand has been something that chefs have built on, raising the profile of regional and local produce as they do so. This trend also reflects the consumer's growing level of knowledge and demand for quality. Restaurant cuisine is taken seriously for its inherent qualities, making it less of an adjunct to a social occasion and more the prime centre of attention. Degustation menus, in particular, have become a popular expression of this growing interest, where diners can try up to 15 or more dishes in a succession of tastings with accompanying wines.

Australian Aborigines practice a number of ways in which foods are prepared and cooked, including roasting in the fire and steaming underground (but not traditionally including the use of an oven as such). Meats such as crocodile, snake, kangaroo, emu, fish, crab, and crustaceans are all roasted over coals. Much "bush tucker" is gathered and eaten raw in the form of berries, grubs, or fruits. Since Aboriginal peoples are hunter-gatherers, moving from location to location in search of food and water is a way of life conducive to eating, as in the islands, according to when the food is available and where it is abundant. In much of Australia, where pockets of traditional Aboriginal cultures still exist, these practices continue to be incorporated into daily routines.

In the contemporary world, by contrast, there are numerous social and practical problems confronting remote Aboriginal communities, not least of which is the question of the basic adequacy of their diet, contributed to by Western-style foods that have significantly altered eating patterns and certainly played a role in the poor health standards that have developed. Aboriginal people are already the worst off Australian citizens in relation to life expectancy, and at least some of the discrepancy in the statistics can be accounted for by poor diet, including the consumption of refined and processed foods, as well as drug and alcohol abuse.

Somewhat ironically, in fashionable city eateries in Australia, bush food has gained a certain kudos in recent years: *quangdongs*, ryeberries, bush plums and tomatoes, bush basil, lemon myrtle, and many other mostly indigenous species of plant have enjoyed new culinary status as gourmets and chefs alike hunt down these products to add a special something to their latest creations. In New Zealand, the trend is similar, with many native plants known to the Maori turning up on elite restaurant dining tables. While a small number of restaurants have been dedicated to the advance of bush food, focusing sometimes exclusively on native products, this trend has been of minor commercial and cultural significance. The Australian public is conservative by nature, and even something like kangaroo meat, which is widely sold, and served in restaurants, is by no means a national favorite. Bush food appears to be more of a fad than a movement of lasting importance. Nonetheless, many people, not merely chefs, have become better-educated about bush foods (and their health properties), and access to them has been facilitated through advances in production, marketing, and retailing. Indigenous communities have also benefited in some cases from the sale of foods from their traditional lands, while most of the interest taken in these essentially boutique items comes from elsewhere in the world.

Whereas in countries with long-lasting culinary heritages, such as China, France, or Italy, the influence of other culinary cultures is muted, in Great Britain, Australasia, and to an extent the United States, a much greater variety of dishes representative of cuisines from other nations is available. This can be explained partly by the fact that, when it comes to food, increasing numbers of consumers appear less tied to tradition; this is reflected in their wide-ranging food choices. Moreover, without the strong social bonds that food culture reinforces in traditional societies like those of the Pacific Islands, the absence of such food-based culture leaves consumers somewhat freer to choose according to whim, fashion, or personal preference, rather than conforming to the demands of the group.

The presence of a varied islander and Maori culture in New Zealand makes its food culture visible as well as edible, and therefore adds to the sense in which it actively contributes to both the symbolic and material constitution of community identity. Typically, in New Zealand, this might take the form of a hangi, but Maori food culture is increasingly gaining a profile through mediums like the Internet. Numerous festivals and a general revival of interest in Maori cookery have taken place. Whether this is a mainstream trend is doubtful. White New Zealand has historically taken little interest in Maori food. Ingredients such as mutton birds (the still flightless young of the sooty shearwater), various shellfish that bear Polynesian names like pipi, *tua tua*, and toheroa (*Amphidesma ventricosum*), all being clams, and *kina* (sea urchin) are vernacular terms familiar to most New Zealanders; yet, only the clams have attained wide popularity.

The hangi style of earth oven cooking has been through phases of decline and rebirth that have followed those of Maori culture itself. In New Zealand's largest city, Auckland, home to more Polynesian people than any other urban area inside or outside Polynesia, enterprising businesses have sought to capitalize on the blending of tradition and convenience. The hangi always involves work and hours of preparation, but the "eco-hangi," an above ground oven made from a converted beer keg, is gas-fired, and can be bought on the Internet.[22]

NOTES

1. Helen M. Leach, "Cooking without Pots: Aspects of Prehistoric and Traditional Polynesian Cooking," *New Zealand Journal of Archaeology* 4 (1984).

2. Leach, 48.

3. Asesela Ravuvu, *Vaka I Taukei: The Fijian Way of Life* (Suva: University of the South Pacific, 1983), 24.

4. Ravuvu, 22.

5. On Maori hangi see David Burton, *Two Hundred Years of New Zealand Food and Cookery* (Wellington, NZ: Reed, 1982), 1–3; Gwen Skinner, *The Cuisine of the South Pacific* (London: Hodder and Stoughton, 1983), 74–75. Also see How to make a Hawaiian imu, http://hawaiiankava.com/imu/imu%20how%20to,%20p7.htm.

6. P. A. Sopade, "Mumu: A Traditional Method of Slow Cooking in Papua New Guinea," *Boiling Point* 38(April 1997): 34–35.

7. Leach, 53.

8. D. E. Yen, "Indigenous Food Processing in Oceania," in *Gastronomy: The Anthropology of Food and Food Habits*, ed. Margaret L. Arnott (The Hague: Mouton and Co., 1975).

9. Paul Alan Cox, "Two Samoan Technologies for Breadfruit and Banana Preservation," *Economic Botany* 34, no. 2 (1980).

10. Gerd Koch, *The Material Culture of Tuvalu* (Suva: Institute of Pacific Studies, 1981), 77.

11. Rob Rickman, Peter Henning, and Glen Craig. *Under the Mango Tree: The People, the Palate, the Pleasures* (Coolangatta, Queensland, 2005), 41.

12. Koch, 78.

13. Mrs. Thomas Lascelles Iremonger, *Our Daily Bread and Fifty Recipes in Gilbertese, Ellice and English* (Suva: Government Press, n.d.).

14. Susan Parkinson, Peggy Stacy, and Adrian Mattinson, *Taste of the Pacific* (Auckland, NZ: David Bateman, 1995); Susan Parkinson and Peggy Stacy, *A Taste of the Tropics* (London: Mills and Boon, 1972).

15. Gwen Skinner, *The Cuisine of the South Pacific* (London: Hodder and Stoughton, 1983); Rafael Steinberg, ed., *Pacific and Southeast Asian Cooking*, Foods of the World Series (New York: Time-Life Books, 1970); Jennifer Brennan, *Tradewinds and Coconuts: A Reminiscence and Recipes from the Pacific Islands* (Boston, MA: Periplus Editions, 2000).

16. R. J. May, *Kaikai Aniani: A Guide to Bush Foods, Markets and Culinary Arts of Papua New Guinea* (Bathurst, NSW: Robert Brown & Associates, 1984); Rachel Laudan, *The Food of Paradise: Exploring Hawaii's Culinary Heritage* (Honolulu: University of Hawaii Press, 1996).

17. Mike Hosken, *Cuisine Faim Facile en Nouvelle-Calédonie* (Noumea: Éditions Footprint Pacifique, 2005).

18. Rob Rickman, Peter Henning, and Glen Craig ("Three Loose Coconuts"), *Unforgettable: A Coconut Cookbook* (Tweed Heads, NSW, 2004); Rob Rickman, Peter Henning, and Glen Craig ("Three Loose Coconuts") *Under the Mango Tree: The People, the Palate, the Pleasures* (Coolangatta, Australia, 2005).

19. Another notable early exception was Philip E. Muskett, *The Art of Living in Australia* (London; Melbourne: Eyre and Spottiswoode, c. 1893), which

included 300 Australian cookery recipes and accessory kitchen information by Mrs. H. Wicken.

20. *Australian Cookery of Today Illustrated*. Melbourne: The Sun News-Pictorial, c.1950s.

21. On Australian cookery, see Michael Symons, *The Shared Table: Ideas for Australian Cuisine* (Canberra: AGPS Press, 1993); Michael Symons, *One Continuous Picnic: A Gastronomic History of Australia*, 2nd rev. ed. (Melbourne: Melbourne University Press, 2007).

22. On New Zealand's cooking see David Veart, *First, Catch Your Weka: A Story of New Zealand Cooking* (Auckland, NZ: Auckland University Press, 2008); Tony Simpson, *A Distant Feast: The Origins of New Zealand Cuisine* (Auckland, NZ: Godwit, 1999); David Burton, *Two Hundred Years of New Zealand Food and Cookery* (Wellington, NZ: Reed, 1982); Eco-Hangi, http://www.eco-hangi.co.nz/The%20Eco-Hangi.htm (accessed April 11, 2008).

4

Typical Meals

The average Pacific Islander's daily fare has been substantially altered over the last half century (post-1945), and continues to change in significant ways into the 21st century. The widening influence of the globalized food industry, the transition to a cash-dominant economy, urbanization, ethnic pluralism, food aid, and the changing prestige of foods represent the interconnected forces involved.[1] This has meant that the typical meal of islanders can no longer be defined with reference to a core number of natural foods, cooked simply, and conforming to culinary traditions hundreds of years old. Today, there can no longer be a meal that is considered typical: islanders have embraced variety, and have also changed their lifestyles to the extent that not only are the foods consumed different, but the circumstances of consumption have also changed. Westernization has brought with it linked phenomena: new time pressures, more disposable income, a widening range of imported foods, and more and more opportunities to eat at different times and in different places. Such conditions have eroded traditional foodways simply by virtue of removing the possibility of engaging with them on a daily basis, as was once the norm. Thus, growing staple crops like taro and yam has become a thing of the past in urban areas, but if purchased (in the town or city market), they are also more expensive compared with imported alternatives like rice or pasta. Poorer communities and villages still grow some of their own food and raise animals for consumption, but their typical meals are nonetheless a blend of old and new. Even rural diets, therefore, and the meals that constitute them, are supplemented by bought goods, including white bread, white rice, noodles, flour, sugar, and tea, as well as highly processed products like soft drinks, snack foods, biscuits, confectionery, frozen foods including cured and processed meats, and vegetables, as well as precooked meals, canned and dried foods, condiments and sauces. All of these are standard fare in supermarkets around the world, but are prestigious in much of the Pacific.

Such foods have made a big impression, turning the traditional everyday meal into a bought meal, or convenient and ready-to-eat, in many instances. Ease and convenience, especially in the urban areas, has already won out over taking time, effort, and skill to prepare a meal, while, rather predictably, products trade on the promise of delivering home-style goodness. The New Zealand-based company, Fishers, markets a number of "original family recipe" frozen sausage and meat products, typically found in supermarket freezers, products that actively market tradition using names like "Traditional Frankfurters," "Traditional Smoked Saveloys," and "Traditional Breakfast Sausages."[2] Sausages of various sorts like these are very popular in Fiji and elsewhere in the Pacific. Taste, price, and ease of preparation must account for some of the popularity.

Interestingly, when the modern grazing urbanite is compared with the average Pacific Islander of the past, they seem to have quite a bit in common, at least superficially. Both eat on the run and take food as they find it, or not, as the case may be. Snacking, with less focus on formal meals as such, is a major Western trend, affecting Pacific Island peoples as much as those in other countries. With adequate means, a consumer can find food dispensed around the clock in a range of venues. In the past, self-sufficiency was a way of life in the islands, and part of this involved snacking, because finding things to eat during the day was a normal part of life. But these people had no choice, and there was a natural order to the way meals were taken and what composed them. Much of the food was collected, caught, or otherwise procured directly, and all things being equal there was more vegetable than fish and more fish than meat. The main traditional foods were eaten fresh, cooked, dried, or fermented for the purpose of typical everyday meals. Fresh food was consumed most frequently, and fermented food least often. Today, in outlying islands, islanders still lead this simple way of life based on finding enough to eat. A typical Tokelauan meal may be as simple as fresh slices of coconut and raw fish, washed down with the coconut's liquor, and buds, leaves, grubs, berries, and various fruits can all be savored as the opportunity arises. Cooking, therefore, tends mostly to be for family or communal gatherings. Snacks eaten during the day do not infer the use of the *umu* (underground oven), the whole community eating together, or feasting, and include dried foods, also used in emergencies brought about by food scarcity. As in the city, then, snacks are represented by all the incidental foods that fall outside communal meals, and include items like fruit (for children), leftovers from the previous day's evening meal (taro, coconut, or today, cassava and rice) and perhaps a little meat or fish (tinned, dried, fresh, or cooked). Some of these foods may have been cooked in the *umu*.

Consequently, "meal" is not a word that easily translates into island languages because eating food together is, primarily, a social rather than a culinary or gastronomic event (although these aspects are still important). Primarily, the meal gives expression to social relationships. An islands meal is not defined in a purely material sense as a selection of certain foods presented in a certain way to be consumed at a given time. It is an opportunity to connect to a greater social order and honor one's relationships within it. Meals, therefore, are not seen as separate events that punctuate life, but as part of a continuum of intertwined social activities. To eat well (that is, to consume a lot of food) expresses well-being in a clear and unambiguous fashion: "I am happy because my community is well provisioned; therefore I will eat as much as I can to show respect to the host and because there is an abundance to be shared." Abundance is also the sign of the provenance and blessing of God. Indeed, potlatch (the conscious wasting of food or other material goods), and the presenting of more than was necessary, was a traditional form of acknowledging the overall wealth and power of the community. At the same time, modesty and humility are often expressed in relation to food. In the Tokelau Islands, large and small meals are equally referred to as "a bit" or "a bite." Humility is seen as a great virtue, and this is expressed when talking about food.[3]

Thus, there is a great deal bound up in the politics of meal-taking that has an effect on what gets served as a typical meal. During the day, if tending plantations, fishing, or hunting and gathering, islanders' lunch can involve roasting at-hand root vegetables in a fire or, in Fiji, eating fresh sugarcane. Cooked food can also be prepared and consumed at one time, which makes sense for practical reasons: foods never last long in the tropical heat before becoming unsafe to eat. But leftovers from the night before do well as snacks for the next day.

Before dinner in the evening, elders are typically first summoned from their houses, normally by a young member of the family.[4] Traditionally, meals are taken at dusk, by which time the food is cooked and ready to eat. Sometimes, if ceremonial drinks like kava, *yaqona*, or toddy are being consumed, the meal is held off until the men finish their drinking session.

Diners are seated on the eating mat in a particular order. The father or head of the house sits at the head of the mat and, next to him, the eldest son, then the rest of the younger children. Women are first required to serve and, traditionally, are not permitted to share the food at this stage.

Portion sizes reflect the relative status of the diners; again, chiefs, senior males, but also guests, would normally be offered the best and the most of what is on offer. This is an expression of islander hospitality. Eating everything one is given, however, is not advisable, as leftovers are also an important element. They are offered to others later, and are reminders that diners are thinking of those who have not eaten yet and who will eat later. Everyone is also served in an order that reflects the hierarchy: men first, then children, and women last.[5] Food is presented in communal bowls, on banana leaves, or in or coconut leaf baskets. In modern times, the table has usurped the dinner mat, and glass and plastic receptacles are commonplace, although in villages more traditional forms can still take precedence. Women are customarily required to begin eating only after the others have left the eating area, but today these rules are sometimes relaxed. Nevertheless, the hierarchy that is reinforced at mealtimes is typical of how food practices enforce social rules. After the Christianization of much of the Pacific, grace became obligatory, and is nearly always said by the head of the household before the meal.

Evening meals, especially, always involve the consumption of cooked starchy staples. They need to be cooked in the first instance because taro, yam, and cassava all have a level of toxicity that cooking destroys. Fijians refer to taro as *kakana dina,* or "real food," and like with many other islander people, the staple foods have special significance and are normally consumed first. The Fijian term *i coi* is used to describe foods such as fish, meat, fruit, coconut meat or boiled leafy green vegetables (like *rourou, bele,* and *ota*). The reason behind this classification is partly related to the food production process. The presence of starchy foods traditionally indicated the "strong hands" of those who grew and harvested the food. Food acts in this instance to reinforce the social sense of self-worth. The extent to which fish or meat is included and, if served, how much it is appreciated, depends on the community. Coastal peoples can value meat more highly; conversely, inland peoples appreciate fish as a special food. But the staples are what islanders value most. Without this *kakana dina,* they do not consider that they have eaten to any significant degree, no matter how much is consumed. The staples are simply boiled for an every-day meal, whereas, when steam-baked in the *umu* for a special occasion, their eating qualities are also enhanced.

On one level, the only thing that has changed in terms of typical meals is that one starch has been substituted for another. Cassava (*tavioka*, also manioc) has gradually taken the place of taro, yam, and sweet potato in many everyday dishes. It began to be produced in quantity in relatively recent times (brought to Fiji, for example, by the British in the 1950s), and has proved very popular, partly because of its ease of production, but also its cheapness in the market. It is very easy to cook, requiring a shorter period of steaming or boiling than taro or yam. In Fiji, cassava is the most popular everyday food of the Fijian population, particularly those living in urban areas. It is also easy to prepare. It can be curried in a matter of minutes, a regular choice among the Fijian Indian population, but also a popular substitute elsewhere in the region. ("Curry," a generic word for a normally wet dish made with an assortment of spices mostly of Indian origin, including turmeric, coriander, cumin, chili, and asafetida, has become a firm favorite in the Pacific, as elsewhere around the world.) Taro and yams are substantially more expensive than cassava (about $10 Fijian (US $4.80) per bunch, each containing about six or seven corms, the technical name for the root of the taro), which has also made the latter a popular choice, even though nutritionists have pointed out that its food value is not as high as that of taro or yams.

Rice is another imported food that has replaced local starch foods (see chapter 2), but other imports, including fresh fruit and vegetables like onions, potatoes, salad greens, carrots, apples, pears, and oranges have added variety to meals. The range of typical meals, therefore, has increased overall. New foods are being added to the diet all the time, even if the overall quality of a lot of these (processed) foods render them similar in terms of food value. In days gone by, and still today in remote areas, opening a tin of fish or beef might be a daily operation, and adds small amounts of salt, protein, and fat to complement the blander bulk of starch that is almost always a part of the meal, whether in pasta, bread, rice, or cassava. But additional condiments (meat, bottled sauces, ready-prepared foods) are also shifting the balance. The centrality of simple starch foods is being challenged.

Other important staples have remained central to the diet, particularly coconut, its palm known in Oceania as the tree of life. Without the coconut, survival would hardly be possible on many atolls.[6] Coconut provides milk, cream, and flesh. Unripe nuts supply refreshing drinks; the most mature nuts provide a rich cream obtained from squeezing the grated flesh. Coconut milk or cream finds its way into a multitude of everyday dishes. Increasingly, however, canned products are used, which tend to be higher in saturated fats and can contain other additives, including bleaches (whiteners) and preservatives. A typical meal based on starch could include cassava, rice, or potatoes, onions, green vegetables (either taro leaves, *dalo* [Fijian] or hibiscus leaf: *moca* [Fijian] or *chanya ke bhaji* [Hindi]), coconut milk, chili, and tomato. *Miti*, a condiment of coconut milk, chili, and onion might also be poured over fish or vegetables. Some fish, meat, or chicken could be part of the nightly meal, which tends to be the main meal of the day.

TYPICAL MEALS: HOW THEY ARE EATEN

Islanders, like some of their Asian counterparts, eat with the fingers of both hands. Bowls of water are usually provided so that hands can be cleansed intermittently. When food is being eaten, diners need to take care to look around them between mouthfuls, which shows that they are thinking of others and that they care for them. A view of passersby is also important because there is a desire to invite them in to share the food. *Mai kana*, "come and eat," is a common expression used widely in Fiji. It is as much a greeting as an invitation. One can refuse politely without offending, or accept the offer, which will be honored. Guests and those who partake of the meal are expected to show appreciation by making gestures and noises, like eating noisily or nodding the head to show approval. Merely saying that the food tastes good, *kana vinaka na kakana*, is not enough, unless the diner also eats heartily and demonstrates enjoyment with gestures. It is very much the case that actions speak louder than words.[7]

The basic pattern of the meal described continues to be fundamental to islander meals. New foods, the use of tables, chairs, knives, forks, ovens, refrigerators, and even the purchase of ready-cooked meals that might be eaten in front of the television, have not substantially affected the social hierarchy and how it is expressed at mealtimes. The father is still the head of the household. Women are expected to cook (the exception here is that men always prepare the *umu*), and the pecking order is maintained. The staple starches still have symbolic pride of place. Even though substitutes like rice, noodles, and bread have broadened the range of high-carbohydrate food, it is unlikely that they will ever be accorded the same status as that of the traditional crops. The new foods do, however, attract some positive status because they are associated with all things Western; this may seem ironic given that many of the imported foods consumed and relished appear to have significantly less nutritional value than the traditional foods that are being displaced. Desserts are not normally eaten as part of the traditional diet, unless in the form of a pudding or fruit soup consisting of mashed fruit and coconut baked in the *umu* or conventional oven; Polynesians can also add starch to this mixture for consistency.

Today, a typical meal often means a combination of traditional island elements (either foods or techniques) and introduced foods and cooking methods, including the use of electric or gas stoves. In Rarotonga, one can buy a ready-cooked dish of steamed taro with braised brisket and taro greens (*rukau*) in the local market at Avarua (the capital). The brisket is corned and salty, and the greens, cooked in the juice of the beef, are also highly salted. While this dish has its traditional elements, the salty beef is a Western addition that has now, across much of the region, become "traditional." In the pre-Western era, this dish would have included a smaller amount of meat or fish, and markedly less salt, something which was not available except when occurring naturally in foods (and which could be added using seawater during cooking), and without the chemical nitrites associated with corning. A further mutation of this dish involves the use of canned corned beef, which also includes high amounts of saturated animal fats. Indeed, canned meat is now a staple. Supermarkets throughout the Pacific stock this imported product (from New Zealand and Australia) in a range of sizes up to 25 pounds.

Breakfast

Today the pattern of eating, as well as what is eaten, is certainly changing. While it was customary in the past to have a meal in the morning and another at night, different patterns have emerged in both rural and urban contexts. Today, the normal urban, rural, and village breakfast of native Fijians consists of bread (with or without margarine) and sweet tea, reminiscent of the working class diet in 19th-century Britain. In country areas, this aspect of the diet is potentially less varied than in urban areas, where the range of purchasable foods is broader. The same trend is also widely evident elsewhere in the Pacific. Other Western foods have become popular, like cereals, but purchase depends on available cash. For most, these foods are treats.

Lunch

Sandwiches are typical fare for lunch in country areas. Children still snack on fruit (banana or plantain), but increasingly, snack foods, biscuits, cakes, soft drinks, and other junk food are impinging on the traditional diet. As elsewhere in the world, lunch has also been affected by the pressures of work. If time is limited, then there is the choice of bought foods from take-out businesses.

Dinner

Given the many rules and taboos that apply to food consumption in islander cultures, a typical dinner at home in a traditional village on Namu, in the Republic of the Marshall Islands, for example, would be prepared for a household, which might include a number of nuclear families with sisters in common, and all involved would behave according to the rules of matrilineal obligations and rights. The food would be cooked over an open fire using coconut husks for fuel. Breadfruit would be cooked directly in the coals and the same fruit, fermented, would be cooked in an oven; for everyday convenience this would be an improvised oven made from tin, which would be more economical and less time consuming than the *umu*. Rice would be boiled in a pot. When the breadfruit and rice are ready, grated coconut and perhaps a little meat or fish can be added as condiments. Leftovers, as is customary all over the Pacific, are parceled up and shared out. Thus, in the Republic of Palau (east of the Philippines), commonly eaten breakfast fruits like orange, mango, and banana are not considered real food unless they are taken together with leftover "snacks" in parcels from the previous evening's meal.

A typical dinner meal today in a rural Indian Fijian family would be based on cassava, with the possible addition of spring onions, green vegetables (either taro leaves, *dalo* [Fijian] or hibiscus leaf [*moca* in Fijian] or *chanya ke bhaji* in Hindi), chicken or fish, dahl (made from lentils), coconut milk, chili, and tomato. *Miti*, a condiment of coconut milk, chili, and onion might also be poured over fish or vegetables. Typical meals now include more fried and deep-fried products, sugar, and salt, both as ingredients in processed foods and ready-to-eat products. In 2008, in American Samoa, a chain known as L&L Hawaiian Barbecue, which operates 130 outlets in the United States and 52 in Hawaii, opened what it calls a Drive-Inn, selling out of food in six hours on its first trading day, after feeding 1,000 customers on its *matai* plates, a three-pound lunch plate containing three scoops of rice, two scoops of macaroni salad, BBQ beef and a choice of BBQ chicken or chicken *katsu*. Matai is the Samoan word for chief, and the advertising run by the company promotes the *matai* plate as being fit for a king.[8]

Meals of any kind underline the importance of sharing the vital supply of foodstuffs. Sharing embodies friendship and group solidarity, and also expresses love.[9] When a family eats a meal together, part of that meal might include foods that have been given by relatives in other villages, or in the case of the Cook Islands, Tonga, Samoa, Niue, and Tokelau, it may have been sent from relatives living in New Zealand or Australia. A typical meal is therefore one that has been made possible by a social network that extends beyond those actually present.

Other typical meals are those that reflect a transcultural influence, since island communities depend on imported foods for survival. Fiji imports the vast majority of foodstuffs its people consume, including rice coming from Thailand and Australia. Fiji is capable of producing its own rice but, as with many agricultural products, making land available for plant crops has historically been thwarted by Fiji's Great Council of Chiefs, who can deny leasehold to the land by would-be growers. This occurs because of a persistent although baseless fear within the council that, whether currently used or not, land turned over to agriculture will cease to be owned by the council. While this cultural impediment exists, Fiji remains in the position of having to import much of its food, including fresh fruit and vegetables; these often come, air freighted, from Australasia, adding costs to Fijian consumers. This lack of self-sufficiency in food means that Fiji is at the mercy of fluctuations in world food prices. Such a system also shapes the daily fare of local people. Many growers supply the local market with taro, cassava, yams, leafy green vegetables, ginger, gourds, wing beans, chilies, and various fruits. Markets are vibrant, busy places in the islands where many local people shop and where—in terms of retail supply—traditional foods are most conspicuous. To this extent the markets underpin the community's allegiance to the traditional diet.

Typical Meals in the City

On Friday nights in Suva, street stalls cook barbecue within a stone's throw of the downtown McDonald's. Lamb chops, sausages, and chicken are browned on the high heat of a large metal hotplate, to which Chinese cabbage, onion, chili, teriyaki sauce, and other seasonings are added, seemingly at the whim of the cook in charge. Suva shoppers eagerly consume this fare during their exodus from the city. Fijians and Fijian Indians will both sit down for curry, including *roko* (taro leaves) and, typically, a soft drink. In villages, the accoutrements of dining are still simple, but it is more likely that a family will eat from a plate, at a table, than from banana leaves and seated on the ground. Perceived convenience is seemingly always a factor and a powerful generator of change.

Other dishes that have become popular with tourists include marinated raw fish, which is served in different forms all over the Pacific; the French

Polynesians call this *poisson cru*, the Hawaiians call it *poke*, it is *mororo* in the Cook Islands, and in Fiji, *kokoda*. In this way, local traditions are preserved as something more or less intact in the face of outside, globalizing, influences because it coincides with the foreigner or tourist's taste. To some extent this explains how raw fish dishes, only slightly adapted to suit tourists' tastes, have remained firmly part of the local cuisine. Popular local dishes that do not generally appeal to foreigners (*ariri*, for example, which are sea snails served marinated in coconut and lime juice), remain very much local delicacies. Other products, including fermented foods, have never been popular with foreigners. This has added to their decline in local cultures as well.

The small size and isolation of Oceanic island groups has meant that new ideas and food-related practices, as well as foods, achieve a greater level of exposure that can have a lasting and wide-reaching effect on local communities. Imported food culture in general has left its mark on whole ways of life within a relatively short span of time. Typical dishes, therefore, now must include snack foods, sweet confections like ice cream, doughnuts, cakes, candy, and soft drinks. While not constituting meals in themselves, these foods add significantly to dietary intake and represent an everyday part of life for many locals. Price determines quality in many cases, so there is a high proportion of cheap meat products like sausages or chicken legs available, as well as numerous frozen foods including "crab sticks"—often referred to as "seafood extender"—a processed, reconstituted, and artificially flavored product containing material extracted from seafood, but which trades more on the name *seafood* than on any real resemblance to fish or other marine life. Artificial flavors boost what is seafood in name only. Naturally, these products can be produced relatively cheaply and appeal primarily because of price in island communities where living wages are low, choices (among meat products) are limited, and education about diet and food is not easily disseminated. Cooking tips and recipes are offered on radio and television, as well as through magazines. There is no real evidence that this type of information actually changes attitudes or meals at home, but there must be some uptake among consumers, who are being offered many new options. As disposable income becomes a reality for more, particularly urban, residents, experimentation in cookery becomes affordable and attractive. In this context, meal ideas are often a blend of old and new.

Prawn and Cassava Curry

1 lb. of cooked cassava (boiled in water until soft) and cubed in inch squares

1 c. fresh (or canned) coconut cream

2 Tbs. olive oil

1 tsp. curry powder

1 onion, chopped

2 garlic cloves, crushed

2 tomatoes, chopped

1 green bell pepper, chopped

11 oz. of raw, shelled prawn meat

Coriander

2 tsp. fish sauce (*nam pla*)

Sauté onion, garlic, bell pepper until soft. Add curry powder and prawns and cook until these are just firm. Add cream and cassava. Simmer gently for 5 minutes. Season with fish sauce. Garnish with plenty of fresh coriander leaves. Serve with steamed rice.

Some broad generic influences, in terms of national culinary styles, have emerged to shape typical meals. In Tahiti (French Polynesia) and New Caledonia, a French culinary style is plainly in evidence, while Fiji, Tonga, Samoa, and the Cook Islands, falling as they did under British colonial jurisdiction, bear the traces of the Anglo-Saxon culinary legacy. Minor influences in the form of ingredients include Japanese soy sauce, Indian curry, and American ketchup.

AUSTRALIA AND NEW ZEALAND

Meals have changed very much in Australasia due to increasing variety, income (relative to the amount spent on food), and awareness: both knowledge and a willingness to try new things on the part of consumers. Two trends are worth noting. The first is the growing demand for good-quality fresh fruit and vegetables. The warm climate of Australia favors a long summer menu of salads, fruits, and outdoor entertaining (barbecues), and there has been an explosion in terms of product lines in salad mixes and ingredients for them. Part of this trend is also seen in organic foods. While only 2 percent of chickens farmed are certified organic, the growth in organic product sales has been one the recent success stories of marketing. The other trend, however, is almost the opposite. More popular than ever before are the precooked, heat-and-eat meals that can often go straight from the shelf to the microwave.

Home-cooked meals using fresh ingredients are prepared something like two or three times a week, with the other meals being split between restaurants, fast food, convenience foods liked canned meals, and the newer breed of heat-and-eat products. Other ingredients make cooking simpler and lessen the amount of time one needs to cook. Stir-through sauces that only require heating with the addition of meat or vegetables are now part of the typical day's meal intake.

Breakfast

Breakfast is often eaten relatively quickly, and might be as simple as toast and tea. Toast cannot be mentioned in Australia without someone else saying Vegemite (New Zealanders also have Marmite; both are yeast extract spreads), a perennial favorite and no less a national icon than the kangaroo. Fruit and cereal with yoghurt is a perennial favorite, but so is the cooked breakfast, which has become the mainstay of breakfasting out at cafés, a pastime that is now as much a part of the Australian lifestyle as swimming or cricket. Coffee sales have risen steeply, reflecting the influence still of Italian and Greek immigrants, as well as global coffee culture and broadening consumer demand. Broiled (grilled) bacon, poached eggs, toast, and a fried half tomato is a commonplace choice, while muesli, French toast, fruit salad, muffins, focaccia (Italian-style toasted sandwiches), juices, mineral water, and other drinks are also commonly consumed. Other offerings include various types of fritters (corn or ricotta), specialty sausages, pancakes, and Boston baked beans. At home, cereals, toast, fruit, yoghurt, and the occasional cooked breakfast (often on weekends) prevail as the standard among Australians of European descent.

Lunch

Lunch has become a meal squeezed into the working day, eaten alone, or lingered over as a treat on a special occasion. Weekend lunches can be especially social and, given the often fine conditions, dining alfresco has become an Australian lunchtime tradition. Like countries around the world, variety of choice has changed the way Australasians lunch. Sandwiches and other bread-based snacks are still favorites, as are ham, chicken, beef, and cured meats to put in them. In the cities, Asian restaurants provide cheap and popular choices for lunch, including noodle soups, barbecue chicken, dumplings, yum cha, sushi, and dim sum, and fast food outlets also claim their share of the lunchtime trade. Australasia, unlike parts of Europe, does not shut down in the afternoons for siesta, so lunch tends to be constrained by time and by the responsibility to work. Drinking is normally kept to a minimum if dining out. A beer, or light beer, is acceptable.

Dinner

Less time to cook and only a little time to eat: that sums up the way eating has changed to reflect time pressures. People are shopping more regularly, buying fewer items, cooking less, and preparing more foods that require minimal time. The market caters to this need by providing foods that are ready to go, which also explains the popularity of natural whole foods that only need washing and plating before eating. Long hours of preparation are not fashionable except for the gourmet enthusiast. There are too many choices now to leave many disappointed, and simple techniques have marginalized stews and casseroles. "Salad" has come to refer to any number of ingredients that are minimally prepared before being tossed in a bowl with a dressing. In some cases, carbohydrates are dispensed with altogether as a result, meeting the heath requirements of some. Other foods have long been popular and remain so. Various dishes based on pasta, as well as stir-fries, accommodate the variety of ingredients by offering a generic form of dish that is easily adapted in various ways. The age of the meat and three veg meal is over in Australia and New Zealand as people become more adventurous, time-harried, affluent, and knowledgeable about the food they choose to eat. In 2008 and into 2009, the global financial crisis has hit the spending power of consumers and this means a return to the old standbys to some extent , the cheaper cuts of meat and also "mince" (ground beef steak). This has been a perennial favorite used to make such dishes as shepherd's pie (savory mince with mashed potato on top), Bolognese sauce for pasta, meatloaf, meatballs, and "rissoles" (large meatballs). Using cheaper cuts in hard times is a knee-jerk reaction to rising prices, but also somewhat ironic, since brisket, shanks, trotters, and other traditionally low-priced cuts have increasingly appeared on menus in expensive restaurants in the last decade. Consequently, the prices of some of these items have risen. Fruit, vegetables, fish (and to a lesser extent, meat) in season are still the best option for value, but as consumers move to eat more and more preprocessed or prepared foods, the perception is widespread that these represent the typical meals of the future.

NOTES

1. Jimaima Veisikiaki Lako, "Dietary Trend and Diabetes: Its Association among Indigenous Fijians 1952–1994," *Asia Pacific Journal of Clinical Nutrition* 10, no. 3 (2001): 186–87.

    2. New Zealand-based Fishers Meats, exporter of meat products to the Pacific region. http://www.fishersmeat.com/default.asp (accessed May 21, 2008).

    3. Gwen Skinner, *The Cuisine of the South Pacific* (London: Hodder and Stoughton, 1983), 56.

    4. Asesela Ravuvu, *Vaka I Taukei: The Fijian Way of Life* (Suva: University of the South Pacific, 1983), 28–34.

    5. Ravuvu, 28–34.

    6. John Morrison, Paul Geraghty, and Linda Crowl, eds., *Fauna, Flora, Food and Medicine, Science of Pacific Island Peoples* (Suva: University of the South Pacific, 1994), 171.

    7. Morrison, Geraghty, and Crowl, 171.

    8. "L&L introduces supersized plate lunch," Honoluluadvertiser.com, May 28, 2008 (accessed June 6, 2008).

    9. See Kalissa Alexeyeff, "Love Food: Exchange and Sustenance in the Cook Islands Diaspora," *Australian Journal of Anthropology* 15, no. 1 (2004).

5

Regional Specialties

A remarkable feature of the Pacific region's food culture is that it retains continuity across cultures. In this sense, regionalism, as that term pertains to much larger countries, is meaningless in Oceania, which, although immense in size, shares much in common among its cultures. The use of the earth oven and the dishes typically cooked within it are represented throughout Oceania, including Hawaii and New Zealand. Variations of generic dishes are also a common feature. *Palusami* in Fiji is *lu pulu* in Tonga, for example, but essentially they are the same dish: meat or fish wrapped in taro, then banana leaves, and baked. In Tahiti, a similar dish is made using the leg meat of pork mixed with coconut cream. The mixture is then wrapped in taro leaves and baked in the *ahima'a*, the French Polynesian's term for the *umu*. Wrapping foods in this way is a Pacific-wide style of cookery that is used for both savory and sweet dishes; meat, fish, and taro, but also puddings of sweetened cassava and coconut are typically wrapped in banana leaves before baking. This dish is called *ubai* in Papua New Guinea (PNG), and *vakalolo* in Fiji.

Another dimension to regionalism has come through the marketing of the islands to the world; thus, to some degree, regional differences are exploited to attract business. Food and drink, however, have played a minor role. It is really only at the local level that a variety of dishes and ingredients could be claimed to account for truly regional differences.

Vakalolo

2 lbs freshly grated cassava

10 oz. grated fresh coconut

1/2 a thumb of ginger, grated

7 oz sugar

6 cloves

Mix all ingredients together and wrap in banana leaf parcels. Steam for 40 minutes and serve.

A variation on *vakalolo* is *vakalavalava*, which includes banana. In Tahiti, *poe* is prepared in a similar way, although there, bananas or a mixture of fruits including pineapple, mango, and papaya, are first cooked, then mixed with sugar, coconut cream, and cassava starch (tapioca), and baked into a pudding in banana leaves. Arrowroot starch would traditionally be used to thicken the version of this dish consumed in the Cook Islands, which is known as *poke*. Today, the arrowroot starch comes from Thailand, but traditionally islanders would grate cassava (tapioca), squeeze the juice into a container, and use the fine starch that settled in the bottom as a thickening agent for the *poke*. Arrowroot was also grown in the Cook Islands. Another pudding-like dish made on Raro is *kuru papa*: near ripe breadfruit (*kuru*) are toasted on charcoal, peeled and crushed, and mixed with sweetened coconut cream. In New Zealand and Australia, puddings have tended to follow Anglo-Saxon recipes based on wheat flour. Nonetheless, the influence of the Pacific was felt in other ways. In the following recipe, taken from the *War Economy Cookbook* (c. 1943), the name itself was perhaps chosen to improve morale during the period of rationing.

Pacific Pudding

1 c. flour

2 tsp. ground ginger

3 oz. butter or drippings

1/2 c. Sultanas

1/2 c. syrup, warmed

1/2 tsp. soda

1/2 c. milk

Sieve together flour and ground ginger. Rub in butter or drippings, add sultanas and syrup. Dissolve soda in milk and add to mixture. Steam 2 hours.

Another pan-regional specialty that does not require cooking at all is marinated raw fish, what in French Polynesia it is called *poisson cru* (or *e'ia ota* in Tahitian), in Fiji and New Guinea, *kokoda*, in the Cook Islands, *ika mata*, in Kiribati, *orao ra*, in Tonga, *lei ika*, in Samoa, *oka i'a*; and on Niue, *ota ika*. In Australasia, it might simply be called marinated fish salad, carpaccio (after the Italian style of thinly slicing raw meat) or *poisson cru*, which gives it an air of sophistication. Raw fish (*ota*) is a tradition in many island cuisines and, indeed, varieties of seafood including mussels, oysters, and, a favorite among Maori, *kina*, or sea urchin, are preferred raw, as they are in many parts of the world. In the islands, fish are also eaten raw, after cleaning and scaling; sometimes, fillets are simply dipped in sea water and consumed as a snack. Local variations on raw fish are fermented fish preparations like the Tahitian *fafaru:* chunks of fresh fish are placed in a container (traditionally, a gourd) with sea water and left for days. The water is changed, but the fish ages in this broth, which, by the time the fish is deemed ready to eat, smells "off" to Westerners. But the most popular way is to marinate fish in coconut milk and citrus juice (which over several hours "cooks" the protein in the fish by enzyme action). On Rarotonga, a version is made with tiny turban shell sea snails (*ariri*), and this dish is called *mitiori*. In Fiji, as well as elsewhere, seaweed called "sea grapes" (*Caulerpa* sp., called *nama*) are added to the generic *kokoda* dish. This type of dish has raw fish and coconut (grated, milk, or cream) in common, and usually also citrus juice: lime in Tahiti, but lemon is also used elsewhere. In Fiji, it can also be made using local vinegar, but this is not as highly regarded. In Samoa, by contrast, the fish is often barely marinated (without citrus juice) in thick coconut cream before serving.

Many varieties of fish can be used, although less oily types suit this dish the best. Tuna, snapper, or bass are all good. The rich and creamy-textured moonfish is also favored. Other seafood delicacies like octopus, crab, lobster, and calamari can also be treated this way. In Tahiti, tomato can be added, in Hawaii a version with tuna (aku, skipjack; ahi, yellowfin) is made with sesame oil and seaweed, and is called *poke* (not to be confused with the Cook Islands pudding!). Also used in this dish is another local variant, *inamona*, roasted, crushed kukui (candle) nut, which has been used medicinally for centuries by Hawaiians, but that also adds texture and flavor. Other local versions of marinated fish in citrus juice and coconut involve a slight fermentation that adds another dimension of taste and that contrasts to the natural sweetness of the fish. In Rarotonga and elsewhere in the Cook Islands, *ariri* (or turban shell, a small winkle) is first broken open and its flesh removed to make *mitiori*. Coconut is then grated onto the flesh and the mixture is left to ferment for a few hours or overnight, with finely chopped onion or chives, the whole thing wrapped in paw paw leaves. This delicacy has a slightly crunchy consistency when eaten. A special occasion dish, *mitiori* would not normally be offered on menus in local restaurants or to tourists, who would better recognize *poisson cru*, or even *sashimi*, since this Japanese-style of preparing and serving raw fish dish has also become popular in the Pacific. Specialties like *mitiori* are only eaten once in a while and, even though they would be offered to guests at special occasions, they would not necessarily be to the taste of nonlocals.

Tahitian Poisson Cru

1 lb. firm raw white-fleshed fish or tuna

1/2 c. fresh lime juice, and grated zest of two limes

1/2 c. coconut milk (canned, but better fresh)

2 finely diced tomatoes, seeds removed.

2 Tbs. chives or parsley, minced

1/2 small hot chili, deseeded and finely chopped (optional)

Salt

Cut fish across the grain of the flesh into equally sized 1/2-inch-thick strips. In a stainless steel bowl, combine the juice, zest, coconut milk, and salt. Add the fish, tomato, chives, lime juice, and zest. Gently fold to coat the fish well. Cover and keep chilled or serve straight away. Serves four.

Other regional specialty foods include duck and goat, the latter particularly among the Indian population of Fiji, where goat is farmed for local and export markets. Fiji's hinterland supports goats and pigs, as most of the larger islands do. In PNG, deer and buffalo have also been introduced. In urban areas, meats like pork and chicken can also be special foods, depending on the circumstances of the families involved. In rural areas, pork meat or suckling pig, cooked in the *umu*, is a great delicacy, as it is across the region. In New Guinea, pork fat is particularly relished, although pork meat in general is sometimes consumed when barely cooked on Western standards. Special guests could be offered this fare if attending a feast. This can prove dangerous because ingestion can lead to a sometimes deadly bacterial infection of the digestive tract called *enteritis necroticans*. In the Solomon Islands, bride-price is paid in the form of pig meat. This is not cooked, but butchered ready to be cooked for a feast pending the decision of the betrothed in naming the day of the wedding. Live pigs are also given by the groom to the father of the bride. Consequently, pork is a highly prized food consumed at feasts in the Solomons, among other Melanesian islands, and Papua New Guinea.

PNG has specialties all its own, like the giant tree grub and grubs of the sago palm, a plant which supplies quantities of starch that is processed and cooked in a variety of ways by local people. Sometimes, palms are deliberately cut down and left so that the grubs will form. They can reach 3–4 inches in length and are boiled or roasted before eating. In the markets, sago grubs are also served satay style on skewers.[1] Grubs are also relished in Tonga, where another wood-eating variety called *afato* are a favorite. The same word is used in Samoa, where the grubs are fit food for chiefs. Large *afato* are called *mata mata*. Another term, *moe 'ese 'ese*, means "sleeping apart from one another," which is a sign that the grub has reached a particularly succulent stage of readiness for eating. Traditionally, Maori also used terms to describe different stages of larvae, grub, pupae, and adult development. The Tuhoe tribe call larva *tunga rakau*; when the larvae stops eating it is called *tataka* (pupa stage); prior to chewing its way out of its protective layer, it is called *pepe*; and the flying beetle is known as *tunga rere*.[2] This insect-specific gastronomic terminology is a key to understanding the eating qualities of these traditional delicacies.

Larvae of beetles, moths, wasps, and dragonflies are also consumed in PNG, as are adult moths, grasshoppers, crickets, cicadas, and beetles. In the Sepik River region, some of these creatures are wrapped in sago leaves and smoked before being eaten. The consumption of insects is widespread amongst indigenous peoples worldwide. While not to the taste of most Westerners, eating insects can be very nourishing and is also ecologically friendly. Over many years, people adapt to their environment in such a way that few potential foods are excluded from the diet. In PNG, like Aboriginal Australia, foods are found everywhere where life is supported in its myriad forms. PNG also supports larger prey, like the cassowary, a flightless bird related to Australia's emu. Both are eaten by indigenous people in both countries. In Australia, emu meat is also sold through meat retailers, along with other local meats like kangaroo. The native possum is also a source of food. PNG's extensive biodiversity makes it unique in the region. Literally thousands of potential sources of food can be accessed on this island, which is one of the world's largest.

In the contemporary urban island context, a range of specialty items are used in everyday cookery as well as being represented in the gourmet pages of magazines, now a growth industry in their own right. Suva market is a place where leafy vegetables, many of them introduced, are sold each day and used in a variety of dishes, often in Indian cooking. Leaves of

moca (*Amaranthus tricolor*, variously known as *tubua* or *chauraiya* [Hindi],
Joseph's coat, Chinese spinach, amaranth, or pigweed) are a versatile addition to curries, stir-fries, or as an accompaniment, stewed in coconut
milk or cooked in oil. Long beans (sometimes called snake beans) are also
popular.

To some extent, regional specialties have developed into lasting traditions as the result of contact between East and West. In Hawaii, for example, the influence of American culture and tastes has been dramatic, but
its gastronomic heritage is also the product of diverse cultural influences:
Japanese, Korean, Chinese, Filipino, and Portuguese. Therefore, food
styles and dishes developed as the result of the multiethnic population's
input into local cuisine, tourism, and the Americanization of island tastes.
Beginning in the 1930s, the heyday of grand entertaining, this phenomenon became ever more prevalent until it eventually became synonymous,
at least to visitors from abroad, with what was supposed to be Hawaiian.
Cocktails were a feature of these parties, as well as what became known
as pupu (little dish), savory appetizers that were eaten as hors d'oeuvres
with drinks, typically as an "aloha" starter at a luau. A number of popular
dishes originating from many different cuisines comprise a typical pupu
platter. Eating a lot of pupu constitutes having a meal. Sweet and sour
snacks, deep-fried coconut and sake shrimp, Korean meatballs with soy
dipping sauce, various tartlets, hummus, blue cheese, and other dips, carpaccio, ceviche, and pâté might all be found on the pupu plate. Typically
Hawaiian elements like pineapple, coconut, and various tropical fruits
add to a festive island theme, replete with plumeria (frangipani) flowers,
colorful fruit-laden coolers, punches, and other drinks are presented in coconut shells or hollowed-out pineapple containers. The tradition of pupu
and cocktail parties naturally suited the lifestyle of people on holiday and
for whom socializing was high on the agenda, particularly in an exotic
location like Hawaii.

HAWAII

The influence of outsiders on Hawaiian foodways is quite specific, especially given the long association with the United States. Other people
from many different parts of the globe have also had an effect on the
island group's food culture. Hawaiian cuisine is a creole cuisine, one that
has borrowed elements from various national or regional cuisines and
formed its own style in so doing. Creolization is a constant in the world
of food culture, but Hawaiian cuisine is an excellent example of this process as it typifies Hawaiian foodways as a whole. What makes Hawaiian

food distinctive is not recognizably indigenous in terms of ingredients, techniques, or culinary traditions as such, but is more the result of the cultural mixing pot. Hawaii's traditional foods, were established by the Polynesians who came from the south (the Marquesas and Society Islands), bringing taro and sweet potato. Taro did very well in Hawaii, and the Pacific region's largest irrigated system of paddies for taro production was created there. Poi, made from pounded cooked taro, became a dish of the highest status and was consumed in great quantities at feasts. From Vanuatu comes a variation on poi and *palusami*, called *lap-lap*, a thick cake or pudding made from grated taro, manioc, sweet potato (*kumala*), or plantain (cooking bananas) mixed with coconut milk or cream, packaged in banana leaves and cooked in an *umu*. Depending on how it is preferred, the longer *lap-lap* is cooked the drier it will become.

Fish and some meats (including dog) were also eaten. By the end of the 19th century, Hawaiians were eating salted meat and fish, and potatoes and bread instead of taro, which gradually became associated more with special occasions. Then, especially with the decline in numbers of native Hawaiians, mostly due to disease, immigrants were brought in as indentured laborers to work in the new plantation system that was developing. Chinese, Japanese (Okinawans), Koreans, Puerto Ricans, Portuguese, and Filipinos would all add culinary diversity and variation to the local diet. In the early 20th century, rice was a major crop (the third biggest), small farms and market gardens added a growing number of ingredients to those available, and tofu was produced, along with sake and noodles. Westernization meant bakeries, grocery stores, and restaurants. But standard Western fare and traditional Hawaiian foods, the dominant two styles, failed to cater to the range of tastes represented by the various ethnic minorities. The workers' need for cheap, fast-food alternatives also gave rise to a regional specialty known as the plate lunch: a large serving of rice and meat covered in gravy and eaten with chopsticks. Small vendors and street stalls served this fare and it has remained a style that is recognizably Hawaiian. Regional accents include the use of soy sauce (called shoyu in Hawaii) and teriyaki sauce, which are both much used as condiment and seasoning. A variation on the raw marinated fish found throughout the Pacific region, the Hawaiian version, *poke*, often contains chili, soy sauce, and sesame oil. Other fusion products found in a Hawaiian grocery are an array of snacks and crisps made from bananas, breadfruit, and taro. Paradoxically, for a century or so, the term "Hawaiian" has indicated a multitude of ethnic origins, while the fusion style of food that has evolved as a result of multiethnicity can now claim to be the one thing that holds all of these disparate groups together. Thus, being Hawaiian still means eating Hawaiian, even though Hawaiian identity and cuisine have both been transformed.

SAMOAN LUAU

A part of Polynesia, Samoa shares the term luau with Polynesian Hawaii, where a luau has come to mean a beach party; originally, however, *laulau* was the name given to a dish made with young taro and its leaves and coconut cream, together with a little chicken, pork, or sometimes fish or octopus, and wrapped in ti or banana leaves and baked. The word luau has come to mean a social event in both island cultures, including music and dancing. This is hardly surprising, since food and its consumption have always been an integral part of social gatherings, inseparable from them. It makes sense that luau has come to be synonymous with the celebration of life in the islands of Polynesia and to be identified by tourists with island culture itself.

New Caledonia (NC) has been gastronomically transformed, not by an assortment of ethnic influences, but by the dominance of a major culinary culture, that of France. This illustrates how the total marginalization of indigenous foodways can occur in a relatively short span of time. The native Kanak people of Micronesian descent were forced to give up their agriculture as their lands were confiscated or overrun. The French have long been known for their fine cuisine, and so it is that one can eat well in NC today. At the same time, it is virtually impossible to recognize any regionality here, aside from there being a good supply of fresh fish and other seafood, and a splash or two of coconut cream here and there. There are also some fusion creations to be found in cookbooks, like *frites de manioc*, cassava chips made in the same way as the traditional deep-fried potato chip. There is also *bougna marmite*, a casserole of staple island root vegetables, chicken, and coconut milk, given the name *bougna* to signify that it is cooked in the traditional Kanak way, similar to *umu* cooking. Like all recipes found in cookbooks, however, it is difficult to deduce from these alone whether such foods are prepared with any frequency on the island, or even at all. The impression one gets today, in NC, is of a desire among the French citizenry for recognizably French cuisine, for imported French products, and little more. Although there are local specialty ingredients including *roussettes* (flying foxes), local deer, lagoon and coral reef fish (like *dawa*), crabs and lobsters, *poingo* banana (used in *bougna*), *païta* beans (locally grown haricot beans), *pomme-cannelle* (custard apple, *Annona squamosa*), and locally recognized accents like the use of lime and saffron, the style of preparation is indisputably French. Tourism Web sites

Suckling pig at feast, Tokelau Islands. Courtesy of Michel Blanc.

promote visits to NC using native food, but dishes such as *bougna marmite* are served to create a sense of tradition at special tourist-focused events. Their preparation does not reflect the reality of local foodways today. Some pan-regional influences have fused with French culinary traditions, in minor ways, such as the ubiquitous use of soy sauce. *Poulet au soyo*, for example, contains coriander, ginger, and soy sauce. Similarly *poulet à l'ananas* contains pineapple (which is grown in NC), Kikkoman (soy sauce), and oyster sauce. New Caledonia and Hawaii are very different places from a gastronomic point of view.

AUSTRALASIA

Regionality is only now developing in Australasia, partly as the result of the wine industry's success, but also due to packaging region as a tourist attractor. Wine regions are of course instantly recognizable as such due to the large acreages of vines, which add a verdant, uniform beauty to the country side. But so too is the mythology of wine (its association with history and tradition), its social prestige, not to mention its gustatory attractiveness, all pull-factors for the tourist even without promoting the region as a favorable destination.

Notwithstanding, food and wine have figured prominently in recent marketing promotions of Australian regions, especially since gastronomic, or food and wine, tourists as they are called, have been recognized as a well-heeled group globally growing in number. Even though in reality the development of local cuisine is, in comparison with European countries, still in its infancy, and wine making has a strong focus on export markets, producers, and to some extent, communities, have rallied around the notion of projecting a food- and wine-focused public image of regionality. A larger range of varietal wines are being produced locally (and regionally), one consequence of the globalization of the wine industry. This is also adding further depth to the development of local culinary styles, and to experimentation with food and wine matching in the elite restaurant sector, now a crucial player in regional tourism. Wineries themselves are also driving this change with more and more of them incorporating dining facilities. While by no means a new idea, promotion through the Internet and other marketing avenues coupled with the increase in tourism, interest in gastronomy, and recognition of the demand for lifestyle activities that integrate dining with a tour of the winery, wine-tasting, and even short courses on making wine, are evidence of a new approach to regionality. This strategy has also benefited local communities who, in some instances, have regained a sense of their identity, one that emphasizes the potential to market their local products and services effectively to the world. In the Pacific Islands, regionality and locality are fundamental aspects of tourism marketing, and qualities like uniqueness and authenticity are big attractions for tourists. In Australia (and NZ), this same formula is also working well. There are natural regional differences in climate and terrain from state to state in Australia, but what is similar in all is the degree to which regionality itself has been developed as a primary tourist attraction.

In South Australia (SA), for example, the government has sponsored tourism campaigns stressing food and wine, and is currently investing in tourism that will attract discerning diners from around the world. Settled by free settlers, a process which started in the 1830s, SA has some unique features, including some old food traditions that are not seen elsewhere in Australia. Free settlement (as opposed to transportation) meant, in part, that foodways and traditions arrived more or less intact and were subsequently nurtured in the new land by the early immigrant families, and later, by communities. One area that retained its roots in European cookery was the Barossa Valley, where, beginning in the 1840s, numerous

Prussian Silesians migrated to escape religious persecution. They brought their culinary and gastronomic traditions with them, and today Barossa Valley cooking still has a flavor all its own. German-style butchers produce smallgoods (bacon, ham, sausages, and mettwurst, a fermented style of salami), while cakes, biscuits, and pastries are also made according to time-honored recipes. Festivals, fetes, and fairs are often held to celebrate the common cultural and gastronomic heritage of this region, and a strong tradition of artisan food making has firmly established itself at such events as well as in local retail businesses.[3]

Other regions within South Australia, but also elsewhere in Australia, claim to have food traditions, but in general these are weak. Like in New Zealand, wine culture has done most to strengthen and raise the profile of regions, whereas, up until recently in both countries, history attests to the lack of traditional community foodways and more of a reliance on retail food supplies. There are now virtually continuous overtures to regionality in the media, and recognizing regionality as an important part of individual, community, and national identity is becoming more widespread.

Another boost to the public consciousness about regionality has come through food marketing, some of which is related to winery production, in the form of restaurants, vineyard lunches, or cellar-door food and wine matching classes.[4] But more broadly, the desire for fresh, local, organic, and also biodynamic produce has boosted the popularity of farmers' markets, which have been another key element of what could be called a new culinary regionalism.[5] Farmers' markets further increase the social and business links between small producers (wine and food), restaurant culture, tourism, and the public, adding at the same time an attractive lifestyle dimension to shopping for food. Chefs now pride themselves on sourcing local products from these markets, which are typically within, or within easy access of, urban areas. Artisan foods, vineyard cafes, and restaurants, accommodation (with in-house dining), and, to a growing extent, local food- or wine-related festivals, are building a network of support. Popular television programs like *The Food Lover's Guide to Australia* and *Food Safari* have had plenty of material to choose from that captures regional and local differences in food and cooking.[6] But in general, communities as such still have a way to go in recognizing the potential that active foodways represent.

As in New Zealand, regionality is being developed by the tourism industry as part of what is called "the experience economy," whereby regional produce in particular is showcased to great effect, connecting place and taste in a way that creates an appealing sense of wholeness for tourists. It is a way of commodifying a range of aspects of a particular area and packaging them in terms of region. However, the experience of everyday Australians and New Zealanders is not predominantly shaped by a consciousness of region, even though the celebration of region has become a focus. Adelaide's Hilton Hotel Brasserie, steered by television chef, Simon Bryant, presents what is now a permanent menu called "Seriously South Australian," which constitutes a kind of new regional tradition in itself. The specialties here are the products, including Coffin Bay oysters, Limestone Coast lamb, local almonds, peaches, wild rabbit, and goat cheese, olive oil, and of course many regional wines. Thus, it is not a grassroots tradition of cuisine or community foodways that has prompted such an offering, but rather the lack of such things, and therefore an opportunity to connect regionality with local products in what has proved to be a lucrative commercial move. The manner in which the products are prepared varies according to the creative whim of the chef, and bears no particular relation to local tastes or traditions. Invention is a drawcard in today's climate of consumerism, with diners expecting the new and different in an atmosphere where food has become more entertainment than sustenance, but where regionality can neatly bundle the experience and offer a nostalgic sense of community traditions. In reality, these have only very recently been developed by, in particular, the food and wine producers, restaurateurs, and retailers.

Regionality does have to have some basis to it, and the quality of the foods of South Australia are of the highest standard. SA is the driest Australian state, but the climate, which is often likened to the Mediterranean, favors plants like the olive, and herbs like rosemary, sage, and thyme. Walnuts and almonds grow well, as do stone fruits. One of the major agricultural products is wheat, along with oats and rye. At the same time, the environment also supports a range of grazing stock, including sheep and cattle. Grapes, and in particular shiraz, also called syrah, has been grown in areas like the Barossa Valley, north of Adelaide, and in the McLaren Vale, to the south, for more than 150 years. Adelaide is surrounded on three sides by grape-producing regions, cooler-climate (Adelaide Hills), coastal (McLaren Vale, Fleurieu Peninsula), and inland (Claire Valley, Langhorne Creek).[7] Shiraz from the McLaren Vale regularly wins international prizes and the highest praise at wine shows around the world. South Australia is Australia's largest state producer of wine. Local restaurant culture thrives.

But the specialties of SA are not so much culinary or gastronomic as they are determined by product. Like elsewhere in Australia, particularly in the urban context, "modern Australian" is the adopted cooking style: a cosmopolitan mishmash of flavors, techniques, and ingredients that reflect international more than local trends in cookery and consumer taste, but which take advantage of the best local produce. SA's seasonal, local produce is showcased at the iconic Central Market of Adelaide, where millions flock each year to buy from a huge range of food items. Local fish, meat, fruit (fresh and dried), vegetables, bread, cheese and yoghurt, olive oils, sweets, nuts, wines, and pasta are all sold in the buzzy atmosphere of a vast covered market the size of half a city block. Imported and local produce are sold side by side, but the local goods, now buoyed by the extra prestige that local and organic produce attracts, further highlight the quality and uniqueness of the foods available for sale.

Like the value of regionality for tourists compared to its value for the man in the street, so the cultural value of the market arguably outstrips its functional role. Indeed, in recent years, the market has gradually been losing custom as more convenient ways to shop for food develop. But the tourists never stop coming. The market is more than a retail operation or a convenient and enjoyable place to shop and then meet with friends over coffee or breakfast at one of several cafes inside, adjoining, or near the market. It also provides a venue for cultural exchange, the value of which often goes unrecognized. The numerous stall operators are presently under some pressure from local council, which, in recent years, has raised leasehold fees and made leasing more difficult by shortening the overall leasing periods. There is a feeling that the council would prefer to develop the site's real estate in other ways. The market, however, is a cultural institution that should be supported because of its regional uniqueness and because it is an expression of the South Australian way of life. Investing in this cultural economy makes even more sense in the context of globalization. These culture wars are typical of a country like Australia, where food culture has not been nurtured at the local level. It continues to be undervalued and poorly managed.

Regions and their specialty foods are also a developing aspect of New Zealand's food culture, driven to a large extent by the developing wine industry. The country recognizes 13 wine regions, including the tiny island of Waiheke, where a number of premium wines are produced. Because wine is associated very much with the climate and soil of a locale (known as *terroir*), a sense of regional difference naturally follows. There have been other spurs to the growing sense of place as this relates to food and wine, but the wine industry and its associated culture has galvanized public awareness.

In this context, tourism has also been a driver of regionality as it is elsewhere; an expression of globalization that can have a positive effect on how a community sees itself, but more importantly, how it markets itself to the world. First and foremost this calls for an image, which New Zealand manages well by projecting the natural beauty of the landscape as a backdrop to travel. Food and wine tourism has flowed naturally from this. Tourism also boosts the output of local small producers and food and wine businesses, creating employment and, with it, wealth and community power, in many instances through promoting the uniqueness of the community's foodways. Perhaps ironically, keeping in step with these global opportunities reinforces or reinvigorates social bonds in a way not dissimilar from how traditional food-related practices created community in days gone by. Burgeoning local and often semi-indigenous food cultures now cater to a globalized niche market in tourism. New Zealand's Innovative Chef of Year (2007), Charles Royal, takes gastronomic tours (Mokoia Food Tour) through the New Zealand bush in search of traditional Maori foods, exposing visitors to aspects of Maori culture with which most mainstream New Zealanders would not be at all familiar. Royal is part of a movement that has reclaimed Maori cooking, which, until very recently, had been almost completely overshadowed by adopted Western foods and eating habits among Maori themselves. Royal collects such foods as flax seeds (and does not miss the opportunity to claim that they have health benefits, being high in omega-6 fatty acids), along with the immature fronds of the native New Zealand *pikopiko* fern (*Polystichum richardii*). This food is high in vitamin E, claims the Maorifood.com Web site, representing another appeal to a customer base not necessarily interested in Maori food per se, but attracted by healthy food choice alternatives.

Other developments in the commercialization of local difference are ongoing. Culinary hybridization, a conscious invention blending the old with the new, in this case involves appropriating Western terms to popularize describe bush foods: *Pikopiko* pesto is one of many such examples. Bush pepper (horopito; Bot: *Pseudowintera colorata*) and bush basil (kawakawa; Bot: *Macropiper excelsum*) are two other rediscovered plants that have been branded to capture the imaginations, if not necessarily the taste buds, of tourists and travelers. "Kawakawa and flaxseed pesto," and "horopito hummus" both blend the strange and more familiar, a process typical of hybridization, practitioners of which aim to please as many as possible by delivering exciting, different, appealing, but often also what are touted as very healthy foods to attract the adventurous gastronomic tourist and food enthusiast alike.

NEW ZEALAND'S SEAFOOD SPECIALTIES

A number of native shellfish have lent a distinctiveness to New Zealand's cuisine, both in everyday cooking and for special occasions. *Tua*

tua, a creamy-colored, smooth-shelled bivalve that grows up to about three inches in length, is popular among Maori and pakeha alike. Its flesh is tasty, similar to cockles, but can easily become tough if overcooked. *Tua tua* fritters are made by mincing the *tua tua* through a traditional mincer (food processors can overwork the seafood) and then mixing into a batter with egg, flour, and seasonings. Fried on a low to moderate heat in olive (or vegetable) oil, these appetizers have become an unofficial national dish, especially for those within easy access of the beach where *tua tua* can be found in numbers, buried in the sand at low tide. It is not uncommon to see groups, families, or individuals "tua tua-ing," bent double in the shallows with arms immersed up to the elbow, and with someone else to hold the bucket or bag. There is no real ritual involved in eating the fritters. New Zealanders are fairly casual in their attitude to dining, but still appreciate this native resource and enjoy it greatly. In the old days, but seldom nowadays due to beach fire restrictions, Maori would steam *pipi*, mussel and *tua tua* open on the glowing coals for a feed before heading home. Maori also traditionally enjoyed other varieties of mollusk, like *pupu*, a small spiral-shaped variety with a "cat's eye" protecting the entrance to the shell at one end and a pointed tip at the other; and *kina* (*Evechinus chloroticus*), also called sea urchin or sea egg, is another favorite. During early summer, the sex glands of *kina* become swollen. These are the highly prized roe, traditionally eaten raw by Maori. Wild *kina* are harvested every year in the amount of 600–700 tons, most being sold in New Zealand. Although New Zealand fishermen would like to export *kina* to Japan, where roe can sell for as much as US$200 a pound, problems with quality have hindered the market expansion.

Toheroa (*Paphies ventricosum*), another edible bivalve and member of the clam family, similar to a *tua tua* in shape although somewhat larger in size (up to 6 inches), can claim to be one of New Zealand's greatest ever specialty products, although today, the now legendary toheroa soup is virtually never made, if indeed it is made at all. Millions of the clams were extracted mainly from the west coast beaches of New Zealand's northern North Island, near Dargeville, and in the region of Northern Kaipara. Perennially popular among locals of Northland, but soon sought after far afield, toheroa and in particular, toheroa soup, would achieve something of an international reputation in the first half of the 20th century. Beginning at Dargeville beach around 1905, a total of three factories were set up to can toheroa soup (and concentrate) for export and domestic consumption, and not without good gastronomic reason. One brand touted its toheroa soup concentrate to be of rare delicacy and excellence.[8]

Indeed, toheroa makes a savory soup with a slightly greenish hue, smooth texture, and appetizing aroma. The soup has a natural piquancy, lending itself perfectly to the addition of cream as a finishing touch. It would, and indeed must once have served, as an ideal starter to a banquet featuring duck or game birds, or perhaps venison, as a main course. Toheroa soup has a naturally sophisticated, complex flavor all its own.

The fate of the toheroa, at least in the 20th century, was sealed, it seems, at a dinner in 1921, during which its international gourmet status was assured. During a tour of New Zealand the Prince of Wales, later King Edward VIII, asked for a second helping of the piquant soup made from the unassuming clam. The news of the future king's taste for the toheroa soon spread throughout the Commonwealth. In due course the New Zealand Society, established in 1927 as a dining club for New Zealanders in London, featured toheroa soup on its menus, by which time, in most of New Zealand's hotel dining rooms, the dish had became virtually obligatory, adding the air of class to all those who would "eat like a king," and putting even greater strain on the toheroa beds.

Without adequate legal controls on taking toheroa, stocks naturally diminished over time, although the commercial canning enterprises, resented by the man in the street, were not solely to blame. Fluctuations in numbers of toheroa due to disease, insufficient ocean-borne phytoplankton available for the toheroa to ingest, and other unidentified causes, contributed to the decline in stocks. The public's overfishing of the beds, however, was of major concern to those, including the commercial canners, who wanted legal regulation of numbers taken to be enforced. In 1949, one case was reported of individuals removing over 13,000 toheroa in a single sortie and, by the 1960s, up to 50,000 people could descend on a beach over one weekend, taking countless thousands of the much-admired toheroa.

The canning industry declined along with stocks of the shellfish until its collapse in the 1960s, and taking toheroa from the beaches was totally banned in New Zealand in 1971. Maori have recently regained rights to take toheroa again, but this is carefully controlled. Toheroa soup, once a great delicacy relished by gourmets, is now only a memory for the connoisseur:

Toheroa Soup

For toheroa, substitute *tua tua* or *pipi*

50 finely minced *tua tua* or *pipi*

1 oz. butter

1 onion, finely chopped

1 crushed clove of garlic

A bunch of chopped parsley

1/2 oz. flour

1/2 pint milk

Good squeeze of lemon juice

Salt and pepper

Cream to finish

Sauté onion gently in butter, add garlic, and soften. Add flour off heat and mix until smooth. Whisk in warmed milk and put back on heat, whisking all the time. When sauce thickens and is smooth, turn heat right down.

Add shellfish, lemon juice, salt, and pepper. Bring to simmer point. Remove from heat. Stir in cream and parsley. Serve hot.

Another mollusk, one which is held in particularly high esteem and can still be legally fished, is the paua (*Haliotis iris*), or blackfoot abalone. Paua's dark flesh has a steak-like texture (and some say flavor) when grilled, and is much prized by Maori, who are real connoisseurs of *kaimoana* (seafood). Only 10 paua can legally be taken from the ocean per day, normally by divers who scour the rocks below the tide for their quarry. The large shell is oval-shaped and grows up to about six inches. After the paua flesh has been removed, the shell's interior reveals a most exquisite turquoise color; this is used for cabinet or box inlays and, traditionally, for jewelry and ornamentation.

Seafood abounds in the oceans around New Zealand's long coastline, and one of the oldest and most famous in terms of regionality, particularly post-colonization, is the Bluff oyster (*Tiostria chilensis*), which has been marketed from the southernmost part of New Zealand's Southland District since the1860s. Since 1996, an oyster festival has been held to celebrate the Bluff oyster. It includes both oyster opening and oyster eating competitions, and has attracted up to 3,000 people at this annual event. Rather than being a festival that has developed out of a tradition of local oyster eating, the event has been conceived of and presented to raise the profile of Southland, as well as to encourage investment in the region. This regionalism is less gastronomic than it is commercial, but the culinary and gourmet component is what makes it successful. The festival builds local identity by showcasing a product of which Southlanders are justly proud.[9]

The last of New Zealand's notable regional seafood specialties to mention is whitebait (a term that in different parts of the world means many different things), which is the immature fry stage of several small species of fish that, spawned in sea water, are caught with nets in river mouths during a short season when the fry are seeking to swim back up stream. *Inanga*, varieties of *kokopu*, and *koaro*, can all be in the mix of tiny translucent creatures, the flesh of which is sweet and delicately flavored when cooked in the traditional manner as fritters. Little preparation or time is needed to transform whitebait into a gastronomic treat. One mixes a cup full of whitebait with 1/2 an egg white, a pinch of salt, and some minced parsley. It is fried gently in olive oil until lightly browned and served with lemon and bread and butter. Whitebait is exported frozen to Australia, and is highly regarded there as a gourmet item. The extreme delicacy of the tiny fish, in texture and flavor, makes it unique.

Both Australia and New Zealand have inherited Anglo-Saxon foodways and tastes. Roast lamb and mint sauce, steak and kidney pudding, sausages and mash are all favorites, as well as foods they have made their own like Anzac biscuits, pikelets, pavlova, lamingtons (a kind of plain egg sponge cake, which is then cut into a number of two-inch-long oblongs that are dipped in a chocolate flavored and coloured syrup, then rolled in shredded coconut) and pumpkin scones. But these are national more than regional dishes. The ongoing influx of ethnic migrant groups has also made dishes like spaghetti Bolognese, focaccia (Italian toasted bread sandwich), Greek moussaka, Thai green chicken curry, Malaysian *laksa*, and Chinese dim sum into "Australian" foods over the years . This is truer in the cities than in the country towns and is, in essence, a global trend rather than being specifically local or regional. What does make Australia and New Zealand exciting food cultures today is that traditions are being made anew, and there is no limit to what can happen. New styles, ethnic communities, adventurous producers and marketers, and more people dining out, are driving change and adding to proliferating choices. This is probably a good thing for both countries, since the inherited cuisine and food attitudes of Great Britain, which predominated for so long, certainly never suited Australasia particularly well. Traditions like the meat pie remain firm favorites, however, in both Australia and New Zealand. Given the latter country's colder climate, roasts, puddings, and stews in the British tradition also continue to be a sensible choice, while today the still entrenched tradition of meat and three veg exists as one among many other traditions. A new age of egalitarianism in food culture has dawned that underlines personal preferences above conformity to societal norms. Attitudes toward health, health issues like allergies, ethical, religious and political viewpoints, financial cost, and, when it comes to choice, personal taste, all determine that a diverse range of foods will end up on people's plates will be.

Tokelauan women with baskets of crab and crayfish, prized feast foods. Courtesy of Michel Blanc.

Regionalism has not been a strong culinary factor in this process of change in either Australia or New Zealand; the latter, with a population of just over 4 million, has historically been the more conservative of the two in terms of public taste. In recent years, however, regionalism has developed as a concept to which food businesses, entrepreneurs, producers, and chefs have warmed as a way of promoting quality, difference, and uniqueness as added values that help to promote and sell products. Since at least the 1970s, New Zealand has found that its clean green image gives it a marketing edge, but today it is not only products, but also other forms of public culture, that are pushing regionalism as an attractive product in its own right. A recent television series called *Surfing the Menu*, featuring two chefs, Mark Gardener (NZ) and Ben O'Donoghue (Australia), exemplifies this trend. The two travel and cook their way around both countries and, during their brief stops, regionalism is developed in relation to particular products rather than being described in terms of an established cuisine or local cooking style. This reflects both the lack of any grassroots culinary regionalism and the desire to create one.

The cooking style showcased on the program is very much of the international celebrity chef variety, in both its form and appeal; still, regional touches, matched to themes of lightness and freshness, set off this culinary internationalism. Tuna ceviche with aromatic salad would be at home nearly anywhere (including the Pacific Islands), while tuna tartare Niçoise, another variation on the raw fish theme, seems more at home in the Mediterranean climes of South Australia where, incidentally, export quality tuna are farmed at Port Lincoln for the Japanese market.

NOTES

1. R. J. May, *Kaikai Aniani: A Guide to Bush Foods, Markets and Culinary Arts of Papua New Guinea* (Bathurst, NSW: Robert Brown & Associates, 1984).

2. Wendy Pond, "Parameters of Oceanic Science," in John Morrison, Paul Geraghty, and Linda Crowl, eds., *Fauna, Flora, Food and Medicine*, Science of Pacific Island Peoples (Suva: University of the South Pacific, 1994).

3. Angela Heuzenroeder, *Barossa Food* (Kent Town, SA: Wakefield Press, 1999).

4. See special issue of *Cuisine* magazine, *Wine Country 2009*, which surveys New Zealand's 13 wine regions and local food producers, farmers' markets, restaurants, cafes, and, where applicable, food and wine festivals. For more information on New Zealand's food and wine scene, see *Cuisine* magazine's Web site, http://www.cuisine.co.nz/.

5. Sally Hammond, *Guide to Farmers' Markets: Australia and New Zealand 2007* (Mosman, NSW: RMW Classic Publications, 2007).

6. *The Food Lovers' Guide to Australia* (SBS Television) http://www.sbs.com.au/food/show/food-lovers-guide/ (accessed January 27. 2009).

7. Barbara Santich, *McLaren Vale: Sea and Vines* (Kent Town, SA: Wakefield Press, 1998).

8. Brian Murton, " 'Toheroa Wars': Cultural Politics and Everyday Resistance on a Northern New Zealand Beach," *New Zealand Geographer* 62 (2006), 25–38.

9. Kristy Rusher, "The Bluff Oyster Festival and Regional Economic Development: Festivals as Culture Commodified," in *Food Tourism around the World: Development, Management, and Markets*, ed. Colin Michael Hall et al. (Oxford; Boston, MA: Butterworth Heinemann, 2003).

6

Eating Out

Western-style types of foods, including fast foods, have made the idea of eating outside the traditional eating regime more acceptable in island communities. This is partly because, as old ways of life change to adapt to different aspects of modernization (transport, communication, urbanization, and new technologies), patterns of eating, dining, and cooking naturally change accordingly. For islanders, immigrants, and certainly for tourists, eating out is now accepted as being an individualistic, recreational pursuit that is predominantly driven by impulse and desire rather than being expressive of traditional, community, or social values. While the old ways persist, they are also challenged.

What does eating out signify for island peoples in Pacific Island communities today? Undoubtedly, there is some prestige associated with Western foods, even with those that may seem less than appetizing to Westerners. Tinned fish and meats (notably corned beef) are still highly valued by islanders, and have been incorporated into local foodways. Conversely, Westerners have seldom deigned to eat islander food unless it is in an appropriated form, "dumbed down" or made to conform to international gastronomic trends, but suitably exoticized for customers seeking something authentic. Pacific style, as far as food is concerned, tends to conform to the idea of a sophisticated barbecue, with grilled fish, seafood and steaks, salads, tropical fruits, and cocktails dominating. Values like ease and convenience, together with the broader influence of Western-style economics, also fuel consumption and further promote the widening variation of consumer choices. This, in turn, has instigated major changes to eating habits in the islands. Eating out takes several forms, represented by restaurant culture, fast food, and cafe cultures at one extreme, and by roadside stalls, kava shops, and market fare at the other. One can drink piña colada or toddy, Coke or coconut milk. Variety highlights the choices now available between traditional and imported styles of food. The major factor that governs consumption, however, is cost. The market, therefore, is split between provision for the everyday supply of foods (supermarkets, food outlets) and restaurants and resorts that charge prices way beyond what locals could afford.

Nonetheless, eating out at restaurants and other food outlets in the Pacific region has become an increasingly popular mode of meal taking over the past few decades, particularly in the growing urban areas. It has in some cases replaced, but almost always, displaced, traditional food consumption patterns; the types of foods consumed, when they are consumed, and the meaning associated with consuming them have altered accordingly. Taro, such a meaningful and socially significant food in the region, can now be bought as a fast food snack (McDonald's makes a taro pie), all but entirely removing the traditional significance of the food by turning it into a commercialized product, designed for the individual eater and not necessarily for the group. This trend toward the individualization of dining habits is an important social factor to consider with regard to eating out in the islands because it represents a radical shift away from the structured meanings and symbolism that various foods had at most communal and family meals in the past. While such meals are still enjoyed, eating out, and the casualization of dining that this has instilled in island culture as a whole, have had a profound effect on both attitudes to eating and on the diet. Other factors that have influenced the tendency to eat out include urbanization, increasing levels of disposable income, the presence of convenience and fast foods, and the culture-wide adoption of the Western lifestyle.

Traditionally, commensality, or the act of eating together, has a very specific meaning, or rather a constellation of meanings, in Pacific Island communities. Food and eating are a powerful means of communication. Eating in public—the traditional equivalent to eating out—communicates to the wider community that the correct social relations are being observed, because these are always reflected in the dining etiquette and behavior associated with meal taking. There are many, many strictly observed social rules that apply to behavior in the context of eating in public. In Fiji, as elsewhere, a ritual wedding meal (called *kanavata*, or "eating together"), for example, symbolically celebrates the social act of marriage and demonstrates the willingness on the part of those present to reinforce local custom and marital law by dining and eating together in the traditional way.[1] Men and women dining together make a public statement about their sexual relationship by acting according to the codes set down. Meal eating, in general, enforces these codes throughout the region as part of a ritual, whereby men are customarily seated higher at the table than women, who, as a mark of respect and acceptance of the wider, everyday social norms, must wait to eat until after the men have finished. The traditional subservience of women to men is reflected at mealtimes.

But today, eating in public, at social events or just out, has taken on Western meanings that have tended to erode the strict traditional hierarchy enforced at meals. This casualization of eating out and the watering down of traditional symbolism related to food has not been the collective choice of islanders themselves, who have largely been unable to alter the ongoing Westernizing of the Pacific region. Notwithstanding, islanders have readily adapted to these changes in diet, dining, and consumption patterns, and in many cases have willingly adopted Western foods, which have naturally appeared appealing, but also had an acknowledged status by virtue of being Western. Novelty value, acquired status, and the simple fact that a lot of the new foods have found ready consumers among island populations have led to the explosion in eating out, which, apart from the traditional events that honor the old ways and foods, has become a casual affair for most islanders. Fast food, or street food, snack food products, supermarket options, and vending machines maintain the ongoing transformation of the Pacific island diet. The change also reflects, of course, that islanders are willingly becoming Westernized, being influenced by Western fashions for all consumer goods, driving cars and watching television, shopping in supermarkets, and eating in cafes and restaurants.

One of the most noticeable imports that has made a difference to islanders' food culture in recent decades has been fast food. The success of fast food in the Pacific is somewhat controversial because, as fast food, it appeals to low-income people (most islanders), and therefore has been linked to health problems like obesity in Western countries as well (see chapter 8). It is, however, indisputable that fast food is popular in the islands and commercial providers include the big global chain restaurants like McDonald's and KFC. But "fast food" really means processed foods, products that are made and retailed within an industrialized (the mechanization-standardization of a food product's manufacture) and post-industrialized (the global management, marketing, and media exposure given each product) system of production and consumption. The micromanagement of the entire manufacture and retailing operation of fast food is truly revolutionary, and its process has been replicated by the supermarket system; supermarkets are full of highly processed and ready to heat and eat fast food. McDonaldization is the name given to this now globalized mode of maximizing profit by means of standardization and of maintaining the lowest possible production and service costs. Today, chain store franchises selling all manner of goods are also McDonaldized.[2] For islanders, the products of these global operations have the glamorous appeal of the completely novel, served up in seemingly ultramodern venues replete with colorful décor and signage, uniformed staff, and friendly smiles. Culturally, fast food restaurants represent a way for islanders to step out of their everyday identity and be Western in a manner that does not threaten their own conventions because there are no particular social rules that need to be observed. Aside from the obvious appeal of the food itself, there is a sense of freedom on offer that is arguably one of the attractions of fast food for islander consumers.

The popularity of fast food among islanders is growing. Most of the largest cities and towns, including Honolulu, Port Moresby (PNG), Noumea, Suva, Apia (Independent State of Samoa) and Nuku'alofa (The Kingdom of Tonga's capital), have their global fast food chains like KFC and McDonald's. Tonga is the exception here because, in the 1990s, it chose not to allow KFC and McDonald's franchises to open in the country as a result of King Taufa'ahau Topau IV's edict that Tongans should lose weight (see chapter 8). However, Tongans do have a product called Country Fried Chicken (deep-fried chicken pieces), a franchise that began in 1994, and which Tongans (and other islanders) have taken to with a passion. Such fare is among a growing number of cooked food options that are now available to islander consumers.

Aina Haina McDonald's was the first in Hawaii, opening in 1968. Other Americanized locales or territories (Guam, American Samoa) also naturally have these more familiar brands, while in other places, local laws have played a role in slowing the advance of fast food culture. The township of Avarua, on Rarotonga, capital of the Cook Islands, has no multinational food and beverage groups like McDonald's or Starbuck's, and hotel chains like the Hilton and Sheraton have struggled to gain a commercial foothold there. The lack of business opportunity or consumer demand is not the issue, however; rather, it is the local land-related laws. In fact, Cook Islanders love their KFC—one of the largest KFCs in New Zealand, at Auckland International Airport, is the point of departure for thousands of buckets of fried chicken in the course of a year, which leave with islanders returning or visiting home on regular flights to Rarotonga—but on Rarotonga, land ownership is tightly controlled by communities of families led by the *ariki* (tribal chiefs), who make it more or less impossible for non-Cook Islanders to own land. This means that investment in the region is rendered problematic for companies that do not wish to invest in land they cannot own outright or lease only for a given period.

There are therefore certain disincentives to providing food and beverage outlets in the Pacific, but these must be understood in the cultural context rather than as a reflection of lack of desire for new foods on the part of islanders. In general, eating out at restaurants, fast food outlets, and other food service facilities (food halls, street food, and vending machines) increases in step with the ongoing Westernization of the economy and retailing infrastructure of the islands. Chains like McDonald's are also known to adapt to local differences in food preferences, and has therefore introduced distinctive "island" products. Its taro pies were first sold in Hawaii in 2005, but are also available in Fiji. These are similar to the company's apple pie product insofar as they feature the same deep-fried pastry crust and come in the same shape. Inside, however, there is a taro paste filling. This is one way in which local diets are altered, perhaps adding to the conception that McDonald's is becoming a little bit islander at the same time. But far outweighing the cultural merit of any concession paid to local gastronomic tradition is the fact that such chains have been responsible for the introduction of myriad product lines; they have boosted islanders' reliance on the cash economy by providing what are perceived as cheap meals; they have increased the importation of processed foods and food products; and they have further entrenched the degree to which islanders regard eating fast food as maintaining a degree of cultural capital. These factors have made for the success of fast food in the islands.

Dining out on fast food and shopping in supermarkets are the two points at which islanders connect most regularly with Western food and foodways. At the other extreme, in the expensive high-end restaurant and catering market, eating out has assumed an entirely different character. At this end of the market, it is tourism, now an essential economic activity for island communities and livelihood, that has driven change. The globalization of the tourism industry—and another example of McDonaldization—at the level of resort dining has a fairly standardized appearance. Fiji's Vatulele Island resort, for example, features alfresco dining with views of a lagoon, and serves a selection of world cuisines: Californian, Thai, Japanese, Pacific Rim, and Indian. Fresh ingredients are advertised as being flown in daily from Australia and New Zealand. Seafood is central to what is offered, and this is very often the case region-wide. This is how global tourism marketing understands the Pacific, and there-

fore also standardizes island cuisine. In terms of style, it is not so much islander cuisine as it is an international cuisine that is recognized instantly
by the well-heeled tourist.

Looking at particular examples of Pacific food culture today, it is clear
that this packaging of products has become highly sophisticated and increasingly sensitive to the desires of consumers. In relation to food, trends
to consider are creolization and hybridization, terms that denote the
blending and adapting of traditional foods in ways that incorporate new
foods and techniques that typically originate elsewhere. This process has
also created real economic opportunities for islanders. The tourism industry has been particularly effective in "re-badging" island destinations
through food-related marketing that emphasizes particular values that
appeal to would-be tourists. This hybridizing typically involves linking
culinary styles and particular dishes with the professional skill and experience of a celebrity chef, and may also include describing foods in terms of
their supposed health benefits, or political and ethical status, for example,
as organic, fresh, Fairtrade, or local. The more serious diner-out has an
increasing opportunity to sample not only the best local or just caught
seafood and freshly picked fruit, but also a variety of indigenous foods,
locally grown vegetables and herbs, including organic products, or other
foods that are grown with minimal environmental impact.

On Turtle Island (Nanuya Levu, a privately owned Fijian island), for
example, French-born chef, Jacques Reymond, a long-established celebrity chef in Australia, is touted as the resort's food consultant. The cuisine
is described as the result of nature's bounty, including fresh seafood and
organic fruits and vegetables that are reportedly sourced locally from the
resort's own four-acre garden. A variety of fish, "just caught by local fish-
erman," is also promised in the resort's marketing material. The romantic
notion of a Garden of Eden where foods are easily accessed is strongly suggested in such advertising, but not without irony. Evoking the dream of
an idyllic setting where foods are always present in abundance is an image
that supports an industry in part responsible for the marginalization and
erosion of islander livelihoods, local economies, and traditional lifestyles.

Recent endeavors do point in a new direction, however, with collaborative arrangements being made more frequently between resort owners and local islanders, increasing local input and boosting employment,
skills levels, and revenue. Changing political, ethical, or ideological views
have not been responsible for this sea change, but rather the key shift
toward lifestyle and experience tourism that now plays such an important
part in tourism growth around the world. The recent development of local
island economies through collaborations between tourist resorts and local

food producers, therefore, has been a real success story for islanders and their environment. The new demand for ecotourism, coupled with the pressure felt by resort owners over damage caused to coastlines, coral reefs, and fishing grounds through the overuse of beaches and reefs, climate change, run-off from farmland, and effluent disposal, has spurred action and played into the hands of locals, who have been keen to get involved in projects that can help restore some ecological balance as well as putting dollars in their pockets.

In the hinterland of Fiji's Coral Coast region, for example, growers have successfully diversified from subsistence agriculture, and now produce a range of produce that is sold to the coastal resorts nearby. This means that resorts, to their advantage, can advertise local produce as a feature on restaurant menus, or even cite their saving of "food miles" (a measure of the carbon footprint of imported foods) if the ethics of environmentalism is deemed a tourist drawcard. Whatever the reasoning, the fostering of such enterprise has so far been of real benefit, particularly on the smaller outlying islands, where transport costs and quality control can be even more of an issue. At Matava resort on Kadavu Island, south of Viti Levu, the proprietors boast an extensive organic vegetable garden that supplies the resort's kitchens: coconuts, pineapple, paw paw, guava, banana, mangos, lemons, melons, avocados, mandarins, eggplant, tomatoes, lettuces, cucumber, zucchini, carrots, cabbages, pumpkin, capsicum, radishes, cassava, coriander, basil, sage, and oregano are all listed as being produced. Waste is also recycled in what is described as an extensive composting system, and seeds are raised in a seed house for planting in the garden. This information, provided on the resort's Web site, is an attractive lure, especially for the growing numbers of ecotourists who want to see where their food is coming from, perceive that it is good for them, and ensure that it is not adversely affecting the environment. Waibulabula (Living Waters) was developed as a collaborative effort between local Fijian villages and resort complex owners also on the Coral Coast. Waibulabula focuses on treating wastewater by creating series of heavily planted shallow lakes, in which phosphates and other damaging chemicals are used by the plants as the water flows through.[3] In some cases, these new collaborations attract input from agencies such as the Secretariat of the Pacific Community, which help with the development of gardening and agriculture, advise on the threat of pests, and assist with strategies and planning. Education, economy, and employment can all benefit from these developments in global tourism.

Selling the unique food products of a locality, region, or as examples of an artisan food heritage is another feature of tourism world-wide, and this can potentially involve many local people in exploring, reappraising, and reengaging with their own sometimes forgotten or sidelined culinary-cultural knowledge. While there is nothing particularly new about "natives" staging their own history for the pleasure of bemused or curious tourists (postcards of "cannibal feasts" were very popular in the early 20th century, for example), the new economic and cultural rationale of selling food culture, in particular, represents another recent departure that offers important opportunities for the revitalization of native foodways and environments, and puts more than a new face on eating out.

Restaurant and catering have created many jobs for islanders, both at the production and consumption ends. Islanders supply locally sourced fish, seafood, vegetables, and fruit to the restaurant and catering trades. They have also found employment in the tourism industry service sector (if not directly in restaurant and catering). While locals may not often enjoy what tourists experience while dining out, they are nonetheless part of the scene and are earning a living. By and large, islanders do not eat out in restaurants unless they are low-budget establishments. Culturally, individualized eating of this kind is not particularly attractive to islanders, but cost is the main impediment. This draws attention to the noticeable inequity that exists in the tourism industry. Typically, driving along any stretch of road in the islands will mean passing a walled, ocean beach-fronted resort replete with all the conveniences and luxuries that Western culture can offer. Oasis-like, these resorts seem oblivious to all around them and, certainly more than a world away from the half-naked kids selling fruit piled in neat mounds in the dust on the other side of the road. Running past the manicured lawns, fluttering flags, and gleaming signage of the resort, these fruit vendors do not seem to notice that here, abruptly, the First World meets the Third World. This is a commonplace phenomenon; it is particularly noticeable in places like Rarotonga and Fiji, but also exists on many outlying islands where locally based islanders have long since given up their subsistence forms of living and moved elsewhere, squeezed out by sprawling resorts. Private islands have also increasingly turned themselves over to exclusive tourism operations, including fine dining. Seldom do locals profit from these places although, recently, there have been opportunities in the supply of local produce, which has been a growing drawcard for discerning tourist-diners.[4]

The Cook Islands provides an example, however, of where tourism has been a lifesaver for a struggling economy in the Pacific region. In the diverse food products and choices for eating out that it offers, there is a clear indication of how a tourism-aligned island economy provides a diverse range of food service operations. In 2006, the population of the Cook

Islands was 14,000, which represented a decline of 30 percent since 1975. With dwindling economic prospects for islanders at home, and for the tiny nation as a whole, after the collapse of all the major export businesses that had developed over the years, many islanders have sought there fortune elsewhere, particularly in New Zealand. Island nations still have to struggle to compete in economic terms with global competition and the foreign ownership of local resources. This is a battle they can never win, but one in which they have learned how to compete with some success. Tourism offered to the Cooks (as they are called by locals) what may have seemed the only hope and opportunity for many islanders to survive. Now visited each year by 85,000 tourists, all of whom need to be provided with daily food and drink during their stay, the Cooks, and particularly its main island, Rarotonga, have developed a range of dining-out options. The venues where eating out is at its most conspicuous include some of the best real estate in the islands, which now accommodate resort and dining complexes. Ocean sunset vistas form a glorious background to eating, drinking, and relaxing in such venues, where decks and poolside recreation areas, virtually on the beach, often include bar and dining services. In the township of Avarua (the only town on the island), and at many other locations around the island (one 16-mile road runs around the periphery of the island), restaurants cater to a wide variety of tastes. Generic Italian-, Chinese-, and Mediterranean-themed restaurants compete with many fusion-style eateries that serve eclectic blends of local and imported cuisines. Inventive fusion dishes like taro root lasagna, popular in both Hawaii and the Cook Islands, or cannelloni stuffed with taro leaves, suggest the ways in which local foods can be incorporated into foreign cuisines.[5] But, as is the case with incorporating other indigenous ingredients from other parts of world, the presence of local foods is often suggestive more than constitutive, an intriguing garnish more than a central element. Tourists are mostly skeptical diners by nature, preferring things they recognize, and only wanting exoticism in small doses. Mostly, local ingredients become part of a typically Western style of contemporary cuisine: crumbed pork fillet with sweet potato mash and paw paw coconut sauce, for example. An element of attractiveness appeals to the customer's desire to eat local in a dish described as such, while the foods themselves, with the possible exception of the sweet potato, may be anything but.

Cafes, and now Internet cafes, are popular places for coffee and meals among visitors who are also eager to call home, contact friends while on holiday, or simply surf the 'Net. These serve the normal variety of cafe food that could be found almost anywhere in urban centers around the world. Boutique food outlets have also appeared on Rarotonga. Globalization has meant that more and varied products can be sourced, and so it is possible to buy French cheeses, truffle oil and wines, handmade Italian pasta, and exotic imported herbs and spices. This availability, and to some extent, new demand, from tourists has also had an impact on the local restaurant scene, which, for such a tiny island, is quite diverse. Not only the restaurants, but also take-out and fast food outlets, cafes, resorts, bars, and supermarkets all cater to those who, broadly speaking, desire to eat out. Most retail food outlets would like to count on the tourist dollar, and although the fast food chains have realized the potential for islander consumption, they also realize that tourists like a taste of home while on holiday, and buy take-out. And, as the laws of commercial enterprise dictate, prices are equated with what customers (mainly tourists) are willing and able to pay rather than by consideration of what locals can afford. Eating venues, therefore, are mainly designed for visitors, and often give visual representation of the perennial themes associated with an island lifestyle: a sunny, beachfront position, overlooking the water, the inclusion of local artifacts (carvings, paintings, tapa cloth, printed cloth) as decorative features, a breezy atmosphere, and easy-going service. Also mandatory are the typical range of cocktails, small appetizers (pupus, in Hawaii) and various islands-themed dishes. Island Nights are also a perennial favorite on Rarotonga, as elsewhere in the region. Usually held twice weekly, for an all-inclusive, prepaid sum, diners get their meal, drinks vouchers, and a show, normally featuring island music and dance. Islanders have a strong musical tradition, and many are accomplished drummers, guitarists, or ukulele players, as well as dancers. Traditional costumes, including grass skirts, necklaces of flowers and shells, make for a colorful night's entertainment as the backdrop to eating and drinking. The foods served at such gatherings cater very much to Western tastes, but naturally include local delicacies like fish, shellfish, crab, and tropical fruit. Steaks, fries, and other commonplace Western foods are also offered. These events are very much for the tourists. In terms of what an event like this costs, tourists used to cheap food and accommodation prices in parts of Asia, for example, would find the Pacific region to be a comparatively expensive place to eat out. Of course, high costs are partly the result of supply costs. Given that the spread of eating venues in the islands has been predicated in the past on the availability of a range of imported products, eating out means eating more expensive imported foods and drinks.

Tourism has changed the face of eating in the islands in terms of what is available and how much it costs. But the overall effect of the growth of tourism on the economy of the Pacific region also needs to be measured

Indian sweets on display.

in terms of wealth generation and employment, although the effects of tourism, or the lack of it, differ markedly from place to place. Smaller island states like Nauru, for example, have struggled to get their tourism image right.

Perceptions of what tourists want in the way of food and drink tend to be determined by current tourism trends and how the tastes of tourists are thought to conform to international food styles and aesthetics. The tourist may choose an item from a menu of exotic-sounding dishes because it meets their expectation of what island food should be like. But when it arrives, a dish that is colorfully presented, architecturally arranged, and enticingly flavored, might reflect the global taste of that tourist or global trends in the hospitality and restaurant markets more than any particular local food style. Restaurant culture and restaurant menus represent island food in particular ways, according to the specific needs of the restaurant and its customers. Lower-priced establishments tend to offer standardized fare, like burgers, focaccia, pasta, bread-based snacks like sandwiches, wraps (pita bread), and rolls, fries, deep-fried products like spring rolls (served with the globally ubiquitous sweet chili sauce), salads, an assortment of drinks including coffee, juices, smoothies (blended drinks), shakes, beer, wine, and spirits. All these foods are what one might expect anywhere in the Western world. In addition to these foods, however, are other dishes that can be usefully classified according to various themes. Fresh fruit and fish are in evidence everywhere on restaurant menus, but the style of preparation can differ greatly. Common themes have emerged, like cooking fish in coconut milk, but in general, the variety of dishes is international in its appeal, with only a small number of dishes that could genuinely be called local.

LOCAL FOOD

The theme of local food has recently gained ground as a trendy option for discerning diners with a conscience, who recognize the difference in the flavor and quality of foods grown locally instead of shipped in, perhaps having been stored for months prior to sale. They also recognize that there is an ethical difference in choosing to buy local or global: foods that have not only come from far afield but that also have an uncertain, perhaps morally compromised provenance, produced by recourse to unfair labor practices, or with the use of harmful hormones or other chemicals. In this sense, local food has gained a foothold in the marketplace for consumers with a conscience, who see themselves as doing the right thing in choosing to buy products that represent minimal impact on the environment and the lives of the ordinary people who help produce them. Local foods in the islands have been affected by this trend to the extent that particular traditional ingredients like taro, cassava, varieties of seafood, coconut milk, and various vegetable leaves, fruits, buds, and seeds have found their way onto restaurant or resort menus, appealing to a perennial desire for authenticity that the interest in provenance and quality partly explains. The notion is that eating local means sampling the experience of native people by eating local foods, like a seasonal ingredient such as *duruka*, a plant resembling sugarcane and prized for its stem's heart. But how these foods are prepared now differs greatly from traditional cookery methods. Where local foods are offered, even though other items may be *produced* locally but not indicated as such on the menu, styles, techniques, combinations, and modes of presentation best described as hybrid differ markedly from those related to traditional fare. Typically, a nice piece of local fish, say tuna, might be charcoal-grilled and served rare, sliced, with coconut-infused rice, and a ginger-citrus glaze. While fish, rice, coconut, and citrus might all have found their way into a fairly traditional dish using the same ingredients, this "smarter" version appeals to a more international audience who might expect to encounter such a dish on a menu in a stylish restaurant in any major city around the world. In the Pacific, offering such a dish serves to highlight local ingredients to good effect, but without necessarily needing to source local product. Two exceptions would be marinated raw fish (which really requires freshly caught fish), and dishes where the main ingredient is unusual or unknown outside the islands, like *ota* (Athyrium esculentus), a dish made with bush fern, which is simply cooked in coconut milk and seasoned with lemon before serving. This dish, *ota miti*, would appeal to the restaurant diner who wanted to try something different, authentic, or both. Offerings like taro leaf soup, cassava root curry, or chicken baked with mango and ginger exemplify how dishes have evolved as a marriage between local ingredients and Western forms of preparation.

Techniques of cooking that have taken on a local flavor include charcoal-grilling; this was traditionally done using open fires, or the embers they produced, whereas today it is more likely a gas-powered restaurant grill. *Poisson cru* is regarded as local, and it is easy and cheap to make, since fish, coconut, and citrus are all available locally. Without heating being required, there are also no heating-related costs. *Poisson cru* is a widespread favorite, and delicious, but it has partly become a standard because it is so economical and convenient to prepare rather than because of its traditional status as a food among locals.

ETHNIC FOODS

Traditional Chinese food is found everywhere that Chinese communities have been established. The overseas Chinese, as they were once known, cleaved almost religiously to their gastronomic and culinary traditions, no matter how far they roamed from mainland China. In Noumea, today, one can eat a fairly standard form of dim sum, or wonton, beef and black bean sauce, egg foo yung, or chicken chow mein, the same as anywhere else in the West. So far as these dishes represent Chinese food to the world, they have endured, remarkably unchanged, for generations, even in far-flung corners of the globe. In this respect, Chinese food is almost unique in terms of its resilience to influence and its longevity as an international cuisine. In the Pacific region, the Chinese, and as a consequence, Chinese food, have been very successful, in spite of the poor treatment the early Chinese migrants received at the hands of their colonial masters. Given the relative cheapness and high quality of Chinese food, its popularity was almost guaranteed.

Although Chinese did travel into the Pacific during the Ming and Tang dynasties, it was not until the mid-19th century that waves of Chinese

immigrants entered the Pacific arriving in Tahiti, first in 1865–66 as indentured laborers, and later, in the period of 1907–1914, when many of
the families of the workers arrived. Chinese were indentured to many
islands, including Hawaii, Papua New Guinea (PNG), and Western
Samoa. Once established, Chinese immigrants moved into commerce,
market gardening, and restaurateuring as their means of livelihood. Today,
people of Chinese descent make up roughly 10 percent of the Tahitian
population (26,000), and, while still celebrating traditional festivals like
Chinese New Year, including lion dances and fireworks, Qingming (pure
brightness), Kasan (tomb-sweeping day), and the Mid-Autumn Festival
with its traditional moon cakes, they also celebrate Western-style Christmas, New Year, and All Saints' Day (known as Toussaint). They also
take part in French Tahitian celebrations, the most important of which
is Heiva. For Heiva, the Chinese mainly provide mobile snack bars and
game stands, but also watch as spectators. There have been no Chinese-
language schools in Tahiti since the 1960s (when they were closed) and
so, increasingly, the Chinese have become assimilated into the French
way of life. Ethnic Chinese with the surname Xiao are better known as
Sichoix, and Lius are known as Lenfants, both representing a Frenchifica-
tion that has somewhat estranged the Tahitian Chinese from their Chinese homeland. Many Chinese have intermarried with Polynesians over
the years and so, as French citizens, these Chinese also describe themselves as Polynesians of Chinese ancestry, and include taro and other local
ingredients in celebratory banquets. In contrast, Chinese restaurant food
has not changed much, and while at times reflecting local tastes, it would
still be recognized the world over as generically "Chinese." Chinese communities flourish in New Caledonia (French Polynesia has around 10,000
Chinese), Fiji (5,000), Hawaii, Vanuatu (300), PNG (1,500), the Solomons (900), New Zealand (140,000), and Australia, where about 500,000
people are of Chinese ethnic background. In some cases, the Chinese
began life in the islands because of foodstuffs. In Fiji, on Levuka, during
the 1870s, Chinese returning home from the gold fields of Victoria, Australia, found work exporting bêche-de-mer, and other foodstuffs. Today,
many Fijian Chinese work in commerce and market gardening. Chinese
restaurants are also popular, as they are in Tonga and Samoa, and anywhere an island's food business might thrive. Chinese food products have
also influenced Pacific food culture; in particular through soy sauce, that
versatile product that seasons and flavors at the same time. It is to be
found everywhere in the region.

Around 50,000 people of Chinese descent (but far fewer of other Asian
groups) live in New Zealand, and Chinese restaurants and food importers

Typical Fijian Indian budget restaurant fare.

were a long-term feature of the port city of Wellington until the 1980s, when generational and economic change meant the closure of many such establishments. Less commonly represented in the Pacific are Asian cuisines including Thai and Vietnamese (now commonplace in Australia, where 150,000 Vietnamese, many of whom were refugees, now reside).

Indian food, and the epicenter of Pacific Indian cuisine, Fiji, means Southern Indian food (little tandoori, for example, a Northern Indian tradition, is to be found), and there are many cheap and cheerful curry houses there that vie daily for local and tourist trade. The prices are low and the fare is often based on an assortment of meat, fish, and vegetable curries of varying spiciness, dahl, pickles and fresh chili. Indian restaurants, exhibiting a greater diversity of regional Indian and Sri Lankan cuisines, are also well represented in Australasia.

The influence of Asian cuisines in general can be viewed as limited to a few ingredients and a certain number of restaurants, since there is little ethnically home-grown food culture as such in the islands, but Asian cooking techniques have greatly affected public food style in the Pacific, as they have across the globe. Stir-frying, which involves the preslicing of numerous ingredients before speedy wok cooking, has perfectly adapted itself to restaurant service. Various forms of rice or noodles and rice form the natural accompaniment to what is a limitless range of possibility in terms of ingredient combinations. Fish sauce, soy, hoisin, and teriyaki sauces, chili (and various chili-based curry pastes), sesame oil, ginger, garlic, Asian green vegetables like bok choi or *choi sum*, spring onion, coriander, and lemongrass are typically used to accent stir-fried dishes based on meat, fish, or vegetables, and tofu. The technique is economical, fast, and readily adapted to incorporate new taste ideas and ingredient combinations.

Other ethnic influences in the region are Italian, a remarkably popular cuisine on Rarotonga, for example, perhaps because of the taste for Italian among the mainly New Zealand tourists who visit the tiny island. Italian restaurants in the Pacific are not the result of Italian immigration, but rather of the popularity, relative ease, and convenience of the cuisine itself. Tinned tomatoes, dried pasta, salami or prosciutto, and hard cheeses are all reasonably readily transported and long-keeping foods. The use of various forms of pasta, a range of simple sauces, fresh meat, seafood, vegetables, herbs, and soft cheeses, plus basic cooking skills allows virtually

French *patisserie* in Noumea.

anyone to prepare rudimentary Italian dishes. Pizza, originally perfected in Naples, has found its way into the Pacific, not as a representative of the regional Italian tradition that created it, but as just another appropriated, generic food style turned fast food.

Japanese-style foods like sushi and sashimi are also popular, as they are around the world. In the tropical Pacific, however, Japanese cold foods, in particular, which also utilize raw fish and other fresh, uncooked ingredients, have been very successful. French cuisine completely dominates in New Caledonia and French Polynesia, although even there one can find Chinese eateries.

Hawaii presents perhaps the most eclectic blend of traditions even though, today, its cuisine is highly Americanized. Japanese, Chinese, Hawaiian, and Portuguese are among the influences that have affected the most Hawaiian of eating events, the luau. Dishes like teriyaki chicken and dried beef "Hawaiian" style (*pipi kaula*), *lomi lomi* (salmon cooked with tomato and onion), are as traditional as *poke* (raw fish salad) and poi (baked taro paste). A medley of gastronomic influences has shaped Hawaii's dining culture. Today, as in many urban centers world-wide, Chinese, Indonesian, Japanese, Korean, Philippine, Thai, and Vietnamese restaurants are popular there. Portuguese sausage and a form of deep-fried doughnut (*malasadas*) have become Hawaiian standards. Hawaii also has its own hybrid favorites, like *loco moco*, a dish that goes back to the late 1940s, consisting of white rice, a hamburger patty, a fried egg, and gravy; this dish also has a number of variations.[6]

TIKI CULTURE

At the point where Pacific food becomes something unique to the islands, but where its form and ingredients used originate elsewhere, is a process oddly reversed in appropriated forms of Pacific culture, including food. The origins of the most conspicuous form of appropriated Polynesian/Pacific culture is known as tiki culture, after the emblematic carvings of human form that range in size from monumental totem to ornamental jewelry. Maori customarily wear small greenstone (jade) tiki as neck pendants, while similar forms carved in wood also adorn their architecture (door lintels, etc.). This style of carved totem, large and small, would become the basis of a whole decorative style of interior design, a central feature of what were originally bars, clubs, and restaurants. Tiki culture is the name given to this Polynesian décor and aesthetic, the invention of which goes back to the 1920s, and to Los Angeles's Coconut Grove nightclub, which opened in April 1921. The décor there was conspicuously Pacific, and included numerous palm trees overhanging the dining tables, and cocktails, which also became synonymous with tiki.

The onset of the Great Depression in 1929, in one sense, aided the development of tiki culture. The island aesthetic was taken up and developed by Ernest Gantt, a one-time bootlegger with no real prospects who, after having traveled for several months in the South Pacific, realized an opportunity to open a bar in McCadden Place, Los Angeles, in 1934. He called it Donn the Beachcomber, and it would become famous for its décor and drinks. Gantt decorated his small bar with tiki ornaments he had collected from the islands, including nets and even bits of wreckage from old boats. The original setting of the bar, the personality of the host, and, importantly, his ability to mix drinks—mostly rum-based cocktails, a drink style that would later become synonymous with Island holidays—assured his success, prompting Gantt to adopt the name Donn Beach. His first cocktail was called the Sumatra Kula, made on a base of rum, the cheapest spirit then available, imported from the Caribbean. Beach is also attributed with the invention of the mai tai, which means "good" in Tahitian, and again is based on rum with the addition of curaçao and fruit juice. A restaurant followed the bar in 1937, serving what customers thought was very exotic fare, but which was in fact based on Cantonese cuisine, which in this context became associated with the Pacific.

After World War II, Beach opened a branch of Donn the Beachcomber in Hawaii, where he spent the remainder of his life, adding to his reputation with the invention of a total of 84 drinks.[7] These included the Zombie, an alcoholically potent cocktail, which was popularized at the 1939 New York World's Fair. Beach's tiki culture included thatched roofs over the bar area, "rain" supplied by a hose outside that would spray the roof, dim lighting, and an abundance of Polynesian tokens and gewgaws.

Probably the most well-known example of tiki culture today is Trader Vic's restaurant chain, which has about 25 outlets distributed around the globe. In 1936, inspired by Donn the Beachcomber and so also South Seas-themed, a French Canadian, Victor Bergeron, changed the name of his popular bar in California to Trader Vic's. The Trader Vic's franchise is still trading on Pacific culture today.[8] At the time it first opened, South Seas island art and culture was already making popular headway among middle-class Americans, who romantically associated it with figures like the French painter Paul Gauguin, who had lived and worked in Tahiti. More recently, at that time, the voyages of Thor Heyerdahl's *Kon Tiki* had also made a big impression, along with various films like Bing Crosby's *Waikiki Wedding* (1937) and later, *South Pacific* (1958). The Coconut Grove (where the Academy Awards were held throughout the 1930s and

'40s) and Donn Beach's association with such acting legends as Marlene Dietrich and influential film barons like Howard Hughes partly explain why tiki culture took off. Tiki culture served to make island holidays an alluring prospect and, from then on, would be sustained and fostered by the growing tourism trade.

Tiki culture also spread in the United States, and became an aesthetic that influenced the design of everyday consumer venues like laundromats, bowling alleys, and trailer parks. Masks, mats, and tiki sculptures also added some South Seas spice to normally mundane interiors. This is the key point about the tiki craze because it highlights how the Pacific Islands were commodified for easy consumption by Western consumers. In the Tiki bars and restaurants, all the kitsch décor was the main plank of a marketing push to get people consuming more alcohol-based drinks. The exotic atmosphere lulled customers into a fantasy far removed from the worries and monotony of their everyday lives. A few colorful cocktails, lounge music with a tropical lilt (an original form of which is associated with the "island sounds" of composer Martin Denny), and Polynesian trappings completed the island scene, which amounted to virtually the opposite of what socializing traditionally represented in the islands. Drinking alcohol seemed to be the main reason for frequenting these venues, and the latest *Trader Vic's Cookbook* contains recipes for 100 different sorts of cocktail, while the foods are described as pan-Asian nibbles, including crab Rangoon and crispy prawns, harking back to the original Cantonese fusion food at Donn the Beachcomber.[9]

Eventually, in the late '70s, the tiki bar craze petered out, although there was a revival in the late 1990s, when, for a while at least, tiki was no longer considered tacky, but another form of retro-chic, along with flared pants and side burns. Contemporary surf culture in California, in particular, has adopted tiki masks and icons as part of the beach lifestyle, while the Tonga Room, at the Fairmont Hotel, Nob Hill, San Francisco, is one of the last, most intact tiki culture bars left in the world, and still has a loyal following. It features live entertainment, dancing, typical tropical cocktails like the mai tai, and a "rain storm" that erupts around the venue's pool. Its restaurant boasts Pacific Rim Asian Cuisine and the décor, as expected, is kitsch Polynesian.

Tiki culture says something fundamental about the West's attitude to the islands, and to Pacific food culture, because it has recycled island culture to suit the tastes of Western consumers, something can also be seen reflected in the West's appropriation of Pacific cuisine (see chapter 3). The cuisine of the Pacific, when attempts to reproduce it have been made, tends toward a predictable and somewhat clichéd use of fruits, fruit salads, coconut cream, and seafood. The Hawaiian snacks known as pupus were also popularized in tiki bars, the consumption of which naturally punctuates the drinking of cocktails over several hours. This is often the fate of food styles and cuisines when they travel; travel makes them subject to interpretation, especially when a dish becomes disconnected from where it originated and from those who prepared it and imbued it with cultural meaning. Foods can take on meaning in a new setting as well, and this is certainly the case with Pacific Island food, which has tended to become exoticized in the West. As such, it has also been commodified, turned into a commercial product no longer clearly representative of the culture that inspired it.

DIVERSITY AND HYBRIDITY: EATING IN THE ISLANDS

Understanding the relationship between traditional and currently changing social and cultural values with regard to food means looking closely at how both systems survive and, in fact, strengthen each other by means of globalization and its effects. Much criticism has been leveled at the "forces of globalization," identified as standardizing and imperialistic, yet in the food culture of the Pacific Islands today, seemingly paradoxically, globalization can also help to encourage and reward the development of indigenous or home-grown foodways, because it creates niche markets for goods and services that have gained a global reach. Interest in local foods, in particular, has developed as the direct result of increasing tourism, itself a marker of the trend toward globalization. Today, Fiji's tourism market is second only to food exports as a fraction of its total GDP. Eating out is a fundamental part of the tourist experience, and is now catered to in an increasingly entrepreneurial manner. It is important to consider, then, that there is more to eating out in the islands than appears in eating venues as such. Infrastructure in the form of home-grown small businesses, in industries like hydroponics, organic farming, gourmet, health, and native food products, and ecotours, which include traditional cooking and harvesting, collectively represent growing diversity in food culture-related products and services that are given broader exposure to the world market through globalization. Eating out encompasses diverse possibilities as a result and, although the full variety of foods on offer may only be available to the wealthier tourist, the cultural influence of diversity on the eating habits of locals may also have longer-term benefits in terms of food choices. The largely unchecked influx of Western foods, over the last hundred years, is now being curbed in a small way by the growing demand for quality foods that represent more local-friendly production values like organics and sustainability. If such practices prove to be adopted in the wider region, the diet of locals may be incrementally improved.

AUSTRALIA AND NEW ZEALAND

For many years, Australians, and perhaps particularly New Zealanders, have tended to take the quality of their food for granted. Relatively small populations, fertile lands, a range of tropical to subtropical and temperate climates, good rainfall (although Australia has been in the grip of a serious drought for a decade), and abundant seafood, meat, and dairy products (milk, cheese, cream) have historically provided foods of high quality. The transport of food, more of a cost issue in Australia, safeguarded the ready availability of ample fresh produce in New Zealand and somewhat offset the consumption of processed foods over the years. A good supply of food has been assured, and the cost of fresh food has historically been low (as a fraction of household expenditure). Both countries are also cut off by sea, and needed to establish adequate food supplies that further offset both the need and, for a time at least, the desire for imported foodstuffs. Thus, eating at home was the norm in Australasian culture, as elsewhere in the West, although eating out at public venues like hotels or banquet halls, and luxury food providers, were commonplace from early on. At public dinners and banquets, the foods consumed followed the English model, while in Auckland in the 1850s, people could buy imported delicacies like pickled oysters, hare soup, kippered salmon, Yarmouth bloaters, and champagne. With the gold rushes of the 1860s came many more hotels, which often had opulent and extensive menus. Up until the 1880s, by which time the first refrigerated meat was exported by ship from New Zealand, the steady increase in sheep, cattle stocks, and crops had created a secure and plentiful food source. New Zealanders ate well, and loved their meat, especially. Restaurants were established in the Victorian era.[10] These were frequently based on the French model of service and cuisine. The modern international hotel system of the 20th century cemented French cuisine as the benchmark. Dining out was almost synonymous with eating French food.

At the popular level, tastes remained tied to the mother country, Great Britain, and modes and styles of eating out in Australia and New Zealand also developed in similar ways, although New Zealand was less affected by the cuisines of immigrants than Australia. Both countries retained some of Britain's food traditions and made them their own. The fish and chip shop is a New Zealand institution today, while the pie cart (selling pies laden with mashed potatoes, mushy peas, and gravy), another local adaptation of an older British tradition, is still popular in both countries, although presently pie cart owner-operators in New Zealand are struggling to survive because of health-related local council bylaws.[11] Other local variants have disappeared altogether, like the milk bar (Australia), often American-styled with deco interiors, where ice cream and milkshakes were sold (popular in the 1950s). These were eclipsed by cafes, cafeterias, and the corner store, better known as the deli in Australia, but somewhat different from the delicatessen of Europe or the United States because it also sold everyday items like newspapers and many household goods and groceries. In New Zealand, milk bars were called dairies, and cornered the market for milkshakes and ice creams, but doubling also, as did the Aussie deli, as an everyday grocery-cum-corner store. Pubs (hotels with bars attached) were places to drink, but patrons could also buy pies and "counter meals" (hot meals comprising meat and vegetables). Hotel dining rooms, a limited range of restaurants, and tearooms completed the picture of the options for dining out prior to World War II.

The retention of British standards and styles in Australasia historically hampered change in terms of cuisine. In the early years, hotels, cafes, and restaurants catered to all walks of life, offering European or local fare, but with a predominance of the latter, plain cooking without too much artistry; at the same time, the pub, where beer was sold, became increasingly popular with the working class, which comprised a significant portion of the population. Food, in this context, was more of an adjunct to drink. The influx of 3.47 million European migrants in the wake of World War II was the greatest historical catalyst for gastronomic change, helping to lure stay-at-home eaters out for meals in Australia and New Zealand. In New Zealand, Dalmatians, Serbs, Italians, and Greeks were among those who fled Europe, joining the Chinese immigrants who had arrived in the 19th century during the Australasian gold rushes. Forty thousand Chinese were living in the eastern states of Australia by the 1890s, and naturally brought their foodways with them. Over time, their foods became better-known to Australians and New Zealanders in restaurants that featured predominantly Cantonese cooking.

Over the longer term, the factors affecting attitudes to eating out in Australia and New Zealand have included level of affluence, the industrialization of food processing, retailing, and consumption (supermarkets and fast food), the influence of culinary style as a form of cultural capital, generational change, women's liberation, increased mobility (cars), the influence of the media, and changing drinking habits. In Australasia, a revolutionary shift from eating at home to eating out more often occurred over the last 50 years, a period during which the amount spent on food eaten out of the house doubled (from 25 to 50%). By the mid-1990s, Australians were spending US$10 billion a year on eating out in nearly 20,000 restaurants and cafes, 14,500 takeaway outlets, and 2,600 fast-food outlets nationwide.

Eating out has become the norm and a commonplace activity particularly for city dwellers. Further immigration in the '70s (from Thailand, Vietnam, Indonesia, Malaysia, Korea, Japan, India, and Sri Lanka), and the subsequent loosening of immigration laws, has seen growing numbers of people migrating to Australia, most recently from Africa. Whenever people migrate, they take their foodways with them and, in both Australia and New Zealand today, the food cultures of the various groups can be seen reflected in the range of eating out options. Each culture makes its contribution to food culture in Australia. Sydney boasts world-class Thai, Japanese, and Italian restaurants.

Drinking, an obvious adjunct to eating, was historically dominated by beer and imported wines and spirits. By 1850, there were 48 breweries in Tasmania, the southern island state where cooler temperatures suited the production of hops and barley. Australasians (predominantly men) remain fervent beer fans today, with beer consumption in Australia more than doubling to more than 35 gallons annually per head between 1940 and 1980. In 2004, Australia was the 4th highest consumer of beer in the world, at 133 gallons per head per year. New Zealand ranked 15th at 99 gallons per head.

The next trend in alcoholic beverages to affect beer consumption was the rise in wine production and consumption. Until as recently the 1970s, fortified wines like port and sherry constituted the main output of winemakers in both Australia and New Zealand, with imported table wines being preferred to accompany meals. New Zealand's better off were drinking 66,000 gallons of foreign-made wine annually by 1897.[12] New Zealand once produced its own whiskey, while Australia still makes quantities of "rough" brandy, but also rum, which, in the early days of the NSW colony, was imported from the Caribbean.[13] Today, rum is affectionately known as "bundy," after Bundeberg, a center of Queensland's sugar industry, and a bundy and Coke is a standard pub drink. In part, traditions like rum drinking live on due to the connections they maintain with the past.

But over the last 40 years, it is wine that has made the steadiest inroad and changed the way people dine out as well. The quality of wines has improved greatly, and today Australasian wines compete successfully with the best the world has to offer. Wine is the most popular drink of choice for restaurants, and in an average month 55 percent of Australians of drinking age drink approximately 21 glasses of wine, the highest rate among with New Zealand, the United Kingdom, and the United States.[14] Eating out has driven the love affair with wine, with even modest restaurants offering a broad range of wine choices. In the 1960s and 1970s, in both New Zealand and Australia, wines were either red or white, and dry or sweet. Today, even the simplest wine advertisement carries mandatory tasting notes, sommeliers study hard to learn the finer points of wine tasting, and consumers continue to explore new varietal wines and styles, experimenting with taste. Currently, pinot grigio, *viognier*, sangiovese, and pinot noir are all examples, but primitivo (red grape from Apulia), the origin of the zinfandel varietal of California, aglianico, and fiano (all Italian grape varieties) are also being grown, as wineries micro-tune their production to accommodate cooler climate options according to location. The wines that result are currently gaining a foothold in the market, illustrating a growing diversity helped along by consumer interest. With a growing range of tastes emerging, expert wine and food pairing has become a growth industry. Many of the lesser known Italian wines are proving perfect for food pairing—understandably so—but it has been a slow evolution to reach this stage in Australasia. Tasting menus are now popular among diners. Domestic consumption of wine in Australia is currently around 105 million gallons per annum. In perspective, this amounts to roughly 5 gallons per capita annual consumption, compared to France, at 15 gallons per capita, and the United States, at 2 per head. A proportion of the wine drunk in Australia, as elsewhere, is drunk by restaurant and cafe diners, supplied with wine either in-house or by wine retailers or liquor outlets. Australia also exports more than 132 million gallons of wine per annum.

The distinctive taste profiles of Australasian wines are often collectively described as new world, a term that not only means that the products are literally from the New World (as opposed to Europe, the Old World), but that they are made using up-to-date technology (including stainless steel vats, hydraulic crushers, precision filters, and other automated processes). But as generically different as the wines can be from their old world counterparts, the flavor of Australasian wines no less reflects the *terroir* of the regions from which they come. A crisp, dry, but fruit-intense sauvignon blanc from New Zealand's Marlborough region is a perfect taste encapsulation of the microclimate and the alpine-fed, stony soils that support the vines. Australasian regional wines also have distinctive characters that are increasingly prized by chefs and sommeliers, who take the job of matching food and wine flavors and textures seriously. Dessert wines (stickies) are also a perennial favorite, particularly with Australian diners, and Australia produces world-class sauterne-style wines, muscats, and ports.

In the last decade, canned spirits combined with carbonated mixers have made the biggest impact in the alcoholic beverage market, especially on young drinkers (18–30 years). They are less often partnered with food. The other two drinks that have become major choices with people eating (or drinking) out are coffee and bottled water. Although Australians drink more tea per head of population than Indians (mostly at home), when they dine out, they have coffee. A 15 and 18 percent rise in 2006–2007, respectively, in both these products is indicative of a similar global trend in their consumption.[15]

Today, Australasia has many of the same features that characterize dining out in other highly developed Western nations. Global cities like Melbourne and Sydney, and, to a lesser extent, Auckland, cater to relatively sophisticated urban dwellers with disposable incomes, informed by a multitude of media about foods, both directly (on issues like health) and inadvertently (by advertising and fashion). These consumers are willing to spend more than is absolutely necessary on food for the sake of being hedonistic, or because eating out also means to be seen eating out, and thereby forms part of public social life. Restaurants, bars, cafes, and pubs play a central role in relation to this. Such venues, often themed, provide the backdrop to dining, but food and drink provide more than sustenance, giving the customers a sense of being part of a similar experience, one which, by giving pleasure, also encourages conversation, relationships, and general conviviality. Eating out in this contemporary urban context means far more than eating to live, and conforms more to the opposite, the old gastronomic dictum of living to eat. As well as seeking to please home-grown gastronomes and foodies, urban cuisine caters to the normal mass of incoming visitors and tourists, which also serves to keep restaurant culture up-to-speed with international culinary and gastronomic trends.

The restaurant and catering industry demands constant style innovation. Both Australia and New Zealand have seen a huge rise n the level of conspicuous consumption with regard to food. The cafe phenomenon arose in Australia in the 1950s and continued to grow. In New Zealand, it struck later, in the late '80s and early '90s. Suddenly, cafes popped up as never before, as people watching over a cappuccino became a new urban pursuit. Both countries now both produce many internationally acclaimed chefs and restaurants. The comparative quality and affordability of the prestige foods produced in Australasia is a particular drawcard. Seafood is of excellent quality, and the prices are particularly attractive for visitors from Europe, Asia, or America, who appreciate the great value, matched with quality, of local produce. With access to excellent fishing grounds being a distinct local advantage, the export of seafood (like prawns, tuna, barramundi) fetches top prices in markets like Japan and the European Union, although there is enough locally caught fish and seafood to make available locally, allowing for the best restaurants to give increasingly discerning consumers the quality of product they have come to expect.

In general, Australasia has followed a two-pronged evolution in dining trends: one upward, and one outward, which is to say, high-end dining in the prestige cuisine market is a growth area, with restaurants being sponsored or funded by wealthy business interests more frequently than ever before. Celebrity chefs get the backing of entrepreneurs wishing to invest in a venue that will also conveniently act as a salubrious backdrop to their own social life. In contrast, the outward trend is toward casualization and fast food. The proliferation of cafes and casual eateries in the last two decades has represented a kind of revolution in dining out, one that has met the demand for cheap, good quality food, available in a venue, frequently with outdoor tables, as a choice for consumers who spend more per head on eating out than ever before.

However, with the economic downturn of 2008–09, the trend has already been away from expensive restaurants toward cheaper options. Indeed, the cafe boom of the early '90s can also be correlated with the economic recession at that time, when even award-winning restaurants went out of business due to falling sales. Despite the seeming fluctuation in loyalties between high-end and medium-priced restaurants, and cafe fare statistics suggests that a stable eating pattern has emerged longer-term, and this is dominated by fast food. In Australia today, for every dollar spent on food and nonalcoholic drink, 44 cents (US 33 cents) is spent on fast food, up 2 cents on the year before. In 1977, that figure was 20 cents.[16] Globally, as in the Pacific Islands, there can be no doubt that the consumption of fast food is rising. McDonald's restaurants in Australia numbered 780 in 2009, rising over 10 percent from the previous year. Plans have been made to open 79 new restaurants in the next two years.[17] What is also interesting here is that McDonald's has captured the coffee market with its McCafe, and 24-hour cafes, suggesting a greater penetration of fast food into the consumer eating pattern. KFC sells over a billion dollars' worth of fast food a year in Australia, and 120,000 burgers and 116 tons of chicken each week in New Zealand. With a population of 4 million, that's equal to a weekly ration of a whole chicken breast for every man, woman, and child in the country. Growth in this market has been exponential. In 1980, Australia's the fast food market was only worth $250 million (US$188 million). In the '90s that tripled and, in the first decade of the 21st century, it looks to be doubling again without any sign of abating. Take-out pizza, one of the original dial-a-meal options that had instant appeal in the 1970s, is now a regular option for many busy households, with global brands like Pizza Hut as well as local variants popular with all ages; Domino's Pizza had 434 outlets in Australia in 2009, controlling 50 percent of the market.

Not all fast food, of course, is of the hamburger, fried chicken, or pizza variety (which are high in saturated fats), and much of the growth in fast food in the last decade has been the result of new, healthier lines of foods, including salads and more fresh foods. Chains like Subway (but also thousands of sandwich bars and cafes) have been particularly successful in fresh foods and sandwiches. Other trends include various bars selling one core product with a number of options. Sushi (and sashimi), juice, and frozen yoghurt are among the most significant in terms of market share. Food halls or markets with food stalls have also become a normal part of the urban scene, and must also be regarded as fast food. Any foods and beverages that are convenient (in terms of being available at many different locations, by drive-in, and by phone order) and competitively priced must be regarded as fast food. Department stores, cinemas, and bookstores have also recently begun to incorporate eating and drinking sections for the convenience of customers. Thus, eating out has become a seamless part of the shopping-lifestyle experience, and is also increasingly felt to be less something absolutely necessary and more of an entertainment that can be enjoyed and made to fit in effortlessly with other pursuits or pastimes. In this context, fast food is food that is within easy reach when one is doing something else. Consuming fast food suits the modern lifestyle: eating on the run means not having to think too much about what you eat. In Australasian cities, like in other parts of the world, this means being able to snack anywhere, anytime. As a result, fast food has taken on a broader meaning as a burgeoning range of food outlets intersect more and more with consumers' everyday activities.

At another extreme, in hotels, resorts and higher-priced restaurants, Australian and New Zealand cuisine has embraced eclectic and hybrid styles and a broadening range of ingredients that would represent an intriguing challenge for many consumers. To those with gourmet inclinations, looking for the new and different has become competitive in a way that connoisseurship once was. Today, however, showing that one knows a lot about food and expressing good taste goes much further than the foods themselves. Gastronomic experimentation, the provenance of foods (local, regional, or imported), the food's biological status (organic, free-range, etc.), the consumer's degree of environmental and ethical awareness (the food's carbon footprint), and health issues have also become factors: personal values that also, crucially, act as indicators of the consumer's cultural capital. Restaurant menus, therefore, now embrace a greater range of products that can deliver the added values so avidly sought by the discerning diner.

Another facet of this experience that is a recent development represents a fundamental change in the way foods are presented. Styles of cuisine naturally change over time, but the form the meal takes has recently undergone a transformation. The degustation or tasting menu is now in vogue as never before, but it is a style of presentation that is not only reemerging as the vehicle for the chef's artistry. Rather, the tasting menu phenomenon gives expression to a convergence of changes in contemporary dining culture: increased creative culinary freedom, technological developments, a vastly increased range of ingredients, and a dining public less interested in eating a meal than in sampling, tasting, and experiencing the sensations that go along with that. Affluence plays its part also, since these menus obviously tend to be more expensive than the standard two or three courses.

This development is global, but Australia and New Zealand have both embraced the new culinary zeitgeist. Chefs no longer feel, as they perhaps once did, that they must conform to rules related to traditional cuisines. With patrons' demand for new experiences, the wealth of new foods, and technological wizardry, inventiveness, seemingly for its own sake, is now the prerogative of many chefs.[18] At the forefront of this trend is molecular gastronomy, reflecting improvements in the technology of the kitchen and of machines designed to change the textures and flavors of foods and liquids. Many new ingredients (often sourced globally) reflect the growing interest in having new and exciting flavors.

Eating out, however, has only recently become a phenomenon that appeals to consumers on this level, much like tourist resorts in the islands have only recently adopted environmentally friendly images and begun to serve more locally grown products (especially fruit and vegetables). Increasingly, small producers of foods, including organic and local fruits and vegetables, are selling their produce at farmers' markets, boutique food shops, cellar-door and farm-gate sales, and to quality restaurants.[19] This has also had an effect on attitudes toward food, its quality, and the eating experience, which in a sense represents the opposite of fast food. Taking time to investigate the provenance of a product and to really savor its eating qualities is essentially a slow activity that understandably mirrors the production side of the alternative food industry (small, local producers).

In contrast, speed is all-important for fast food, which, in many ways, is simply the product of the industrialization of food, an inevitable outcome of speeding up all the processes associated with food production and then cutting out everything that incurs costs at the consumption end.[20]

The trend toward incorporating more interesting ingredients is also partly the result of the need for competitive differentiation between increasing numbers of essentially similar consumer goods, a process that has been brought about by the power of global production and marketing systems, as well as by increasingly affluent and savvy consumers. Thus, the food market has been diversifying for years, while the generic quality of products has also been improving. For producers to claim an edge in such a market, added values make all the difference. Packaging, advertising, and marketing all differentiate products (and services) by associating them with one or more values or aspirations. Thus, today, health, origin (provenance), mode of production (organic, pesticide-free, biodynamic), or real taste literally add value to food products because consumers recognize these added values as being desirable and are willing to pay for them when they shop for food or buy a restaurant meal.

An offshoot trend of this value-added dining in Australasia is unique to the region: the incorporation of bush foods into what are often hybridized dishes. A bush tucker platter, for example, could contain offerings like spiced crocodile with wild lime aioli, smoked wallaby with Dijon mustard, kangaroo chorizo (spicy style of smoked Spanish sausage), lemon myrtle curried mussels, and salt bush and pepper leaf calamari (squid).[21] Similarly, in New Zealand, the rediscovery of many of the traditional New Zealand Maori foods has crossed over into mainstream cuisine. Tiny bush fern shoots called *pikopiko*, or sea lettuce/seaweed (*karengo*), might now adorn a *hapuka* steak (local species of groper fish) seasoned with native bush pepper (horopito) in a city restaurant. Although mostly for the curious, or serious, diner, these ingredients indicate that a broader change is occurring in public dining culture.

Minimal numbers of migrants from the Pacific Islands have made Australia their home; in contrast, New Zealand has closer economic, political, and cultural ties to its Polynesian neighbors. Yet, New Zealand has also become home to many more migrants from different countries in the last 15 years, adding significantly to the mix of culinary and gastronomic elements in the food culture.

In the late 1980s, after a number of ethnic cuisines established themselves in the restaurant culture, and after nouvelle cuisine reinstated French culinary aesthetics as a renewed force in the world of elite gastronomy, debates raged over how best to describe Australian cuisine as this was represented by the best and brightest of the new generation of chefs and whether, indeed, there was something genuinely Australian that could be identified in such a way. Modern Australian Cuisine became the standard descriptor on restaurant menus, signifying that quality and creativity were present in more or less equal measure, but little else. Local produce could be a factor in this drive for authenticity, but the argument was largely academic. The only real cuisine that was the result of an organic process of acculturation was the Anglo-Chinese, and restaurants serving this hybridized Cantonese food had become a standard feature of Australian towns and cities by the 1950s. Today, eating out can still mean Chinatown in the larger cities, the local Chinese in a smaller town, or the Anglo-Chinese restaurant in country centers. But to speak of Australian (or New Zealand) cuisine today means to speak of an eclectic contemporary assortment of food styles, informed by trends from elsewhere, maintained by the ready availability of ingredients from markets in all parts of the world and by the individual creative input and willingness of chefs to experiment; by technological changes (particularly related to the efficient and exact thermoregulation of cooking and cooling processes) and by the demand of more and more discerning diners for new sensations that can and do depart from traditional fare in some way. Eating out has perhaps never been more exciting, if excitement is what is sought. The age of the restaurant as a place where signature dishes could be had time and again, year in and year out, has passed. Although restaurants still keep dishes that patrons demand, the trend for the future of Australasian eating out culture, as elsewhere, is to continue to ride the wave of change that, with each passing season, appears to offer more and more creative opportunities and consumer choices.

NOTES

1. Lenore Manderson, ed., *Shared Wealth and Symbol: Food, Culture and Society in Oceania and Southeast Asia* (Cambridge: Cambridge University Press, 1986), 12.

2. See George Ritzer, *The McDonaldization of Society.* Rev. ed. (Thousand Oaks, CA: Pine Forge Press, 2004).

3. Watch a short film on the Waibulabula project, video.google.com/video play?docid=6644216255974733085.

4. Matangi and Yasawa Island in the Fiji islands offer dining experiences that are typically international with the accent on local produce. Yasawa Island Resort and Spa, northwest of Fiji's Viti Levu, http://www.yasawa.com/dining/dining.htm.

5. For a typical menu, see this one from Rarotonga's *The Flame Tree Restaurant*: http://www.flametreerestaurant.com/Restaurants/Cook_Islands/Rarotonga/The_Flame_Tree_Restaurant_rmp=0_IDM=180_IDP=2_idh=10101_Menu___Cocktail_Menu_.html.

6. See James Kelly "Loco Moco: A Folk Dish in the Making," *Social Process in Hawai'i* 30 (1983): 59–64.

7. Wayne Curtis, "Tiki," *American Heritage Magazine*, August/September 2006, http://www.americanheritage.com/articles/web/20060916-tiki-ernest-gantt-don-the-beachcomber-donn-beach-victor-bergeron-mai-tai-restaurant-bar-trader-vic.shtml.

8. Trader Vic's organization, http://www.tradervics.com/.

9. Stephen Siegelman, *Trader Vic's Tiki Party!: Cocktails & Food to Share with Friends* (Berkeley, CA: Ten Speed Press, 2005).

10. David Burton, *Two Hundred Years of New Zealand Food and Cookery* (Wellington, NZ: Reed, 1982), 20–30.

11. Lindsay Neill, Claudia Bell, and Ted Bryant, *The Great New Zealand Pie Cart* (Auckland: Hodder, 2008).

12. Tony Simpson, *A Distant Feast: The Origins of New Zealand Cuisine* (Auckland, NZ: Godwit, 1999), 156.

13. Simpson, 148.

14. Michele Levine and Simon Pownall, "Marketing Wine Industry Outlook: Consumption Demographics," (address at the Wine Industry Outlook Conference, Sydney, Australia, November 25, 2004) http://www.roymorgan.com/resources/pdf/papers/20041201.pdf.

15. Australian Food Statistics 2007, www.daff.gov.au.

16. Mark L. Wahlquist, *Food and Nutrition in Australia* (Sydney: Methuen, 1981), 39

17. Teresa Ooi, "Cash-strapped Customers Flock to Fast Food Outlets," *Australian*, February 16, 2009 (statistics quoted in this article are from Australian market research group, BIS Shrapnel).

18. Michael Symons, *The Shared Table: Ideas for Australian Cuisine* (Canberra: AGPS Press Publication, 1993).

19. See, for New Zealand, the Farmers' Market New Zealand Association Web site, http://www.farmersmarket.org.nz/home.htm; for Australia see The Market Guide Web site, http://www.marketguide.com.au/vic-1.htm.

20. See Ritzer, *The McDonaldization of Society*, 42.

21. Cited in Mukesh Sharma, Mervyn Jackson, and Robert Inbakaran, "Promoting Indigenous Food to Foreign Visitors: An Australian Study," in *Asian Anthropology* 7 (2008): 131.

7

Special Occasions

In the Pacific Islands, special occasions follow the same general pattern as elsewhere in the world. Important milestones in life, including birth (not normally celebrated until the child turns one in Polynesia), coming of age, marriage, honoring a great deed or achievement, paying respect to special visitors or personages, or death (which tends to be marked by a grand feast), are all acknowledged with special meals, particular foods and dishes, and with communal feasting on a grand scale. Whatever is celebrated demands feasting, as does mourning a death. One of the most regular events is the weekly family *umu*, a special occasion because it is where ties are reestablished, hierarchies reinforced, and honor bestowed. It is where family and community expresses their spirituality. To obtain the right foods for the *umu*, a shopping trip to the local food market is indispensable for urban-based islanders, but particularly the strongly Christian Samoans, Tongans, and Cook Islanders, who cater for their families in the traditional style after church on Sundays, preparing the familiar starchy staple foods, plus pork, chicken, and *palusami*, a traditional, indeed generic, dish consisting of taro, coconut milk, and meat (often canned corned beef), that are wrapped and baked in a taro leaf. There are many regional variations.

Feasts, and the celebrations or wakes of which they are a feature, are complex events that express and reinforce the spiritual and philosophical ideals and values of island culture. To this extent, there is an integrated series of stages to a feast involving, typically, a formal welcome from chiefs and elders, a kava or toddy ceremony, toasts, speeches, dances, music, and a lavish, colorful display of food to impress the eye, smiles and gestures of welcome, and an atmosphere of excited expectation. There are basic similarities between feast events across the region. Today, grand events still take place. Commemorations that involve paying respect to ancestors or elders who have passed on are particularly important occasions in terms of holding to tradition. But casualization has also crept into the ways meals are prepared and consumed to mark special occasions. Westernization allows islanders to step away from their formal responsibilities and to celebrate a social occasion for its own sake, without too much pomp and ceremony. It all depends on the occasion.

The great age of feasts now belongs to the past. In 1847, during the reign of King Kamehameha III, a luau (Hawaiian feast) designed to feed 10,000 was prepared, at which 271 hogs, 482 baskets of poi, 602 chickens, 3 whole oxen, 2 barrels of salt pork, 2 barrels of biscuits, 12 barrels of *laulau* (Hawaiian equivalent of *palusami*), cabbages, 4 barrels of onions, 80 bunches of bananas, 55 pineapples, 2,245 coconuts, 4,000 heads of taro, 180 squid, oranges, limes, grapes, and various fruit were prepared for the guests. This sort of grand event is typically what Polynesian hospitality is all about. The bigger the event, the better. In this case, feasting directly expressed the power of the chiefs (kahuna). To display such huge quantities of food at an event of this scale symbolized the economic and political might of the leader. Feasts such as this were frequently held to honor gods, even while, in reality, they conferred greatness and power on the demigod-like figures of the chiefs in attendance. Up to 1,440 pigs were reported to have been cooked at one Hawaiian feast, held over three days, for the dedication of a temple to the war god Ku.[1]

Today, the older belief systems have weakened, as has the traditional power of chiefs, who once demanded that massive supplies of food be requisitioned from villagers. Now, budgetary constraints inhibit the degree of lavishness, even though generosity and hospitality are strongly held values and must be honored. Today, special feasts typically honor guests and foreign visitors, dignitaries, government officials, or even investors, delegates from nongovernmental organizations or bodies like the Secretariat of the Pacific Community, who use such occasions to show support for often struggling communities and to offer help and assistance. The University of the South Pacific and the University of Hawaii, along with other research institutions, also conduct fieldwork all around the Pacific region, and their researchers and administrators are frequent visitors to remote islands, where generous hospitality is shown to them. A large welcoming feast (in Kiribati these are known as *botaki*) on the smaller islands and atolls is simply customary, and a high point on the social calendar of events. Today, banquets accommodate Western guests by being presented on conventional Western-style tables. This facilitates ease of service in a similar way to the Swedish smorgasbord. Guests can walk around the table and help themselves to whatever they desire, before taking their place in the dining area adjacent to the spread. Decorated cloth in traditional patterns adds color to the display of food. Food is displayed in glassware bowls, on trays, and in other convenient ways, rather than being arranged on the traditional banana leaves. In more remote regions, banana palms may not be grown. Typical foods offered at such special occasions would include suckling pig, taro, yams, fish (and, in the old days, turtle) lobster, *palusami*, and sweet potato.

Special occasions, however, while always implying hospitality, are not solely for that purpose. Island life and the life of islanders is marked by important occasions, where feasts are held. In Kiribati, a pubescent girl's coming of age is marked firstly by a quiet, three-day ritual, during which the girl's meals are plain and restricted in size, and her work is limited to simple, everyday tasks, to which she is assigned for long periods. Her aunt, by tradition, gives her dried foods like pandanus and coconut to eat, and she is also offered water, occasionally coconut juice, or fresh toddy. This three-day period, during which the young woman has her first period, sig-nifies that when there is not enough food to go around, the mother feeds her children and her husband before herself. At the end of three days, the young woman shares a meal that breaks her three-day fast with a first-born male from the community. Then the real festivities begin.

While fasting, the girl's parents have been organizing a typical island feast in her honor, at which most of the local community will gather to celebrate the transition to womanhood. In the evening, after the feast, a space is cleared so that the young woman, dressed in red, can dance alone before her family and the community. The performance is tradi-tionally met with warmth and approval because it signifies that the girl has now become a woman. The feast is a traditional part of such ceremo-nies, which are numerous in island culture. Boys also have their rites of passage, marked by feasting within the context of a ritual event. In the Cook Islands, boys are circumcised at about the age of puberty, and when the scar heals, a feast is held to celebrate.

Death is also marked by the staging of feasts, and not only funeral feasts, but also anniversary feasts, are held in honor of relatives, chiefs, and an-cestors. In the Solomon Islands, if a "big man" of the village (a chief or elder) dies, a feast is held in honor of him, but also as a mark of respect to those who may have helped during his illness. In the days before the coming of civilization, the killing of an enemy could also be marked with the actual eating of the dead's flesh, the act of cannibalism, which was meant both to symbolically humiliate opponents and simultaneously transfer their strength to those doing the eating. In these types of events, it is not hospitality as such, but great ceremony, due respect, and all the social rules that apply are followed carefully. Along with cannibalism, the offering of food to the gods was also a common aspect of feasts in days gone by. Both now belong to the past, while feasting and celebration are still very much a part of island life.

Following southern Indian Hindu traditions, a wedding in Fiji will involve three days of celebration: kava drinking, day and night, dancing and feasting. Indian Hindu feasts are vegetarian, whereas Polynesian Fijians would normally kill a bullock for the *umu* and cook it along with other meats, and fewer vegetables. Meat has a high cultural value among Fijians. and must be included. Even the tinned bully beef is regarded highly, culturally speaking, even if it is considered more of an emergency food elsewhere.

One special occasion that stands out in the contemporary context is the reunion of family members, which is a common event among island people, who in many case have greater populations in their adopted countries than in the islands. This is especially true of small islands like Tokelau, Nauru, Niue, Rarotonga, the outlying Cook Islands, and many other scattered island groups. Depending on which countries the island group has ties with, politically or economically, islanders readily travel from home in order to find work elsewhere; also, others return home, to visit or, after varying lengths of stay, to work. A fairly constant traffic of people and goods, including food, flows between Polynesia and New Zealand (Cook Islands, Niue, Tokelau, Samoa, and Tonga), and reunions, a time for celebration and feasting, are important at such points.

Typically, among Polynesians, a homecoming would be celebrated with an *umu*. In practical terms, the *umu* is a great way to cater for numbers. When it is opened, there is no fuss, as all guests help themselves to the abundant food. *Palusami* is always there, along with copious quantities of chicken and pork. To eat a lot is a sign of happiness and good manners, and represents a compliment to the host, who will encourage everyone to eat as much as possible. The informality of such an event, held offshore, as it were, is such that some of the old rules pertaining to mana and *aroa* (generosity to strangers) apply less than does the offering of food as an act of familial love and care. Reciprocity is always implied, and food that is left over is parceled up and taken away after being divided among the family present. Some of this food may later be further distributed to members of the family unable to attend the *umu*. In the context of expatriate Polynesian communities, and now for second- and third-generation New Zealand-born islanders, the spiritual and mythological aspects of the *umu* are less pronounced because of assimilation into the adopted culture. *Umu* for hundreds of people are still not uncommon. A degree of formality still applies today, although the *umu* now lends itself to modern styles of informal, casual dining as well.

Traditional staple foods are still a common feature of feasts and special occasions in the Pacific Islands, or in adopted countries, whenever they are available. Feasts are an integral part of island community life, and many different foods are normally prepared for such occasions. In some traditional cultures, like that of the Trobriand Islands (Melanesian New Guinea), marriage was not marked by a feast at all, whereas death involved a special ritual that entailed the ceremonial division of food. Celebrations or feasts marking a death, while simultaneously celebrating the abundance and provision of food, also took place. In the Trobriand Islands, in years of good harvest or that promise plentiful harvest, the chief announces that a *kayasa* festival should occur. This involves a ceremonial, but also competitive, display of food. This not only means the display of abundance at the feast, but the prior accumulation for show of root vegetables in specially made storage huts.

More elaborate preparations are made at feasts, like the puddings of pounded, cooked taro, pumpkin, or breadfruit that is then mixed with coconut milk (or arrowroot in the Cook Islands), and wrapped and steamed in parcels in the *umu*. Leftovers at any of these traditional feasts are distributed to families to be consumed or passed on to others later.

Feasts were often also held in the past to honor a chief or, as in Tonga, to mark the coming of age of a princess. The feast commonly forms the centerpiece of a whole range of social activities, including sports, singing, and dancing. The feast itself typically takes place outdoors or, in the case of the royal Tongan feast given on the occasion of a visiting warship from Germany in 1978, King Taufa'ahau dined with the guests of honor in an enclosed dining room made from poles draped in fabric and decorated with green garlands of leaves and flowers. The king's table was slightly raised from the ground (18 inches or so), signifying his importance and in honor of his special guests. The majority of invited guests sat on the ground in long lines, facing each other across broad, flat banana palm leaves spread on the ground; the roasted suckling pig, seafood, vegetables, fruits, and starchy staples were arranged on these. Customarily, people eat with their hands. Islanders will say it tastes better that way. This takes some skill, but the reward is that it changes the whole pace of eating and affects the way one thinks about food and its appreciation. It returns a kind of intimacy to dining that knives and forks fail to provide.

In Tonga, at larger feasts held on the village green, guests may be catered for in a number of sittings, but would normally eat in order of rank. Fathers outrank mothers, but sisters outrank brothers. In fact, sisters and brothers must, according to strict custom, avoid each other while dining. Foods are also ranked. The most prestigious part of the pig is its back, esteemed for its deliciousness. *Ufi* (yams) are the highest-ranking root vegetable, as they are in many parts of the Pacific, followed by taro. Ranking is important, because it shows a form of respect and communicates hospitality of the noblest kind. A fish head is also a delicacy that could be offered to visitor or special guest. Some foods would not find a place on the traditional table at all, like cassava, which is regarded as inferior peasant food and has been called the "TV dinner of the Pacific."[2] In the Cook Islands, paw paw is similarly frowned upon and would not be considered fit for the feast table.

Sometimes, the seasonal nature of many Pacific foods means that a feast may include special foods only available at certain times of the year. *Duruka*, a plant that looks like a small version of sugarcane, has a three-month season, from May to July; it is a great delicacy in Fiji served with coconut cream, perhaps greens, onion, chili, and sometimes fish. Other seasonal delicacies include sea worms, called *balolo* (Fijian), of the *Nereis* genus, which are only available during the month of October (*Vulai balolo lailai* in the traditional Fijian calendar means month of many *balolo*). These grow to about 6 inches in length and are no thicker than a 1/16 of an inch. In the past, the growing and harvesting of foods was governed by the traditional astrological calendar. Also during October, in the last quarter of the moon (late October to early November), billions of eggs appear on the surface of the water above the coral reefs, produced by coral polyps, the shells of which combine to make the coral reef itself. Samoans go out on this special night to gather the eggs, known as *palolo* (*Leodice viridice*), a species of annelid, which they then fry and consume at a feast that continues until the *palolo* catch has gone. They are a great delicacy.[3] They are also harvested for consumption in Fiji and Vanuatu, but are not widely known outside this relatively small area of the Pacific. Their flavor has been described as being wonderfully delicate, like caviar, and a gourmet's dream.[4]

Kava, also known as *yaqona* in Fiji, is a mild narcotic and relaxant made from the roots of a pepper shrub (*Piper methysticum*), and has been an indispensable part of hospitality and the formal acknowledgement of visitors in the Pacific Islands for hundreds of years. Today, kava powder, made from the dried root of the plant, can be bought in the market, like the one at Sigatoka, in the north of Fiji. Piles of the stringy roots can be bought alongside the powdered form. Kava sessions are still popular among males, but the drink also forms an important part of wedding celebrations, for example, among Fijian Indians.

Traditionally, in Fijian culture, kava welcomes visitors and forms the focus of a formal ritual. In Fiji, the drinking ceremony is preceded by the sounding of the lali drum. When the *yaqona* (Fijian version of kava) is drunk in a single draft, the hosts cry "*maca*," which means "the cup is drained," and all clap their hands. In Western Samoa, as elsewhere, a large wooden bowl is used in which the powdered kava root is mixed with water. Traditionally, however, the root was first chewed to allow the enzyme action of saliva to increase the potency of the drink. It was once common to see many villagers chewing kava root through the day, making ready for the drinking ceremony. The resulting expectorant was then strained (through layered strands of hibiscus fiber) before being served to guests in polished half-coconut-shell cups (called *bilos* in Fijian). Vanuatu has many varieties of the plant, and it is thought that, from this region, kava spread through New Guinea, Micronesia, and Polynesia. Kava has a slightly peppery flavor; some say it is also reminiscent of licorice, others of rhubarb and magnesia. It is the most important ceremonial drink in many parts of the Pacific region. The flavor is not strong compared with that of alcoholic beverages.

The love of fish and seafood is apparent anywhere one goes in the Pacific region, and no feast for a special occasion would be complete without a fine selection of fresh seafood. At a *magiti*, the Fijian word for a grand feast, visitors and different sorts of delegations from various countries, institutions, and agencies are formally welcomed with a *magiti*, which might traditionally be followed by a night of dancing and singing called a meke. *Magiti* start with a kava ceremony, where the kava is prepared and passed around to be shared. An oration follows before the feast that, subject to availability, would certainly include crab (coconut or mangrove crabs), king prawns, sea urchin, giant clams, octopus, and, among the fish, great trevally, mahimahi, tuna, red snapper, and *wahou* (Cook Islands; *walu* in Fiji). Any specialty items are treated as important tokens of hospitality, and are happily offered to guests and visitors.

MANA, *AROA*, AND *MANAAKI*

An important traditional Polynesian concept to emphasize in relation to special occasions and feasts of this kind is mana. Understanding the meaning and place of mana in islander culture reveals how the outward display of wealth and abundance, and the hospitality bestowed on guests, also serves an important spiritual purpose. Mana itself is not explicitly celebrated and, to outsiders, it may not appear obvious that it is mana that shapes the design of events. Nonetheless, mana gives meaning to all facets of the event. When people meet to celebrate, it is at carefully chosen places that will best attract mana; they eat carefully chosen foods, exchange special gifts, display abundance in the form of foods, feast heartily, and extend lavish hospitality, in part because all these things potentially add to mana.

Mana connotes power, prestige, authority, spirituality, and the supernatural.[5] This means that, in Pacific island cultures, there is much more to feasting than merely celebration. At its core, mana upholds the key values of love, hope, and generosity, and therefore it is easy to see how providing and sharing food had a traditional role to play in expressing mana at special occasions. Mana does not exist on its own, according to its own laws. It can be added to or lost for human beings, according to the will of the gods. Mana must be worked for, and accumulated, and acts can also diminish the mana of a person, place, event, or action. If a chief holds a feast in honor of a visiting group, the abundant display of food also attests to the amount of mana that he has personally accumulated. This reflects well on him because the abundant display is material proof of his mana. The choice of site for such a feast is not made on the basis of whether there is a good view or sufficient shade or shelter, as may be the case for Westerners, but on the basis of whether it has the requisite amount of mana associated with it. How this is determined could relate to such factors as historical incidents that render one site more sacred than another. Mana can also be inherited from ancestors, so individuals can be born with it; land, and therefore the control of that land, attracts mana; and great achievements also bring mana. In this sense, mana is a powerful force that is inherent in the land, people, gods, all actions and material things, as well as intentions, feelings, language, and expression.

A feast needs to be understood as an event where mana is very much to the fore in acts of display, choice of venue, abundance of food, and the authority of the chiefs and dignitaries, all of which are structured around the central guiding principles of love, hope, and generosity. These aspects are also expressed through the Polynesian concept, *aroa*. *Aroa* represents an attitude of generosity to strangers, an idea which is akin to the Western notion of hospitality, a word that in English conflates strangers and guests with generosity in the form of food and shelter. Similarly, *aroa* implies certain obligations, principally that of reciprocity, whereby a kind act to a stranger today will bring a kind act in return sometime in the future. This economy of reciprocal hospitality applied in premodern Europe as much as it still does in most Pacific Islander communities. Clearly, investing in this way in human relationships has proved fundamental to maintaining social order over time.

These two concepts, mana and *aroa,* are at the heart of the Polynesian concept of hospitality. There is, therefore, more to special occasions and traditional feasts than meets the (Westerner's) eye. Special occasions that focus on celebration and feasting always acknowledge, pay homage, show respect, and dignify cultural associations and community links. They honor neighborly agreements and loyalties, and above all enforce the commonly held values relating to mana and *aroa.* The survival of the traditional form of the feast today, even after Westernization's impact on indigenous foodways, attests to these deep-seated cultural values. No matter what changes take place, hospitality and generosity, the display of abundance, sharing, love, kindness, and hospitality still imbue special and festive occasions. Perhaps because of these deep links with the cultural past, the ceremonial form of the feast, in particular, has altered little. While feasts can differ in terms of the degree of formality observed, or required, at the most formal of these events traditional foods and methods of preparation, the laying out of the meal on the ground, presented on banana leaves, the precedence in presentation of offering of the choicest foods to important visitors first conforms to and thereby honors the traditional model, as well as those present as guests, and serves to preserve a unique cultural identity.

In Maori culture, the term *manaaki* is used to describe love and hospitality (*manaakitanga*) towards others. It also remains an important aspect of Maori culture in the contemporary world, particularly now that ecotourism and tourism in general facilitate the expression of *manaaki* in a way that enhances intercultural communication, creates jobs for indigenous people, and fosters traditional values. To some extent, Maori hospitality can go too far, especially in the commercial arena, which is outside the system of mutual obligation. Of the few Maori restaurants that have operated in New Zealand, studies have shown that some of these suffered economically due to excessive generosity. Free feeds for special guests ("cuzzies")—an inclusive rather than exclusive rule of thumb—led to serious financial shortfall.[6]

Given this context of islander hospitality and the extent to which it structures and invests in human relationships, the feasts that accompany particular celebrations take on new meaning. The piles of yams and *kumara* (sweet potato) that were accumulated for feasts were not only there to be cooked and eaten, but also to impress, to symbolize that mana had been accumulated and that, in Maori culture, that *manaakitanga* was being offered. Islander hospitality represents a point of cultural contact between hosts and guests, who are supporting each other through the enactment of mutual obligation.

AUSTRALIA AND NEW ZEALAND

Australian Barbecue

The origins of the barbecue, affectionately called the barby by Aussies and Kiwis, are not to be found in Australasia, even though it has become an iconic meal of national significance in both countries. Australia Day (January 26) holiday celebrations customarily take the form of a barbecue, where family and friends can socialize in the open space of a backyard, or frequently, in the suburban setting, on the deck, participating in what is perhaps one of the most relaxing and easy-going meals imaginable. The beauty of the barbecue is precisely that it takes place outdoors; if the weather is hot, as it frequently is in Australia, under the shade of an awning, an umbrella, or trees. The food is presented in smorgasbord style, although there are no real rules as far as the layout is concerned, as long as everyone finds something enjoyable to eat and has a good time. In this sense, the food is not really the focus, but rather the excuse for getting together.

The barbeque says something quintessential about life, or rather, lifestyle in Australia, because it symbolizes simple pleasures, including simply cooked and prepared foods, relaxed fun, and care-free living. Of course, this is one of the reasons why Australians, in general, enjoy the barbecue because, as a nation, Australia is known for its easy-going casualness in terms of attitudes, lack of snobbery (in relation to conspicuous consumption), and the way in which people tend to take a "no worries" approach to most things, including dining. This makes the barbecue a perfect format for casual Australian lifestyles. To some extent, the barbecue has even made inroads into more traditional food events, like Christmas dinner, and it seems predictable that people should want to eat food outdoors in the summer heat (rather than the northern winter). In fact, eating outdoors, at a picnic, to celebrate Christmas was commonplace in Australia into the 1890s. Old photographs and engravings depict groups casually enjoying a Christmas spread; children play, others read or lounge on the grass. This casualness is a hallmark of Australian dining, but the tradition of Christmas was to change soon after. The rising middle classes, who typically aspire to what they regard as a more elevated social rank, adopted a more British style of Christmas celebration, which, in fact, was a hybrid of German and English traditions in many ways. The Christmas tree was German, and the turkey had come from the United States: both became symbols of the new Australian Christmas. More important than this, however, was that from the eminently sensible casual affair of dining outdoors during such a hot time of year, Christmas dinner migrated indoors, where it could better emulate the British model. As a result, until well after the end of World War II, Christmas dinner was routinely served hot, inside, a l'anglaise: gravy, bread sauce, plum puddings, and all the other trimmings.[7] Given the hot climate, this must have seemed the oddest of customs to the waves of immigrants and refugees who arrived in the 1950s, as it did to the generation of baby boomers who grew up in the '60s and '70s. By the '80s, things were changing. The influence of Asian cooking styles, the product of hot and tropical climates, suited Australia far better than the Anglo-Saxon culinary tradition. The '80s and '90s also saw a shift in style and a new health consciousness. Fish became as popular, if not more so, than turkey, as barbecuing and the outdoor style of casual dining to some extent reclaimed Christmas, giving an Australian flavor more in keeping with the current lifestyle and climate of Australians. Celebration Aussie-style has further been casualized by adopting the barbecue as the cooking technique and the smorgasbord as the format for presentation. Naturally, the Anglo-Saxon tradition of preparing a winter roast has been a lasting tradition, but today it has definitely lost ground to both these styles, better suited to climate and season.

The barbecue's origin is no doubt prehistoric, even though the term, coined in the 17th century, comes from the Spanish barbacoa, meaning a raised platform of sticks for smoking or drying meat. It was named after devices of this kind were noticed in use by native peoples in the newly discovered Americas. The buccaneer, William Dampier (1651–1715), is the earliest known person to have used the term, first in 1699, to describe a raised framework of sticks, not for drying or smoking meat, but to be used to sleep on. Dampier sailed across the Pacific, landing in northwestern Australia in 1688 and again in 1699. It seems unlikely that he made the first Aussie "Borbecu" (as he called it) during his visit. Rather, a combination of factors may have contributed to the barbecue's origins in Australia. First, in colonial Australia, vast areas of land were being explored and pioneered. Eating in that context often meant cooking outdoors, around a fire. The "jolly swagmen," as much as the pioneer graziers and landholders, would have cooked in the open on many occasions, and this bush tradition is nostalgically recalled in the form of the contemporary barbecue.

Characteristically, such an event involved billy tea (tea brewed in a round, deep-sided tin that was hung from a length of branch suspended by two forked branches over the fire), damper (bread made using baking soda as a raising agent and baked in a typically three-legged iron pot in the coals of the fire), and, of course, the roasting or grilling of meat over the fire itself, a method that remains the basis of the barbecue. Baking a roast in the modern oven is not the same as proper roasting, which uses the direct heat from flames or hot coals and embers.

The barbecue takes many forms and uses a variety of fuels today, but the design and purpose are more or less the same: either a metal hotplate or slatted grill is fired from beneath to a heat that will sear meat quickly, often to the point of creating smoke, part of the reason why barbecues are best outside. Thus, there is then a sense in which the barbecue is simple, and this explains why men and not women have assumed the role of "barbecue king" in Australia, as indeed elsewhere (the barbecue is perhaps equally popular in New Zealand, although the wetter, colder climate in the latter country has prevented it reaching quite the same iconic status). There is no suggestion here that men are simple as such, but rather that they enjoy the simple pleasure the barbecue affords. It also occurs outdoors, stereotypically the man's domain. Indeed, men get in touch with a sense of masculinity that the barbecue reinforces, the sort that requires some chest thumping, red meat eating, and getting a bit dirty: men man the barby with tongs in hand, courageously breathing in smoke as they turns slabs of splattering steak and strings of "snags" (sausages) for those waiting. Yes, there is something of the (imagined) life of the cave man reenacted each time the barbecue is fired up. The elemental things in life, fire, meat, and drink, are celebrated. Cold beer is the drink of choice (and Australians tend to like their lager beer, in particular, very cold), as it is refreshing on a hot day, and also because of the male tradition of beer-drinking in Australia. The male bonding, or mateship, of the pub or sport field finds its domestic corollary in the barbecue.

The barbecue has taken varying forms in recent years, extending the casualization of dining that is present in the food culture more broadly. Although, at its core, the barbecue still revolves around the grilling of meat, mostly steak, sausages, and, traditionally, lamb chops, fish (especially salmon and prawns), marinated vegetables and kebabs, specialty cuts of meat and poultry, also often marinated, add to the diverse possibilities suggested by the form of the barbecue. At its simplest, the barbecue might only involve buttered bread and sausages, which, if there are children involved, will be duly laid out on the buttered bread and coated in commercially made tomato sauce, and the whole eaten as best as possible, as a sort of sausage roll. A simple salad could be the accompaniment, but this is probably for the adults. Beyond these bare requirements, depending on the occasion and he number present, the barbecue can become more complex in terms of foods offered.

Often, guests will bring a plate: numerous kinds of salad (potato, tabouli, and pasta salads are standards); dips like hummus, baba ganoush, *taramasalata,* and pesto; bruschetta and other snacks, and any number of made-up dishes using summer vegetables like beetroot, tomato, cucumber, and lettuce. Australian foodways have absorbed Middle Eastern, Asian, and European influences, and the barbecue's easy-going format means that ratatouille and green chicken curry could end up on the dining table along with the sausages (also called bangers) and steak.

A greater sophistication of food and more drinks to choose from has also been reflected in changing barbecue style. Traditional Australian wines to serve have been shiraz (excellent with grilled red meats) and chardonnay (with chicken and fish), although in recent years a greater and greater abundance of choice now reflects the aggressive marketing of new wine varietals and rapidly developing wine trends. Italian and Spanish reds (*nebbiolo, temperanillo*), as well as whites like sauvignon blanc and *pinot gris* (Italian, pinot grigio) add to the diversity of styles available to match with barbecue fare. And judging by the profusion of potable barbecues of various sizes on sale, from balcony hibachis to enormous outdoor kitchens, the Australian love of the barbecue will not abate anytime soon.

Above all, however, it is precisely this adaptive capability of the easygoing barbecue that means it can accommodate changing tastes. This also makes it attractive to a great number of Australian citizens. Given Australia's multicultural status, everyone can potentially invest the barby with a little bit of their own culture. Like its nationalistic American counterpart, Thanksgiving, the barbecue can be a celebration of nation, as on Australia Day (January 26), when lamb is the traditional meat of choice, but for most Australians it has simply become an everyday part of the culinary and cultural landscape. Like "the roast," another Australian tradition, and an event in itself, the barbecue connects people in a way that reflects honest simplicity of taste, cooking, and sociality, serving a similar social and cultural purpose as the open-air feasts of the islander nations. The barbecue is perhaps as honest a gastronomic reflection of contemporary Australian taste as one could expect to find.

NOTES

1. Patrick V. Kirch, "Polynesian Feasting in Ethnohistoric, Ethnographic, and Archaeological Contexts: A Comparison of Three Societies," in *Feasts: Archaeological and Ethnographic Perspectives on Food, Politics, and Power,* ed. Michael

Dietler and Brian Hayden (Washington, D.C.: Smithsonian Institution, 2001), 179.

2. Solomoni Biumaiono, "The Cassava Invasion Continues," *Mailife*, April 2008, 48–54.

3. Rafael Steinberg, ed., *Pacific and Southeast Asian Cooking*, Foods of the World Series (New York: Time-Life Books, 1970).

4. Jennifer Brennan, *Tradewinds and Coconuts: A Reminiscence and Recipes from the Pacific Islands* (Boston, MA: Periplus Editions, 2000), 274.

5. Tracy Berno, "When a Guest Is a Guest: Cook Islanders View Tourism," *Annals of Tourism Research* 26, no. 3 (1999): 659–60.

6. Shirley Barnett, "Manaakitanga: Maori Hospitality, A Case Study of Maori Accommodation Providers," *Tourism Management* 22, no. 1 (2001): 84–85.

7. Cherry Ripe, *Goodbye Culinary Cringe* (St. Leonards, NSW: Allen & Unwin, 1993).

8

Diet and Health

Diet and health in the Pacific region are important issues because concerns have been mounting for some decades about the diet-related illnesses that have had significant effects on the health of islanders. The occurrence of Western diseases, in particular obesity, heart disease, hypertension, and diabetes (Type II), has risen dramatically. All have been linked to changes in diet as well as lifestyle. But there are other issues as well. Food security, which affects the health of whole communities, has become a problem that has been exacerbated in recent times by the global recession, which has added significantly to rising food prices.

In some cases, this is offset by aid. The Northern Mariana Islands has a population of about 70,000, about 8,000 of whom receive food stamps each year. In 2006, 7,000 received stamps, but in the early 1990s, this number was only 1,000. Dependence on financial aid of this kind does nothing to boost self-sufficiency and self-sustainability for islanders, making them more dependent and vulnerable, as they are less likely to cope long-term with fluctuations in world economic trends.

Food security is a serious problem that can have long-term effects on health. In October 2008, Fiji's agriculture minister, Joketani Cokanisiga, claimed that 289,000 people in Fiji, or roughly 34 percent of Fiji's population, live in poverty. Poverty is one of the prime factors contributing to inadequate diet and, consequently, poor nutrition and illness. Cokanisiga also urged children and young people to encourage their parents to plant food crops in their backyards.[1] Dependence on imported foods, like dependence on aid, brings negative health outcomes.

The stereotypical image of islanders with beaming smiles, scantily clad, in robust good health, perhaps matched the social reality of the precontact Pacific world at some stage. The robust and happy islanders James Cook described may also have been just as they appeared. But the notion of "happy, healthy natives" has clearly been exaggerated. Even the firsthand missionary reports that described some of the early meetings between islanders and Westerners in detail can be misleading. Although they testified to good health among native people, the missionaries often had less than adequate information because illnesses and deaths among native people were often kept secret from outsiders, being subject to strict laws of tapu that forbade "others" from attending the sick or dying.

Today, adequate hospital treatment and Western medical care are available, but the long-term effects of diet-related illness is another issue entirely because health also relates to lifestyle. Lifestyle has certainly changed, but is also very difficult to influence in terms of educating individuals to make sensible food choices, as the latter are still governed by traditional attitudes to health and well-being. The West has brought medicines and vaccines that have improved the quality of life through the treatment of curable diseases, but a new threat has emerged for which there has so far been no medical solution: overeating of the wrong foods. In the past, physical exercise and hard work would have had a positive effect on weight gain and the overall health of islanders, and indeed, authorities today are underlining the importance of exercise now that sedentary work and relaxation regimes dominate due to a combination of factors: cars that ferry people around, appliances that render all sorts of manual work redundant (including cooking), and media, including television, that demand a certain amount of inactivity on a daily basis. TV also influences consumer choice for imported, fast, and convenient foods, thereby exacerbating the problem of weight gain.

In general, to be fit and healthy demands taking part in sports or exercise in gyms to offset the effects of total calorie intake, especially when eating too much of the wrong sorts of foods: those high in saturated fats, cholesterol, sugar, and salt; also those that incorporate highly processed ingredients and artificially created chemical additives. In traditional Pacific communities, tending taro plantations, climbing coconut palms, building seacraft, weaving, making tools and fishhooks, fishing, cooking, building and repairing dwellings was the norm. In fact, everything that the community needed had to be grown, made, or found, or chased and caught by that community. Work and diet, therefore, were profoundly re-

Move for Health billboard in Lautoka, Fiji.

lated, and exercise was vigorous. But work of this type is now more or less a thing of the past in the islands. By contrast, the knowledge that exercise helps keep the calories in check, and the added awareness of what foods do (in terms of bodily health), is commonplace wisdom for many Western people, who are comparatively well-educated about the relationship between food, weight, exercise, and health, despite the obesity epidemic. But this is not the case in the islands, where changes in the diet and, particularly, the increased intake of saturated fats, sugar, and salt, have drastically affected health despite education programs encouraging islanders to exercise and eat healthy foods.[2] It is the cultural mindset that precludes the success of programs of this kind. Islanders have traditionally found larger body size to be attractive and a sign of well-being, even success. According to custom, the chiefs were often the biggest people in the tribe, only partly because it was their privilege to eat more food. Consequently, Polynesians in particular can carry a lot of weight in terms of body mass. This penchant for corpulence is naturally abetted by the types of foods now commonly purchased in the islands. To Polynesians, size matters. The bigger one is, the healthier one is; in terms of diet-related illnesses, however, this belief has been a disaster. Among Hawaii's ethnic groups, indigenous Hawaiians have the highest rate of heart disease, cancers, strokes, diabetes, and suicides. Where the Polynesian understanding of food and eating and its relation to well-being meets Western convenience foods is where the problems start. It is a tragic mismatch of food cultures.

A reasonably balanced diet of root and green leafy vegetables (taro leaves, edible hibiscus, fern, and watercress are all high in phytochemicals and antioxidants), fruits, fish, and a little meat was the norm for islanders in the past, which meant that they were largely free from the killer modern diet-related diseases (high blood pressure, diabetes, and heart disease). High in fiber and low in fat, the predominantly vegetable diet, with the addition of some meat and fish, evolved around sustainable practices and those that were designed to meet seasonal food shortages. The fermenting of breadfruit, which can be harvested all year round, was one way of making sure there was something to eat when food was short. Food was always shared. When there was a surplus, it might be celebrated with a feast, where the chiefs would take the lion's share, but everyone would eat as much as they could, partly as a sign of respect. This was the cultural norm. Eating to excess in this way is still considered an acceptable practice in islander culture, only now, sedentary lifestyles have brought serious health implications.

The issue of declining health has been of concern among leaders, researchers, and academics for decades, being linked more broadly to the effects of urbanization and the adoption of a Western-style economy, diet, and lifestyle. This began to occur more rapidly after 1942, when the Pacific became a region involved in World War II. Catapulted into the 20th century, the Pacific Islands' lifestyle changed rapidly. The first Western explorers to the Pacific brought infectious diseases, but the second wave, initiated by American and allied servicemen, created permanent infrastructure, telecommunications, and, after the war, a globally linked cash economy that subsequently contributed to a new range of food-related diseases: tooth decay, diabetes, hypertension, and obesity among them. These are all still of growing concern for Pacific islanders.[3]

Lifestyle change was part of the problem and eventually, by the early 1980s, initiatives were put in place to establish the development of food and nutrition policies in Pacific Island nations. Today, research and aid, local bodies and agencies, help to promote health, and people are encouraged both to exercise and eat healthy food. The current state of islander health is deteriorating, however, and understanding why this is the case requires looking at both historical and contemporary circumstances. In the past, dietary needs were not always met due to drought, cyclone, or periods of bad weather that affected fishing; today, islanders suffer less at the hands of the environment (although global warming is now an issue, particularly for low-lying islands) than they do from overconsumption of foods that are always available, a system that is virtually the opposite in terms of inputs and outputs when compared with the subsistence-style living of the past.

Everywhere one goes in the Pacific there are signs of health problems: overweight, high consumption of fats, carbohydrates, and deep-fried meats, doughs and fries, refined sugar in cookies, snacks, cakes, and soft drinks. But although detrimental health outcomes can be directly related to the consumption of these foods, it is not a lack of education or information that is primarily to blame. There are cultural reasons why islanders have adopted Western foods and why they eat them seemingly without the concern that some Westerners show.

This is a problem linked to diet and to changes in lifestyle, as islanders have increasingly adopted desk jobs and other semisedentary occupations. Coupled with the fact that an exercise culture does not exist in islander traditions, the impact of Westernization has been severe in this context. Other important factors have also had an impact. Cyclones and hurricanes regularly expose rural people to certain foods in the form of aid, including white flour, butter, cooking oil, rice, sugar, and canned food. In countries like Fiji, diverse ethnic groups naturally have led to a multitude of available food products. To some extent, this is similar in other parts of the region. Imported foods have gained a social status because they are exotic, and the lingering perception is that they are more affordable by the wealthy, appearing more prestigious on that basis alone. In addition, the globalization of the world economy has produced a greater reliance on manufactured and processed foods, and a tendency to grow food for export rather than for local consumption. This suggests another generic cause, that is, the shift to a cash economy, which not only provides consumers with the cash to buy imported products, but also makes it unlikely that they will grow their own foods for consumption; more likely, their crops would be sold for cash.

Aside from these aspects, eating until one cannot eat any more is a traditional sign of well-being. What one eats is symbolically important (taro, yam, the head of a fish, or turtle), but so is how much is eaten. The opposite probably holds for the idealized Western slimmers' diet, where food intake is directly correlated with body shape and weight. This idea makes little sense in traditional island cultures. Some of the imported foods that are considered prestigious, like bully beef, also happen to be high in salts and saturated fats. Other foods are considered light food, and are therefore eaten in quantity. Bread and noodles, for example, are a good source

Bully beef, an unhealthy favorite.

of energy, but also have little fiber and, in the case of bread, have a high glycemic index.[4]

White bread and sweetened tea have become staples in the islands, and are now standard breakfast fare for the poor in urban and rural areas. But not all the foods that are considered to compromise good health are imported. Islanders have a fondness for fat-rich foods, and pork fat and coconut cream are examples. Samoans are known to drink coconut cream—as a drink, more or less straight from the can. This is considered a treat and enjoyed greatly. In the past, pork and coconut cream were special foods that would not have been eaten every day, but now that they are available on an everyday basis, along with many other foods including snack and fast foods, and the consumption of these potentially harmful products has increased. It is very much a cultural issue because, while in the West, public awareness of the dangers of high fat consumption is widespread, a similar awareness of the heath impact of certain foods is far less well-known to island peoples. In this sense, the place of food in culture is uncomplicated by expert advice.

Adding to the current alarm among researchers is that cheapness and convenience are major factors contributing to dietary change among islander populations. Additionally, the high cultural status of fat-rich foods in the past continues to make such foods desirable today in many different forms. Of those foods high in fat, sugar, and salt, or otherwise highly processed or of comparatively low quality—(Fiji has a cookie-manufacturing industry) by far the biggest influence on health via changing diet has been through the importation of Western foods and Western eating habits. Fast food of one kind or another is available throughout the region. While islanders have not taken to all of the West's favored fat-based foods, including dairy foods like milk and cheese (the expense of these imported items certainly has something to do with this), islanders still manage to consume high levels of cholesterol in the form of saturated animal fats. Bully beef (corned beef) and lamb flaps, both having been considered traditional favorites in Polynesia for many years, are extremely high in fats. While, culturally, this is regarded as good, with regard to health it has been a disaster. Coupled with what has become an easy-going island lifestyle, where active physical labor in the fields is no longer a way of life, weight gain and heart disease are on the rise across the region. More subtle changes have also undermined the traditional diet, which was mainly comprised of high fiber vegetables and fruits. The taro, one of the highest-status crops and foods, is also nutritionally superior to cassava, which in the last half century, along with rice, gradually displaced taro and yam as a cheap everyday alternative starch. Taro contains higher percentages of trace elements like magnesium, potassium, iron, and calcium.[5]

The whole world, it seems, is battling the current obesity and diabetes epidemics (overweight can contribute significantly to diabetes), but the problem for Polynesian peoples in particular also relates to the cultural value they associate with carrying more body weight. To be of larger proportion is traditionally a sign of well-being (a measure of health in Pacific cultures). Additionally, fatty foods like deep-fried foods, unknown in the Pacific before European settlement in the region, are currently growing in popularity, as is the use of imported cooking oils, which can add significantly to calorie intake depending on what is being fried (or cooked). With fat still regarded as a status food, so many more foods are on the market that not only have a high fat content, but that also contain poor quality fats known to be detrimental to health, like trans fats and saturated fats. Ironically, processed coconut and palm oil, so often used in commercially made snack foods and biscuits because of their stability in warmer conditions (thus maintaining good keeping properties for the products they are in), were, at least in the case of coconut fat, a healthy mainstay of the island diet in the past. Unprocessed coconut cream, flesh, and juice are a healthy option, high in essential minerals and antioxidants. Now, a popular gift to bring home to the Cook Islands from New Zealand is a 50-piece bucket of KFC chicken purchased at Auckland's international airport.[6] No wonder that when *Forbes Magazine* published figures on the world's fattest countries, it listed a total of 9 Pacific countries in the top 10.[7]

Studies have shown that, given an adequate supply of traditional foodstuffs, islanders were mostly physically healthy in the precontact period, and certainly were as compared to today. But during two separate waves of globalization, in the post contact period (1800–1950) and from American and global forces in the post-World War II era, islander health has declined. Globalization now often means higher prices for food items, which rise in price according to global rather than local demand. Cassava, for example, has become a popular substitute for more traditional and now more expensive root crops, but recently the biofuel industry has put upward pressure on the global market for cassava because it is one of the plants used to create alternative fuel. There is not much islanders can do about this global pressure, and few of the players in the biofuel market would even be expected to consider the associated health implication of rising prices for cassava.

Three waves of globalization, over a broader time period (the first being the Austronesian expansion into the Pacific) brought people, plants (some noxious), animals (some pests), foods, and diseases, as well as new attitudes, values, systems of food production, and patterns of consumption. All of these can potentially affect health. But health can only really be meaningfully understood with regard to Pacific Island communities if cultural attitudes are considered closely. This means that there can be no easy answers in terms of attributing absolute causes for the lifestyle diseases that now afflict island communities, including heart disease, diabetes, high blood pressure, cancer, and tooth decay. These illnesses and conditions do not *only* have biological causes. No matter how strongly statistics can verify the relationship between introduced Western foods and the prevalence of certain symptoms, health (in the Pacific) encompasses cultural, environmental, social, psychological, and physiological factors that play an important, indeed a primary, role. For the Gogodala communities of PNG, for example, the belief is that people develop strength, called *kamali*, and achieve growth, *apela gi*, from their clan and family. Physical robustness is understood to be a product of these relationships, not merely resulting from the eating of foodstuffs. More generally, in Polynesian culture, (including Samoan, Tongan, Cook Islander, and Maori), eating a large quantity of food, which is a normalized practice in these communities, is also strongly related to social identity and brings with it the endorsement of one's peers. Eating a lot is not equated with greed, as it can be in the West, but almost its reverse: the social display of consumption as an expression of well-being and an endorsement of social obligation. To eat a lot is to exercise one's power. Historically, this would partly have developed due to fluctuations in food supply, so that when food was plentiful, it was over eaten. But this practice has flowed through into postcolonial times, when more than enough food is available all the time from shops and supermarkets. In Fiji, with its majority Indian and Fijian populations, hunger strikes have occasionally been used as a political tool. While Indians may see starvation in this context as a viable and effective means to assert social power (as it was under Gandhi's leadership in the Indian subcontinent), to Fijians this form of protest only elicits pity. Food, not the lack of it, connotes for them a fundamental value that cannot be transgressed in this way. This explains why Polynesians are always feeding each other, making gifts of food, feasting, and making sure everyone has enough—which often means a lot to eat.

Traditionally, in many instances, such overeating was not associated with the illnesses to which excessive weight contributes in the West today. The traditional Hawaiian diet was made up of approximately 75 to 80 percent starch, 7 to 12 percent fat, and about the same in protein. While corpulence was customary and considered prestigious (according to his status, the king would eat the most at feasts), the diet was also high in fiber and low in fat; the starchy staples of breadfruit, taro, cassava, yams, and kumara that typically formed the basis of Pacific Islanders' diet certainly helped to maintain health by lowering the risk of modern diseases like obesity, stroke, and cancer, all of which are closely linked to diet in the West. Traditional green leafy vegetables also provided valuable nutrients and vitamins. Island peoples developed their own forms of medicine using plants and other substances in the precontact period and, as an extension of food culture, this represents one of the ways in which the edible environment furnished the means of controlling illness.[8] Postcontact, not only did traditional forms of curative prove less effective against Western diseases, but the introduction of new foods (and drugs) changed eating habits, thereby influencing health. From a nutritional perspective, the intrinsically healthy nature of these foods can only partly account for the well-being of native peoples, since it is the symbolic place of foods in social life that also maintains the health of individuals and community alike. To comprehend what this means in the cultural context requires looking beyond the literal qualities of food-as-nutrient and understanding how the growing, cooking, and provision of food are powerfully nurturing practices in the Pacific region.

Currently, there is understandable concern for the high incidence of diabetes, heart disease, and obesity that afflict islander populations but it is not Western types of foods and eating patterns, alone, that are the main cause. A genetic predisposition for diabetes (strongly linked to obesity) among Pacific islanders has been identified due to the fact that, traditionally, they would store food as fat when food to eat was plentiful; as a result, they were better able to survive times of scarcity and long voyages at sea. A large body mass in this instance was adopted as a practical measure.

Being fat in the Pacific Islands, however, also has specific cultural meaning that complicates any simple medical explanation that might be offered regarding the health perils of obesity. To have a body of larger proportions in Samoan or Tongan society actually corresponds to being healthy, especially when considering this term as an expression of well-being. Fatness carries a culturally positive meaning in particular island communities. If medical advice recommends losing weight as a means of avoiding, say, heart disease, this may have a counterproductive effect given that overeating is an integrated social act signifying abundance, generosity, hospitality, and good health. The consumption of high-fat, high-sugar content imported foods, does not necessarily have anything to do with food preferences or perceptions of nutritional value; therefore, lowering consumption must be achieved through cultural as much as medical means. Western-style educational programs focused on diet and consumption levels alone and initiated in response to diet-related diseases are not necessarily effective in changing habits.[9] Similarly, medical technologies may have little effect, as Western medical concepts and equipment are both inappropriate for the Pacific nations. Special attention must be paid to diet and health in their social and historical context, as well as in relation to the values upheld and expressed through Pacific Island food culture.

Similar to the way in which islanders view food production, preparation, and consumption as expressive of a whole way of life, so too does health traditionally relate to community sharing and caring more than it does to maintaining the physical body. In Maori culture, sustaining the *wairua* or essence of the community is paramount. This is what Westerners call today holistic medicine. There is ample evidence and documented practices related to the curative properties of island plants as well. Medical knowledge among the islanders was well-understood and well-implemented. Thus, health needs to be understood in terms of well-being, a concept that spans four broad areas: physical, social, mental, and spiritual health.[10] The issue of islander health cannot be separated from food culture as a whole because health, like food, relates to all other aspects of social life. Rather than being the standbys that they are in Western countries, canned meat (particularly corned beef, in Polynesia) and tinned fish, for example, are regarded as prestigious, special, but also healthy foods. Consequently, corned beef is frequently gifted among islanders and featured at events like weddings, funerals, feasts, and other special occasions. This sense in which corned beef is equated with health also relates to the whole community more so than it does to the individual, whose active demonstration of involvement in a particular eating culture is confirmed by the consumption of this product. But, tragically, the prolonged *cultural* popularity of canned corned beef in Tonga and Samoa (supermarkets commonly carry 25-pound tins) has contributed to rising heart disease rates. At the same time, criticism has also come from the islander community itself. Artist Michael Tuffery (born 1968, resides in NZ), has constructed several life-size steers, with horns, made entirely of empty corned beef cans identical to those exported to the islands. The pieces confirm with irony that the powerful meaning of food, unambiguously emphasized in this instance because metaphorically it takes the form of "bull," a well-known expression (short for "bullshit") used to refer to a lie or fabrication. Tuffery's bulls underline how, in reality, the immensely powerful branding of corned beef, matched only by the cultural prestige accorded it by islanders, continues to symbolize goodness while the food product itself is a real health concern. Any curiosity about the singular commercial or ideological interests at work behind such powerful icons is seldom raised, but as Tuffery's piece emphasizes, the "bull" and the beef are part of the same success story, that of colonialism and the commercial interests it ultimately served. In this context, health cannot be divorced from politics and economics, or from the cultural perspective of island people.

Dietary changes initiated postcontact developed in some unusual ways that illustrate how islander communities made use of introduced foods in their own specific ways, creating new values and meanings not shared by the white men responsible for introducing them. The nation of Tonga, for example, became a centre of whaling in the 19th century. The object of the industry was to extract the whale oil, which, prior to the commercialized production of crude oil, was a mainstay of Western economies. Since whale meat was not consumed by Westerners, and was therefore excess to the production of whale oil and ivory, it was available for local consumption. The popularity of whale meat among the Tongan population subsequently gave rise to a local whaling enterprise. Until the mid-1970s when commercial whaling was banned, tourist guides included information that might alarm the contemporary whale watcher. "You can watch whalers," was the heading used by one widely published and popular tourist guide,

Sunset's, *Islands of the South Pacific*: ". . .you can watch or take pictures of the process from government launches during the whaling season (July through October)," it reports. Describing the process in some detail, the book further states: "once landed [the whale] is killed, flensed [the blubber cut from the carcass], and sold for food to villagers who watch the process from shore and sail out to meet the whalers."[11]

Today, tourists travel to Tonga expressly to watch the whales, not the whalers, although there is more than a little desire on the part of some islanders to resume some form of whaling to supply the small local community with whale meat. There have been dietary and health-related consequences for the islanders who once consumed whale meat but are no longer allowed to do so due to regulations enforced by Australia and New Zealand (both antiwhaling countries). This account encapsulates the complex relations that food and its provision have within a culture, and suggests that care is needed when interpreting the consequences of contact with a preconceived sense of only its ill effects. While the banning of hunting and killing humpback whales in the 1970s was necessary to save a species on the verge of extinction, at that point, commercial whaling was in the hands of large commercialized fleets, not the local whalers who manned Tongan long boats to hunt and harpoon whales. The introduction of whale meat for consumption was seen among islanders as a positive addition.

In 1989 nearly 3,700 tons of sausage, mutton flaps, chicken parts, and corned beef were imported into Tonga to be consumed by Tongans. By 1999, this amount had increased to almost 6,200 tons. That makes 123 lbs per person per annum. Add increases in the consumption of refined sugar and flour to this, and this consumption pattern has clear health consequences.[12] Such change is typical of the kind that have been reshaping islanders' diets since the end of World War II. However, the case of Tonga gives particular cause for concern, since a number of factors seem to have conspired against the health status of this tiny nation. Of its 110,000 inhabitants, over 90 percent of people above the age of 30 are classified as obese. In addition to the conception that big is beautiful, Tongans' love of fatty food has certainly contributed to the problem: lamb flaps with up to 50 percent fat, canned corned beef that literally oozes fat, and roast suckling pigs are great favorites. Week-long religious festivals that involve three feasts a day mean that the very religious Tongans spend a good deal of time celebrating their faith through the consumption of their favorite foods. Lastly, Tongans are not particularly active, preferring to sit around and be sociable with family and friends. It would be a culturally inappropriate misreading of the meaning of the Tongan lifestyle to consider them lazy. They put a great deal of effort in fact into the things they value most.

The country now realizes a need for change, and lamb flaps have recently been banned (as in Fiji) in an effort to curb unfettered fat consumption. An obesity prevention action plan called Project Ma'alahi has been in force, although it has been slow to attract interest. Of more consequence in recent decades has been the example set by the King of Tonga, Taufa'ahau Tupou IV, who reduced his own weight from 460 lbs. in 1976, to 287 lbs in 1997. Ultimately, there would need to be fundamental changes in community values, spirituality, and cultural norms for Tongans' lifestyle to change markedly. Food has proved to be too laden with meaning to be reduced to a question of calories. The effects of mass consumption of bully beef, among other foods of dubious dietary merit, clearly underline how this kind of cultural appropriation has had ongoing health consequences for Pacific Islanders. Historically, Islanders have developed a taste for imported fatty meat products like tinned beef, lamb flaps, and turkey tails, which has led to Pacific islanders being among the most obese in the world. Food importation has exacerbated this problem. High levels and large quantities of carbohydrate (taro, sweet potato, and yam) in the traditional diet also translated into weight gain. Chiefs, in particular, were traditionally obliged to eat a great amount, due to their position of power. King Tupou IV of Tonga (1918–2006) was the most obese monarch in the world, weighing as much as 460 lbs. He loved such Tongan favorites as coconut cream and fatty sheep tails, and at 6 feet, 5 inches tall, embodied the cultural predilection for a fuller figure in imposing fashion. But King Tupou also decreed that the whole country of Tonga should go on a diet and exercise more in order to lose weight, with the king losing over 150 lbs. himself. In seeking a Western remedy to a Tongan problem, the king sought to turn Tonga onto a different cultural track. More recently, royal princesses have continued to campaign for weight loss through exercise.[13] But changing the mindset and behavior of such a closely knit community has proved more difficult than originally assumed, so that, in terms of the body-mass index, Tonga still ranks poorly. The cultural beliefs underpinning the consumption of certain foods continue to shape and reinforce dietary habits. Change is certainly made more difficult because cheap fatty foods are readily available and desirable, but this is doubly the case when a larger body mass is regarded as the most desirable and healthy. The challenge into the future is education, something which has been tried already but without much success. The influence of commercial enterprise and mass media outweigh what can be achieved by traditional means (through extended family) or in schools.

AUSTRALIA AND NEW ZEALAND

While the health issues that relate to island peoples can be identified fairly easily, the complex and complicated relationships of individuals in the urban Australasian context make health difficult to generalize about and even more difficult to sum up. Health and well-being depend on self-image, confidence, and levels of education, as well as physiology; all of these factors differ greatly from person to person. Growing levels of obesity and diabetes are widespread problems, however, across the Western world, and Australasia is no exception. In the past 20 years, the number of clinically obese people has doubled. Approximately 60 percent of Australian adults are overweight or obese, and this figure is set to reach 70 percent by 2010. But other recent spikes in diet-related diseases include a higher incidence of tooth decay in younger children, which is claimed to be caused, at least in part, by the bottled water craze. Drinking bottled water effectively lowers the amount of fluoridated town water consumed (the trace element fluoride hardens the enamel of the teeth). Other causes include a high intake of sugars and other carbohydrates. Links between various forms of cancer and diet have long been made and, like in other Western countries, high red meat intake, lack of fiber, and, more recently, cholesterol, as well as the lack of antioxidants and omega-3 oils (found in fish) have been found to have negative health-related consequences. Constipation and depression are also diet-related and programs of education aim at changing public perceptions of what constitutes healthy and unhealthy foods. In Australia, high-profile restaurateur and writer, turned children's food and health education advocate, Stephanie Alexander has established the Kitchen Garden Foundation. Twenty-seven Kitchen Garden Schools are functioning across the state of Victoria, followed in 2008 by a national program for 190 schools Australia wide. The foundation asserts that "the best way to encourage children to choose food that is healthy is to engage them in fun, hands-on experiences in growing, harvesting, preparing, and sharing such food from the earliest possible age." The Kitchen Garden program connects gardens and kitchens, which are established in schools. Pupils can grow, harvest, cook, and share the foods produced. Cooking classes for children are also becoming popular elsewhere as a method of educating about health that is practical and involving for participants.

But the primary diet-related cause of health problems affecting children and adults in Australasia is overeating in conjunction with a proportionally high intake of refined foods compared with unprocessed plant foods like fresh fruits and vegetables, grains, pulses, and nuts. Hygiene and food safety standards are similar to those of other Western nations, although cases of salmonella poisoning do occur from time to time. Recalls of products and the public health authority control of such occurrences are swift and effective. Alcohol consumption continues to be a problem, particularly with the rise of underage and binge drinking, abetted by the proliferation of ready-mixed spirit-based alcoholic beverages (called "alcopops," or RTDs—meaning "ready-to-drink"—in Australasia), targeted at young adults. Part of the problem is that alcohol is being sold as a fun product and, according to market surveys, 24 percent of 18–19-year-olds interviewed thought there was no alcohol in the alcopops they were asked to taste.[14] Government-funded advertisements now warn of the dangers of this infrequent but excessive form of social drinking, and a recent tax on these drinks designed to curb underage alcohol abuse has successfully lowered consumption levels. Excessive beer drinking (Australian and NZ men are traditionally beer drinkers) has been associated with colon cancer, but also gout, the latter being on the rise among New Zealand Maori and Polynesians, who have been found to be genetically susceptible to the disease. But lifestyle also plays a role. The consumption of shellfish, offal, meat, beer, and soft drinks, popular foods among these groups, has exacerbated the problem. More than 10,000 South Aucklanders of Polynesian descent are thought to be suffering from gout, a painful affliction that causes swollen tendons and joints due to a buildup of uric acid in the body. Untreated, it can lead to diabetes and kidney failure.[15]

As elsewhere in the West, coronary heart disease, hypertension, atherosclerosis, stroke, diabetes, and cancer are the main diet-related threats to human health in Australasia. The link between a high intake of salt, fat, sugar, refined foods, lack of fiber, high alcohol consumption, combined with inactivity, and illness, has been well-known for many decades. Yet the problem is not that the warning messages are not reaching the wider public, but rather that habitual dietary choices are often shaped early in life by a whole range of culturally instilled values and desires, only some, or none of which may be related to a food's health benefits. Food and drink choices are socialized in complex ways that often bypass common sense. Fashion, peer pressure, cost, lifestyle, work-leisure time constraints, and, consequently, the degree of ease, convenience, and immediate accessibility (vending machines, fast food outlets) often dictate what is eaten. Foods are increasingly marketed as fun, or sensational, that is, immediately appealing to the sense of taste. The problem is that the food choices that result from regarding food as something that provides degrees of gustatory thrills are often poor ones with respect to health.

Such cultural issues related to diet and health afflict the islands too, albeit differently. One problem that is shared across the region, including Australasia, is the widening gap between rich and poor. The wealthier members of the community tend to belong to the better-educated segment, while the lower socioeconomic groups have less access to good schools for their children as well as a low income, having the effect of limiting food choice. This does not only occur because there are fewer choices with less money, but also because, when both time and money are short, as is often the case in poorer families, food becomes something of a treat. Treat foods are often seen as Western foods, like KFC or other fast foods. Similarly, cooking is regarded as drudgery, particularly if both parents need to work all day in paid employment. This is a food-related diet issue that is also a social problem. In Australia, rising obesity levels (1 in 4 Australian children are overweight or obese) can now be directly correlated with families from the lower socioeconomic segment of society. Those living in the wealthier suburban areas are not only healthier, eating better (fresher, unprocessed) foods on average; they also exercise more, know more about nutrition and its importance, and, consequently, have lower body-mass indexes. Paradoxically, those wealthier families who have no trouble putting food on the table are less likely to have obese children and more likely to have anorexic ones. Anorexia nervosa continues to be a diet-related disease that also relates to self-image. The important point here is that those with more disposable income, more free time, and better access to information can afford to take advantage of the current trend toward healthier types of foods. They have the time to take an interest, educate themselves, and use food as a form of cultural capital and thereby as a means of self-improvement. In this context, organic and biodynamic foods, local foods, and farmers' markets not only represent widening choices for consumers, but appeal to the latter's ethical outlook, because they communicate a political message, as do so-called green or eco-friendly foods. Production values including social justice and equity are associated with Fair Trade foods and beverages (like coffee) and also appeal to the thinking shopper who is increasingly appreciative of knowing where a food is from and how it is produced: its *provenance*. Ironically, some Fair Trade and other boutique products (often sold at a premium price in Australia) come from places like PNG, with profits going back to support small farmer-producers; not many consumer dollars go to support the poor of Australasia, who cannot afford to "do the right thing" in terms of shopping ethically. It remains a privilege of the wealthy to first take the time to consider the health benefits of one food over another; second, to buy fresh, fair, or unprocessed foods, which are still comparatively expensive, and third, take the time when needed to prepare them. Although some of this healthier produce is now finding its way into supermarkets, where prices can be lower, it is also debatable whether the organic label many of these foods now carry will continue to mean what it is supposed to. Health sells, as do labels. It is not so easy to discern the underlying nutritional qualities of food products from appearance alone. Two tiers of food culture clearly exist in Australasia. One can afford the time, money, and effort to invest in food as something intimately linked to health. For the majority of others, however, food is something that gives immediate pleasure, and the less time or effort spent on buying it, preparing it, and often eating it, the better. This cultural attitude makes solving the serious diet-related health issues in Australasia difficult.

Diet-related health among aboriginal people reveals just how intractable such problems can become. Individual life expectancy among Aboriginal people is significantly shorter (by 17 years) than for the rest of the Australian population. There are about half a million Aboriginal people in Australia, many of whom live in "white fella" communities, including towns and cities. Others still live in remote parts of the country, so diets naturally differ greatly, but lower levels of education and community access to information also work against reforming the diet of Aboriginal Australians. In addition, these native people have had a disastrous relationship with alcohol over the years, which continues to destroy families and communities. With the loss of so much of their traditional culture, generations of Aboriginals have grown up between two completely different worlds, one vanishing before their eyes, the other in many ways inaccessible to them. Food and drink, so much the focus of community life in the islands, has lost its bearings in the contemporary lives of many Aboriginals, who follow the pattern superficially set by the urban world of quick meals, supermarkets, food on the run, and the love of convenience. Nor is there really any option for Aboriginal people who leave the country areas and their traditional roots to maintain much of a bush food culture. As nomadic hunter-gatherers, Australian Aborigines' food culture was inseparable from their values, beliefs, cosmology, and spirituality. Removed from this context, food loses its meaning, appearing new and different in the urban context. Similarly the prestige of Western foods among islanders, for Aboriginal Australians living in centers where they have ready access to food services, eagerly opt for the easiest accessed fast food.

Aboriginal health has suffered greatly through poor diet. Alcohol and drug abuse (gas sniffing has had particularly savage health consequences,

including irreversible brain damage and death) have been an added
consumption-related scourge on health. The lack of access to good housing and, thus, adequate food preparation facilities, also undermines any
chance for change in the short to medium term. Inadequate education
in remote communities (including subjects like health and nutrition), as
well as a lack of skills, like cooking, have worked against the best efforts
of Aboriginal leaders and other groups. To an extent, Aboriginal people
have been forced to forsake their culture and to survive in one that offers
them few opportunities except to keep moving on. In such an environment, food is going to be an immediate, everyday concern, but not one
that can form the kind of meaningful role necessary for a healthy lifestyle
to develop.

Aside from the typically Western diseases that afflict all highly urbanized cultures—cancer, heart disease, stroke, and hypertension—another
increasing, diet-related problem in Australia and New Zealand, as in
other Organization for Economic Co-operation and Development countries (OECD, which has over 100 members including most of the European Union, the U.S., the UK, Japan, Australia, and NZ), is poverty.
Poverty has increased in many of these countries since the late 1980s
and early 1990s, due mainly to the tightening of the welfare system and
the widening gap between rich and poor. As a result, aging single people
and working poor struggle financially to feed themselves. In Australia, 13
percent of adults and 15 percent of children now live in poverty, making a
total of 2.4 million who do not always have enough money for food. Poverty as it effects food acquisition and consumption is called *food insecurity*.
The 1996 Rome Declaration on World Food Security established that
"food security exists when all people, at all times, have physical and economic access to sufficient, safe and nutritious food to meet their dietary
needs and food preferences for an active and healthy life," but poverty has
made food insecurity a mounting problem in wealthy Western countries.
Relief programs have emerged to help educate and provide food. "Foodbanks" (Australia) is a nondenominational organization that operates in
all states in Australia, and demand is growing for this type of service in
New Zealand as well, with the Salvation Army (a Christian agency) now
operating 37 foodbanks around the country, representing growth of over
20 percent in the 2007–08 period. Foodbanks began as a church-run operation, but huge growth in the 1990s brought specialized agencies into
the market. Two million Australians (half of them children) now rely
on food relief each year from providers like Foodbanks. In New Zealand,
Maori and Pacific Islanders are overrepresented among food bank users.
As neighborhood deprivation increases, so does the utilization rate of

each ethnic group, with Maori by far the largest minority ethnic group users of food banks.

Other efforts are being made to address the education of children and ethnic groups who face challenges with regard to poverty, social status, circumstances, or situation. The "Foodcents" program in Western Australia began in May 2004 as an educational scheme for Aboriginal and Torres Straight Islanders living in remote areas. A cookbook was produced called *Deadly Tucker* ("deadly," the book's liner notes reveal, is a term meaning "very good, tops, cool" in the local vernacular).[16] The title strikes an ironic chord given the fact that diets of one kind or another can very much prove to be deadly in today's food world, but the message of the book is clear: eat healthy food and exercise regularly. Apart from a few recipes for kangaroo (which is available at many butchers and markets), the recipes are all for basic generic dishes from a number of cuisines: lasagna, curry, casserole, stews, soups, hot pots, and stir-fries. The book is full of clear how-to color picture descriptions of preparation stages and is obviously meant to be used as an everyday cooking aid. Its success depends on access to food and facilities, two of the problems that continue to face the poor and otherwise marginalized members of the community.

NOTES

1. Harold Koi, "34 pc Live in Poverty, Says Minister," *Fiji Times*, October 17, 2008.

2. See South Pacific Foods Leaflets. South Pacific Commission, 1983–1995 (available from SPC).

3. United Nations Development Program (South Pacific Commission), "The Effects of Urbanization and Western Diet on the Health of Pacific Island Populations," *Journal of Food and Nutrition*, 39, no. 3 (1982): 126–129; also Paul Zimmet, "The Medical Effects of Lifestyle in Pacific Populations," *Journal of Food and Nutrition* 39, no. 1 (1982).

4. Jimaima Veisikiaki Lako, "Phytochemicals in Pacific Foods and Related Health Status" (PhD diss., Monash University, 2006), 62.

5. Shailesh Kumar et al., *Pacific Island Foods: Nutrient Composition of Some Pacific Island Foods and the Effect of Earth-Oven Cooking*, vol. 2 (Suva: Institute of Applied Sciences, University of the South Pacific, 2001).

6. Kalissa Alexeyeff, "Love Food: Exchange and Sustenance in the Cook Islands Diaspora," *Australian Journal of Anthropology* 15, no. 11 (2004), 68–79.

7. Lauren Streib, "World's Fattest Countries," Forbes.com, http://www.forbes.com/forbeslife/2007/02/07/worlds-fattest-countries-forbeslife-cx_ls_0208 worldfat_2.html (accessed June 8, 2008).

8.   W. Arthur Whistler, *Polynesian Herbal Medicine* (Honolulu, HI: National Tropical Botanic Garden). See section on "Polynesian Medical Practices Today," e-book, www.nsdl.org (2004).

9.   Mike Evans et al., "Globalization, Diet, and Health: An Example from Tonga," *Bulletin of the World Health Organization* 79, no. 9 (2001): 856–62.

10.   Nancy Pollock, " 'Good Food' in Pacific Societies: Transculturation and Selection," (paper presented at the History, Health and Hybridity symposium, Dunedin, NZ, 2005).

11.   Mary Benton Smith, *Islands of the South Pacific* (Menlo Park, CA: Sunset Books, 1966), 89.

12.   Mike Evans, "Whale-Watching and the Compromise of Tongan Interests through Tourism," in *Proceedings of the 1st International Small Island Cultures Conference* (Kagoshima University Centre for the Pacific Islands: The Small Island Cultures Research Initiative, 2005), 50.

13.   See Stefan Gates, *In the Danger Zone*. London: BBC Books, 2008.

14.   *Choice* is a not-for-profit company with 200,000 subscribers, and is the largest consumer organization in Australia. It tests products, including food, and advises on quality, safety, and value.

15.   Craig Borley, "Pacific and Maori Men at Centre of Gout Scare," *New Zealand Herald*, September 03, 2008, http://www.nzherald.co.nz/health/news/article.cfm?c_id=204&objectid=10530250 (accessed November 20, 2008).

16.   *Deadly Tucker* (A cookbook produced as part of the FOODcents for Aboriginal and Torres Strait Islander People in WA Program). East Perth: Western Australia Dept. of Health, 2004.

Glossary

ariki   Tribal chief.

Atiu   One of the Cook Islands, where coffee is now grown.

atoll   Low-lying coral island.

basese   Petiole of taro, blanched and served with coconut, chili, and onion.

bele   Spinach-like leaves of hibiscus commonly used in Fiji. Called *pele* in Tonga and *rukau viti* in Rarotonga.

blackbirding   Term coined in the 1880s to describe the kidnapping of islanders of the Pacific for labor purposes.

botaki   Celebration or party (Kiribati).

breadfruit   Starchy fruit, a staple food of Pacific islanders.

bu   Fijian word for green coconut.

bully beef   Canned corned beef.

buw   Micronesian term for betel nut (the seed of the *areca* palm), a mild intoxicant, which is chewed and turns the saliva red. It turns the teeth black with long-term use and is also popular in Palau (FDM), and in the Solomon Islands, where it is called *bia blong*.

copra   Dried coconut flesh.

corms   Botanical name for taro root.

duruka in lolo   Fleshy white stem cooked in coconut milk, likened to asparagus in Fiji.

'eke   Octopus (Cook Islands Maori).

fai kakai   Tongan pudding made from cassava, similar to the arrowroot-based *poke* of Rarotonga and the breadfruit based *po'e* of Tahiti.

fale kai   Dining house (Tonga).

FSM   Federated States of Micronesia.

gari vakalolo   Crab in coconut curry.

geregere   Astringent drink made in PNG from the fruit of coastal varieties of pandanus.

governor's plum   (*Flacourtia indica*) Small tropical purple-red fruit with orange-yellow flesh. Its flavor is similar to that of a plum. Grows wild on Rarotonga.

hakari   Banquet (Maori).

hangi   Maori word for *umu*.

i'i   Tahitian chestnut (Cook Islands Maori).

ika   Fish (Cook Islands Maori).

kahuna   Chief.

kanavata   Eating together (Fiji).

kapai   Fine or good (Maori). Also the trade name of a popular, large arrowroot biscuit exported from NZ to the Pacific region.

kakoda   Raw fish marinated in coconut milk (Fiji).

Katsu   Japanese-style fried chicken popular in Hawaii

kava   Mildly mood-altering drink made from a pepper bush, *Piper mythisticum*. Important drink in Pohnpei, Fiji, Vanuatu, and Tonga. Ceremonial use only in Samoa.

kayasa   Competitive display, involving food (sometimes), dance, and special dress (Trobriand Islands).

kumala   Sweet potatoes (Tonga and Fiji).

kumara   Sweet potatoes (New Zealand Maori).

kuru   Rarotongan for breadfruit.

kuru papa   Cooked breadfruit mixed with coconut cream.

lap-lap   National dish of Vanuatu, a pudding made from plantain bananas, breadfruit, roots or tubers, which are grated and packaged in leaves, then cooked in the *umu*.

lolo   Coconut cream (Fiji).

lovo   Fijian word for *umu*.

magiti Fijian feast.

mana Energy, power. Intangible spiritual and moral force that can be accumulated through good acts. Condition must be carefully created, attitudes cultivated, and relationships respected if *mana* is to be attracted.

manioke Cassava or manioc (Tonga).

maitai Famous cocktail associated with the islands.

mayi Generic Aboriginal term (or cognate of), usually meaning plant food. Term used for bush food in Dampierland, northwestern Australia.

miti Mixture of coconut milk and water, with minced onion, salt, and chili, commonly used as a condiment for fish in Fiji.

nama "Sea grapes," a species of seaweed (Fiji).

okolehao Hawaiian spirit made from the roots of the ti plant.

oppot Specialty of Chuuk (FSM), made by alternating layers of banana leaves with pieces of ripe breadfruit, weighting it all down with stones and leaving it for months before eating. Particularly useful on long sea voyages.

ota miti Young fern leaves served with coconut, onion, and chili.

palolo Reproductive segments of the neiris sea worm, a delicacy in the islands.

palusami Fijian and Samoan equivalent of *rukau*.

pandanus Indispensable food plant on many atolls, yielding fruit and starch.

Papahanaumoku Earth mother. Originally a drinking vessel also fashioned from the gourd (Papa) by Pataka (Hawaii).

pataka Food storehouse (Maori).

papaya Tropical fruit, the same as paw paw.

pe'epe'e Coconut cream, obtained by straining grated coconut (Samoa).

peito Cooking house (Tonga).

peke peke Coconut cream (Tonga).

pia Arrowroot flour.

PNG Papua New Guinea.

po'e Tahitian word for a similar preparation to poi but made with breadfruit.

poi   Hawaiian word for mashing taro; later the word for the finished product, mashed cooked taro root. Poi is available ready-made from the supermarket.

poisson cru   Raw fish marinated in lime juice and coconut milk (Tahiti).

poke   Polynesian (Cook Islander) term for arrowroot starch and fruit (usually paw paw) or pumpkin-based pudding.

pongipongi   Tongan kava-drinking ceremony.

pupus   Hawaiian-style canapés, made fashionable in the 1930s, and often utilizing dainty morsels of fish, sometimes smoked, and shellfish.

Rata   Demigod, maker of canoes. His father and uncle are eaten by a giant clam with which Rata does battle, retrieving the bones of his relatives after killing the clam (Tahiti).

Rongo   God of cultivated foods (New Zealand). God of cultivated foods and harvested seafood (Raratonga and Mangaia, Cook Islands).

roko   Taro leaves (Fiji).

rourou   Taro leaves cooked in coconut cream.

rukau   Taro, but also the name of a dish made from layered taro leaves with a filling of tinned corned beef and onion (Cook Islands). Sometimes other meat (cooked beef brisket) can be used.

sakau   Like kava but much stronger; before serving it is strained through hibiscus bark. Made in the FSM (Pohnpei, Chuuk, Yap, Kosrae), it is drunk ceremonially, but also available in bars.

SPC   Secretariat of the Pacific Community (formerly the South Pacific Commission).

superphosphate   Petrochemical-derived fertilizer.

Tangaroa   God of the sea and the progenitor of fish and canoes (East and West Polynesia, NZ).

tapu   Meaning forbidden, restricted, but also sacred (Polynesian). Origin of the English word *taboo*.

ti   (*Cordyline fruticose*) Starchy rhizomes of this woody plant, which grows up to 13 feet tall, are very sweet when the plant is mature. Eaten in Polynesia as food or for medicine. Ti leaves are used to wrap food.

tiki   Name given to a décor and style themed around Pacific artifacts and motifs, popularized in U.S. bars and restaurants from the 1930s that also featured exotic cocktails and lounge music.

toddy   Potent drink made from fermented coconut juice.

tu'i tu'i Rich.

umu Underground oven, but also the name given to the social event to which to *umu* is integral.

umukai Feast (Cook Islands).

ura Freshwater prawns (Cook Islands).

urura Great trevally, a favorite fish in the Cook Islands.

uto Coconut foam taken from the shooting nut.

utu Variety of mountain plantain, often roasted (Rarotonga).

vi puaka "Mango for pigs." Derogatory term for paw paw among outer Cook Islanders.

viti Fijian name for Fiji.

Wakea (Skyfather) and Papa (existed in the form of a gourd from which Pataka fashioned the world. The lid became the heavens, its juices the clouds, and rain and its seeds became the sun, moon, and stars).

yaqona Fijian word for kava.

Resource Guide

WEB SITES

Australia market guide http://www.marketguide.com.au/vic-1.htm.

Australian Food Statistics 2007 www.daff.gov.au.

Captain Cook's journals http://www.archive.org/stream/threevoyagesofca04cook/threevoyagesofca04cook_djvu.txt.

Eco-Hangi http://www.eco-hangi.co.nz/The%20Eco-Hangi.htm.

FAO Key trade statistics (food imports and exports) http://www.fao.org/es/ess/toptrade/trade.asp.

FAO South Pacific Foods http://www.fao.org/Wairdocs/X5425E/X5425E00.htm.

New Zealand Farmers' Markets http://www.farmersmarket.org.nz/home.htm.

South Pacific Community (SPC) http://www.spc.int/corp/.

South Pacific Community Food Leaflets http://www.fao.org/Wairdocs/X5425E/X5425E00.htm.

VIDEOS/FILMS

Family Footsteps. Documentary about a Tongan woman's return to Tonga that illustrates the pecking order of Tongan social life as it is played out during mealtimes. http://www.abc.net.au/tv/documentaries/interactive/family-footsteps/tonga/.

How to make a Hawaiian imu http://hawaiiankava.com/imu/imu%20how%20to,%20p7.htm.

Making lap lap in Vanuatu http://www.youtube.com/watch?v=P6l5lsW7DhI.

Melanesian Bougna (New Caledonia) http://www.youtube.com/watch?v=TVpLIBciMO0.

Waibulabula project http://www.video.google.com/videoplay?docid=6644216255974733085.

Selected Bibliography

GENERAL

Bailey, J. M. *The Leaves We Eat.* SPC Handbook 31. Noumea, New Caledonia: South Pacific Commission, 1992.

Burton, David. *Two Hundred Years of New Zealand Food and Cookery.* Wellington, NZ: Reed, 1982.

Campbell, I. C. *Worlds Apart: A History of the Pacific Islands.* Christchurch, NZ: Canterbury University Press, 2003.

Cooper, Chris, and Colin Michael Hall, eds. *Oceania: A Tourism Handbook.* Buffalo, NY: Channel View Publications, 2005.

Couper, A. D., ed. *Development and Social Change in the Pacific Islands.* New York: Routledge, 1989.

Denoon, Donald, Philippa Mein-Smith, and Marivic Wyndham. *A History of Australia, New Zealand, and the Pacific.* Malden, MA: Blackwell, 2000.

Flynn, Dennis Owen, Lionel Frost, and A.J.H. Latham, eds. *Pacific Centuries: Pacific and Pacific Rim History since the Sixteenth Century.* New York: Routledge, 1999.

Howe, K. R. *Vaka Moana, Voyages of the Ancestors: The Discovery and Settlement of the Pacific.* Honolulu: University of Hawaii Press, 2007.

Howe, K. R., Robert C. Kiste, and Brij V. Lal, eds. *Tides of History: The Pacific Islands in the Twentieth Century.* St. Leonard's, NSW: Allen & Unwin, 1994.

Irwin, Geoffrey. *The Prehistoric Exploration and Colonisation of the Pacific.* Cambridge: Cambridge University Press, 1992.

Kahn, Miriam, and Lorraine Sexton. "Continuity and Change in Pacific Food-ways." Special issue, *Food and Foodways* 3, no. 1 and 2 (1988).

Kirch, Patrick Vinton, and Jean-Louis Rallu, eds. *The Growth and Collapse of Pacific Island Societies: Archaeological and Demographic Perspectives.* Honolulu: University of Hawaii Press, 2007.

Kittler, Pamela Goyan, and Kathryn P. Sucher. *Food and Culture.* 5th ed. Belmont, CA: Thompson Wadsworth, 2008.

Lal, Brij V., and Kate Fortune, eds. *The Pacific Islands: An Encyclopedia.* Honolulu: University of Hawaii Press, 2000.

Oliver, Douglas L. *Oceania: The Native Cultures of Australia and the Pacific Islands.* 2 vols. Honolulu: University of Hawaii Press, 1989.

Pollock, Nancy J. *These Roots Remain: Food Habits in Islands of the Central and Eastern Pacific since Western Contact.* Honolulu: University of Hawaii Press, 1992.

Rapaport, Moshe, ed. *The Pacific Islands: Environment and Society.* Honolulu, HI: Bess Press, 1999.

Scarr, Deryck. *The History of the Pacific Islands, Kingdoms of the Reefs.* South Melbourne: Macmillan, 1990.

Secretariat of the Pacific Community (SPC). *The Fruits We Eat.* SPC Handbook (not numbered). Noumea: Secretariat of the Pacific Community, 2001.

Secretariat of the Pacific Community (SPC). *The Staples We Eat.* SPC Handbook 35. Noumea: Secretariat of the Pacific Community, 1999.

Skinner, Gwen. *The Cuisine of the South Pacific.* London: Hodder and Stoughton, 1983.

Steinberg, Rafael, ed. *Pacific and Southeast Asian Cooking.* New York: Time-Life Books, 1970.

Stenson, Marcia. *Illustrated History of the South Pacific.* Auckland: Random House New Zealand, 2006.

Symons, Michael. *One Continuous Picnic: A Gastronomic History of Australia.* 2nd rev. ed. Melbourne: Melbourne University Press, 2007.

Walter, Annie, and Chanel Sam, eds. *Gardens of Oceania.* Canberra: Australian Centre for International Agricultural Research, 2007.

Walter, Annie, and Chanel Sam, eds. *Fruits of Oceania.* Canberra: ACIAR Editions, 2002.

HISTORICAL OVERVIEW

Beaglehole, Earnest. *Social Change in the South Pacific: Rarotonga and Aitutaki.* Aberdeen, UK: George Allen & Unwin, 1957.

Burenhult, Goran. *New World and Pacific Civilizations: Cultures of America, Asia, and the Pacific.* St. Lucia: University of Queensland Press, 1994.

Campbell, I. C. *Worlds Apart: A History of the Pacific Islands.* Christchurch, NZ: Canterbury University Press, 2003.

Connell, John. "'The Taste of Paradise': Selling Fiji and Fiji Water." *Asia Pacific Viewpoint* 47, no. 3 (2006): 342–50.

Cooper, Chris, and Colin Michael Hall, eds. *Oceania: A Tourism Handbook*. Clevedon, UK; Buffalo: Channel View Publications, 2005.

Dening, Greg. *Islands and Beaches: Discourse on a Silent Land*, Marquesas, 1774–1880. Carlton, Victoria: Melbourne University Press, 1980.

Fernández-Armesto, Felipe. *Near a Thousand Tables: A History of Food*. New York: The Free Press, 2002.

General Staff Issued under the Authority of the Commander of Land Forces S. W. P. A. *Friendly Fruits and Vegetables*. 1st ed. Melbourne: Arbuckle Waddle, 1943.

Harris, Graham. "Nga Riwai Maori: The Perpetuation of Relict Potato Cultivars within Maori Communities in New Zealand." In *Vegeculture in Eastern Asia and Oceania* (JCAS Symposium Series No 16), ed. Shuji Yoshida and Peter J. Mathews. Osaka: Japan Centre for Asian Studies, 2002.

Howe, K. R. *Vaka Moana, Voyages of the Ancestors: The Discovery and Settlement of the Pacific*. Honolulu: University of Hawaii Press, 2007.

Howe, K. R. *Where the Waves Fall: A New South Sea Islands History from First Settlement to Colonial Rule*. Sydney: George Allen & Unwin, 1984.

Kiple, Kenneth F., and Kriemhild Coneè Ornelas, eds. *The Cambridge World History of Food*. Cambridge: Cambridge University Press, 2000.

Kirch, Patrick Vinton, and Jean-Louis Rallu, eds. *The Growth and Collapse of Pacific Island Societies: Archaeological and Demographic Perspectives*. Honolulu: University of Hawaii Press, 2007.

Kittler, Pamela Goyan, and Kathryn P. Sucher. *Food and Culture*. 5th ed. Belmont, CA: Thompson Wadsworth, 2008.

Knapman, Bruce. "Capitalism's Economic Impact in Colonial Fiji 1874–1939: Development or Underdevelopment." *Journal of Pacific History* 20, no. 2 (1985): 66–83.

Koch, Gerd. *The Material Culture of Tuvalu*. Suva: Institute of Pacific Studies, 1981.

Lal, Brij V., and Kate Fortune, eds. *The Pacific Islands: An Encyclopedia*. Honolulu: University of Hawaii Press, 2000.

Low, Tim. "Foods of the First Fleet: Convict Foodplants of Old Sydney Town." *Australian Natural History* 22, no. 7 (1988): 293–97.

Maude, H. E. *Of Islands and Men: Studies in Pacific History*. New York: Oxford University Press, 1968.

Maude, H. E. *Slavers in Paradise: The Peruvian Labour Trade in Polynesia, 1862–1864*. Canberra: Australian National University Press, 1981.

McLintock, A. H. *An Encyclopaedia of New Zealand*. Wellington, NZ: R. E. Owen, Government Printer, 1966.

Oliver, Douglas L. *Oceania: The Native Cultures of Australia and the Pacific Islands*. 2 vols. Honolulu: University of Hawaii Press, 1989.

Rapaport, Moshe, ed. *The Pacific Islands: Environment & Society*. Honolulu, HI: Bess Press, 1999.

Secretariat of the Pacific Community (SPC). "Food Crisis: An Opportunity for the Pacific." Statement issued at the World Food Summit '08, held in Rome, Italy. Reproduced in *Pacific Magazine*, June 5, 2008.

Simpson, Tony. *A Distant Feast: The Origins of New Zealand Cuisine*. Auckland: Godwit, 1999.

Symons, Michael. *One Continuous Picnic: A Gastronomic History of Australia*. 2nd rev. ed. Melbourne: Melbourne University Press, 2007.

Thaman, Randolph R. "Deterioration of Traditional Food Systems, Increasing Malnutrition and Food Dependency in the Pacific Islands." *Journal of Food and Nutrition* 39, no. 3 (1982): 109–21.

Yoon, Carol Kaesuk. "Alien Species Threaten Hawaii's Environment," *New York Times*, December 29, 1992.

MAJOR FOODS AND INGREDIENTS

Diamond, Jared M. *Guns, Germs, and Steel: The Fates of Human Societies*. New York: W. W. Norton, 2005.

Dixon, Jane. *The Changing Chicken: Chooks, Cooks and Culinary Culture*. Sydney: University of New South Wales Press, 2002.

Gary, Lamora Sauvinet. *The Pacific Hostess Cookbook*. New York: Coward-McCann, 1956.

Morrison, John, Paul Geraghty, and Linda Crowl, eds. *Land Use and Agriculture*. Science of Pacific Island Peoples. Suva: University of the South Pacific, 1994.

Parkinson, Susan. *Cooking the South Pacific way: A Professional Guide to Fiji Produce*. Suva: Tourism Council of the South Pacific, 1989.

Pollock, Nancy. "Food Classification in Three Pacific Societies: Fiji, Hawaii and Tahiti." *Ethnology* 25, no. 2 (1986): 107–17.

Pollock, Nancy. " 'Good Food' in Pacific Societies: Transculturation and Selection." Paper presented at the History, Health, and Hybridity symposium, Dunedin, NZ, 2005.

Ragone, Diane. "Breadfruit Storage and Preparation in the Pacific Islands." In Shuji Yoshida and Peter J. Mathews eds. *Vegeculture in Eastern Asia and Oceania* (JCAS Symposium Series No 16) Osaka: Japan Centre for Asian Studies, 2002.

Skinner, Gwen. *Simply Living: A Gatherer's Guide to New Zealand's Fields, Forests and Shores*. Wellington, NZ: Reed, 1981.

Whistler, W. Arthur. "Ethnobotany of Tokelau: The Plants, Their Tokelau Names, and Their Uses." *Economic Botany* 42, no. 2 (1988): 155–76.

COOKING

Australian Cookery of Today Illustrated. Melbourne: The Sun News-Pictorial, c. 1950s.

Brennan, Jennifer. *Tradewinds and Coconuts: A Reminiscence and Recipes from the Pacific Islands*. Boston, MA: Periplus Editions, 2000.

Burton, David. *Two Hundred Years of New Zealand Food and Cookery*. Wellington, NZ: Reed, 1982.

Hosken, Mike. *Cuisine Faim Facile En Nouvelle-Calédonie*. Noumea: Éditions Footprint Pacifique, 2005.

Laudan, Rachel. *The Food of Paradise: Exploring Hawaii's Culinary Heritage*. Honolulu: University of Hawaii Press, 1996.

Leach, Helen M. "Cooking without Pots: Aspects of Prehistoric and Traditional Polynesian Cooking." *New Zealand Journal of Archaeology* 4 (1984): 149–56.

Matenga-Smith, Taiora. *Cook Islands Cookbook*. Auckland, NZ: University of the South Pacific, 1990.

Muskett, Philip E. *The Art of Living in Australia*. Melbourne: Eyre and Spottiswoode, c. 1893.

Ravuvu, Asesela. *Vaka I Taukei: The Fijian Way of Life*. Suva: University of the South Pacific, 1983.

Rickman, Rob, Peter Henning, and Glen Craig ("Three Loose Coconuts"). *Unforgettable: A Coconut Cookbook*. Tweed Heads, NSW, 2004.

Rickman, Rob, Peter Henning, and Glen Craig ("Three Loose Coconuts"). *Under the Mango Tree: The People, the Palate, the Pleasures*. Coolangatta, Queensland, 2005.

Simpson, Tony. *A Distant Feast: The Origins of New Zealand Cuisine*. Auckland, NZ: Godwit, 1999.

Sopade, P. A. "Mumu: A Traditional Method of Slow Cooking in Papua New Guinea." *Boiling Point* 38 (April 1997): 34–35.

Steinberg, Rafael, ed. *Pacific and Southeast Asian Cooking*. New York: Time-Life Books, 1970.

Symons, Michael. *One Continuous Picnic: A Gastronomic History of Australia*. 2nd rev. ed. Melbourne: Melbourne University Press, 2007.

Symons, Michael. *The Shared Table: Ideas for Australian Cuisine*. Canberra: AGPS Press, 1993.

Veart, David. *First, Catch Your Weka: A Story of New Zealand Cooking*. Auckland, NZ: Auckland University Press, 2008.

TYPICAL MEALS

Alexeyeff, Kalissa. "Love Food: Exchange and Sustenance in the Cook Islands Diaspora." *Australian Journal of Anthropology* 15, no. 1 (2004): 68–79.

Lako, Jimaima Veisikiaki. "Dietary Trend and Diabetes: Its Association among Indigenous Fijians 1952–1994." *Asia Pacific Journal of Clinical Nutrition* 10, no. 3 (2001): 183–87.

Morrison, John, Paul Geraghty, and Linda Crowl, eds. *Fauna, Flora, Food and Medicine*. Science of Pacific Island Peoples. Suva: University of the South Pacific, 1994.

REGIONAL SPECIALTIES

Hammond, Sally, *Guide to Farmers' Markets: Australia and New Zealand 2007*. Mosman, NSW: RMW Classic Publications, 2007.

Heuzenroeder, Angela. *Barossa Food*. Kent Town, SA: Wakefield Press, 1999.

May, R. J. *Kaikai Aniani: A Guide to Bush Foods, Markets and Culinary Arts of Papua New Guinea*. Bathurst, NSW: Robert Brown & Associates, 1984.

Murton, Brian. " 'Toheroa Wars': Cultural Politics and Everyday Resistance on a Northern New Zealand Beach." *New Zealand Geographer* 62 (2006): 25–38.

Pond, Wendy. "Parameters of Oceanic Science." In *Fauna, Flora, Food and Medicine*. ed. John Morrison, Paul Geraghty, and Linda Crowl. Science of Pacific Island Peoples. Suva: University of the South Pacific, 1994.

Rusher, Kristy. "The Bluff Oyster Festival and Regional Economic Development: Festivals as Culture Commodified." In *Food Tourism around the World: Development, Management, and Markets*, ed. Colin Michael Hall et al. Oxford: Butterworth Heinemann, 2003.

Santich, Barbara. *McLaren Vale: Sea and Vines*. Kent Town, SA: Wakefield Press, 1998.

Simpson, Tony. *A Distant Feast: The Origins of New Zealand Cuisine*. Auckland: Godwit, 1999.

EATING OUT

Kelly, James. "Loco Moco: A Folk Dish in the Making." *Social Process in Hawai'i* 30 (1983): 59–64.

Levine, Michel, and Simon Pownall. Roy Morgan Research Pty Ltd. "Wine Industry Outlook: Consumption Demographics, Market Segmentation, Trends and Opportunities." Address at the Wine Industry Outlook Conference, Sydney, Australia, November 25, 2004, http://www.roymorgan.com/resources/pdf/papers/20041201.pdf.

Manderson, Lenore, ed. *Shared Wealth and Symbol: Food, Culture and Society in Oceania and Southeast Asia*. Cambridge: Cambridge University Press, 1986.

Neill, Lindsay, Claudia Bell, and Ted Bryant. *The Great New Zealand Pie Cart*. Auckland, NZ: Hodder, 2008.

Ritzer, George. *The McDonaldization of Society*. Rev. ed. Thousand Oaks, CA: Pine Forge Press, 2004.

Sharma, Mukesh, Mervyn Jackson, and Robert Inbakaran, "Promoting Indigenous Food to Foreign Visitors: An Australian Study." *Asian Anthropology* 7 (2008): 121–34.

Siegelman, Stephen. *Trader Vic's Tiki Party!: Cocktails & Food to Share with Friends*. Berkeley, CA: Ten Speed Press, 2005.

Symons, Michael. *The Shared Table: Ideas for Australian Cuisine*. Canberra: AGPS Press Publication, 1993.

SPECIAL OCCASIONS

Barnett, Shirley. "Manaakitanga: Maori Hospitality, A Case Study of Maori Accommodation Providers," *Tourism Management* 22, no. 1 (2001): 83–92.

Berno, Tracy. "When a Guest Is a Guest: Cook Islanders View Tourism." *Annals of Tourism Research* 26, no. 3 (1999): 659–60.

Biumaiono, Solomoni. "The Cassava Invasion Continues." *Mailife*, April 2008.

Brennan, Jennifer. *Tradewinds and Coconuts: A Reminiscence and Recipes from the Pacific Islands*. Boston, MA: Periplus Editions, 2000.

Kirch, Patrick V. "Polynesian Feasting in Ethnohistoric, Ethnographic, and Archaeological Contexts: A Comparison of Three Societies." In *Feasts: Archaeological and Ethnographic Perspectives on Food, Politics, and Power*, ed. Michael Dietler and Brian Hayden. Washington, D.C.: Smithsonian Institution, 2001.

Ripe, Cherry. *Goodbye Culinary Cringe*. St Leonards, NSW: Allen & Unwin, 1993.

Steinberg, Rafael, ed., *Pacific and Southeast Asian Cooking*. New York: Time-Life Books, 1970.

DIET AND HEALTH

Alexeyeff, Kalissa. "Love Food: Exchange and Sustenance in the Cook Islands Diaspora." *Australian Journal of Anthropology* 15, no. 1 (2004): 68–79.

Borley, Craig. "Pacific and Maori Men at Centre of Gout Scare." NZHerald.co.nz, September 3, 2008. http://www.nzherald.co.nz/health/news/article.cfm?c_id=204&objectid=10530250 (accessed November 20, 2008).

Deadly Tucker. A Selection of Recipes from the FOODcents for Aboriginal and Torres Strait Islander People in WA Program. East Perth: Western Australia Dept. of Health, 2004.

Evans, Mike. "Whale-Watching and the Compromise of Tongan Interests through Tourism." In *Proceedings of the 1st International Small Island Cultures Conference*. Kagoshima University Centre for the Pacific Islands: The Small Island Cultures Research Initiative, 2005.

Evans, Mike, Robert C. Sinclair, Caroline Fusimalohi, and Viliami Liava'a. "Globalization, Diet, and Health: An Example from Tonga." *Bulletin of the World Health Organization* 79, no. 9 (2001).

Gates, Stefan. *In the Danger Zone*. London: BBC Books, 2008.

Koi, Harold. "34 pc Live in Poverty, says Minister." *Fiji Times*, October 17, 2008.

Kumar, Shailesh, William Aalbersberg, Ruth M. English, and Praveen Ravi. *Pacific Island Foods: Nutrient Composition of Some Pacific Island Foods and the Effect of Earth-Oven Cooking*. Vol. 2. Suva: Institute of Applied Sciences, University of the South Pacific, 2001.

Lako, Jimaima Veisikiaki. "Dietary Trend and Diabetes: Its Association among Indigenous Fijians 1952–1994." *Asia Pacific Journal of Clinical Nutrition* 10, no. 3 (2001): 183–87.

Lako, Jimaima Veisikiaki. "Phytochemicals in Pacific Foods and Related Health Status." PhD diss., Monash University, 2006.

Morrison, John, Paul Geraghty, and Linda Crowl, eds. *Fauna, Flora, Food and Medicine*. Science of Pacific Island Peoples. Suva: University of the South Pacific, 1994.

United Nations Development Program (South Pacific Commission). "The Effects of Urbanization and Western Diet on the Health of Pacific Island Populations." *Journal of Food and Nutrition* 39, no. 3 (1982): 126–129.

Whistler, W. Arthur. *Polynesian Herbal Medicine*. Honolulu, HI: National Tropical Botanic Garden, 1992.

Zimmet, Paul. "The Medical Effects of Lifestyle in Pacific Populations." *Journal of Food and Nutrition* 39, no. 1 (1982).

Index

Abalone, blackfoot, 147
Abbot, Edward, 109
Abduction, 23
Aboriginal Australians: alcohol
    consumption, 80, 213; contact
    with European settlers, 44–45;
    contemporary eating habits, 112;
    food, 47, 44, 48, 80, 81, 82, 213;
    earth ovens, 91; education,
    214, 215
Adelaide Hills, South Australia, 142
Afato, 135
Agribusiness, 29
Ahi, 133
ahima'a, 90
Ahim a'hima. See umu
Aitutaki (Cook Islands) 34; food
    dislikes, 70. *See also* Cook Islands
Alcoholic spirits, 21, 175; alcohol
    consumption, Australasia, 211
Alexander, Stephanie, Kitchen
    Garden Foundation, 210
Alite, 98
America, influence on diet, 31;
    influence in Hawaii, 136;
    ketchup, 127

American Samoa, 31, 124; School
    Lunch Programme, fast food, 154;
    SPC, 33
Amway company, 49
Anglo-Saxon culinary legacy:
    Australia and New Zealand, 148,
    171; Fiji, Tonga, Samoa, and the
    Cook Islands, 127
Anorexia nervosa, 212
Anzac biscuits, 148
Apia (Independent State of Samoa),
    diseases, 25; fast food, 154
Ariki (tribal chiefs), 154
Ariri, 126, 133
Aristologist, 109
Arrowroot, 3, 4, 34, 64, 106, 132, 187
Aruhe, 9
Asian cuisine, 52, 71, 108, 128
Auckland, New Zealand, 113, 154,
    171, 175, 204, Polynesian
    population, 42; Samoan
    population, 61
Australia, 3, 43, 62, 72, 135, 164;
    barbecue, 192; breakfast, 128;
    chicken, 71; commercial power,
    31; degustation menus, 112;

dinner, 129; fishing concessions to the United States 74; foodways post World War II, 77, 78, 79; industrial food, 48; lunch, 128; meals, 127–29; multicultural food, 111; population, 42; pudding, 132; regionalism, 53; restaurant cuisine, 111–12; rice exports, 125; vegetable exports to Pacific Islands, 75; wine, 48
Australia Day, 192, 195
Australian chefs, 111
Australian Colonial Sugar Refining Company (CSR), 30
Australian convicts and food, 45–6
Australian cookbooks, 109
Australian Cookery of Today Illustrated, 110
Australian Government House of Representatives' Standing Committee on Aboriginal and Torres Strait Islander Affairs, 49
Avarua, 123, 154, 159
Avocados, 157

Baking, 28, 103
Bamboo, 48, 103
Banana, 4, 20, 34, 35, 48, 57, 64, 70, 97, 123, 132, 138, 157; Queensland, Australia, 35
Banana leaves, 90, 93, 97, 98, 99, 100, 131, 185,
Barbecue, 97, 111, 192–95; Pacific Islands, 151
Bardi people, Australia, 49
Barossa Valley, South Australia, 140–41, 142
Barramundi, 176
Bass (fish), 133
Bats, 15, 90
Beach, Donn, 168, 169
Beachcombers, 19
Beans, 49, 52, 70, 136, 138

Bêche-de-mer, 19, 20, 22, 23, 34; Chinese harvesting of, 164
Beef, 60; Australasia, 78; beef cattle, South Australia, 142; consumption in Australia and New Zealand, 173 "Hawaiian" style, 167; Maori consumption of, 81. *See also* Bully beef, Corned beef, *palusami*
Beer, 128; 211; Australian lager, 194; Maori and Polynesian consumption of, 81, 211
Bele, 70, 120
Bergeron, Victor, 168
Berries, 15
Beverages, Australasia, 175
Bila, 103
Billy tea, 194
Bilos, 189
Biodynamic foods, 212; Australia and New Zealand, 111
Biofuel industry, 204
Bismarck Archipelago, 3, 5
Blackbirding, 23, 24, 30, 50
Boiling, 103
Botaki, 184
Bottled water, 210
Bougna, 90, 97
Bougna marmite, 138
Bowls for food, 101–2
Boyd massacre, New Zealand, 28
Bread, 46, 58, 72–75, 78, 118, 122–23; 137, 201, 202; Australia and New Zealand, 78; baking, 106–7; consumption in Hawaii, 137; damper, 194; focaccia, 148; and health, 202; made with cassava, see *Bila*; Maori consumption of, 81; pita, 161; sandwiches, 128; sauce, 193; with sausages, 194; sourdough, 101; with whitebait fritters, 148
Breadfruit, 3, 4, 13, 20, 49, 86, 99, 102, 124, 132, 187, 205;

cultivation, 9; drying, 98; fermented, 98; leaves, 98, 99; preparation, 64

Breakfast, Australia and New Zealand, 128; breakfast cereal, Tonga, 73; Fiji, 123

Brennan, Jennifer, 108

Brewing, 75; in Tasmania, Australia, 173

Britain, 52; British Empire, 21; food culture, transfer to Australia and New Zealand, 48, 50; introduction of Cassava in the Pacific, 121

Broiling, 89

Bryant, Simon, 142

Buds, 15, 162

Buffalo, 134

Bully beef, 20, 201, 203

Bunya nuts, 80

Burns Philp, 26

Bush food, Australia and New Zealand, 82, 112–13, 144; bush fern, 163; bush onion, Australia, 49; bush pepper, New Zealand, 144; grey saltbush, 47; insect pupae, 81; *Kakadu* plum, 49; Kurrajong nuts, 49; native currants, Australia, 47; native figs, Australia, 47; in Australian restaurants, 112

Butter, 75

Cabbages, 157

Cabbage tree, 69

Cabin biscuits, 75

Cafe culture, 159; Australasia, 172,175; Pacific Islands, 152

Cakes, 103, 126

Calamari, 133

Calcium oxalate, 60

Calla lily, 58

Cambodian immigrants, Australia, 51

Canada, 52

Cancer, 211, 205; Hawaii, 200

Candle nut, 133

Candy, 75, 126

Canned and dehydrated foods: Australia, 31; coconut products, 67, 121–22; fish, 74; fish and meats, 77; meals, 127; meat, 123, 207

Cannibalism, 17, 20, 28, 81, 186

Cantonese cuisine, 168; in Australasia, 172

Capsicum, 75, 157

Carpaccio, 133

Carrots, 157

Cash economy, 75, 155, 200, 201

Cassava (*Manihot esculentai*), 49, 57, 60–64, 90, 103, 120, 121, 131, 157, 162, 188, 203, 204, 205; cassava root curry, 163; cassava starch (tapioca), 132

Casseroles, 103, 129

Cassowary, 135

Catholic church, 26

Celebes Sea, 3

Central America, 57, 59

Central Market, Adelaide, South Australia, 143

Chanya ke bhaji (Hindi), 122

Charcoal-grilling, 163

Chardonnay, 195

Cheese, 75, 78; imported, Australia and New Zealand, 78

Cheong Liew, 52

Chicken, 12, 71, 97, 134, 186; Australasia, 78–9; chicken baked with mango and ginger, 163; cooked in Hawaiian feast, 184; fast food (KFC), 42; introduction into Pacific, 12; organic production of, 127; production of in Australia, 78–79; production of in Fiji

Chile, 4, 8

Chili, 52, 76, 122; chili pepper
    water, 76
China, 59; cooking techniques, 52;
    influence of, 5, 11, 76, 87;
    vegetable exports to
    Pacific Islands, 75
Chinese-Australian food, 180
Chinese food in Australia, 111; in
    New Zealand, 111; in the Pacific,
    163–65
Chinese immigrants, Australia, 51
Chinese plantation workers, 24
Chocolate, 41
Choi sum, 166
Christianity, 26, 28. See also
    missionaries, Sunday
Christmas, 28; Christmas dinner,
    Australia, 192–93
Churaya, 30
Circumcision feast, Cook Islands, 185
Citrus, 25; Australia, 35; citrus juice
    canning, 35; citrus trade, 34
Claire Valley, South Australia, 142
Clams, 113, 145; clam bake, 97
Climate, variations, 15
Cloudy Bay wine, New Zealand 53
Cockles, 67, 69
Cocktails, 168, 169; cocktails,
    Hawaii, 136
Cocoa, 25
Coconut (Cocos nucifera), 3, 4, 12,
    22, 35, 49, 57, 66, 124, 157, 131,
    136, 185; coconut cream or milk,
    36, 64, 66, 67, 75, 76, 90, 97, 98,
    99, 102, 103, 107, 121, 122, 131,
    132, 133, 137, 152, 162, 170, 187,
    202, 203; cooking baskets, 93;
    cutting, 101; fronds, 98, 99, 100;
    husks, 93; oil, 21, 29; palms, 9, 10,
    198; preparation, 66; products, 15;
    shells, 102; as a staple, 121
Coconut Grove nightclub, 167, 168
Coffee, 25, 34, 128, 212; coffee
    consumption, Australasia, 175

Cokanisiga, Joketani, 197
Colocasia, 58, 59
Commercial power, United States,
    Australia, New Zealand,
    France, 31
Community food preparation, 39, 91;
    decline, 104
Conch, 73
Condiments, 75, 76; Asian, 166;
    Hawaii, 137
Confectionery, 58, 75; Tonga, 73
Cook, James, Captain, 9, 13, 17, 198
Cookbooks, 105; and nutrition, 106;
    and social influence, 106; and
    Western leisure culture, 109
Cookhouses, 90
Cook Islanders, 183; Anglo-Saxon
    culinary legacy, 127; culture, 204;
    fish consumption and production,
    74; population in New Zealand,
    42, 97; population in the United
    States, 42;
Cook Islands, 4, 33, 34, 39, 40,
    58, 70, 98, 125, 132, 133, 154,
    158–59, 185, 186, 187, 188, 204;
    arrowroot, 64; breadfruit, 64;
    coconut, 66; diseases, 24; fishing
    concessions to the United States,
    74; leaf techniques, 100;
    missionaries, 27; raw fish, 126;
    tourism, 43
Cooking, definition of, 89; fuels, 85,
    91; hot stones, 5; methods using
    fire, 89
Cooks as servants, 106
Copra, 21, 25, 29, 34, 35; uses of, 26
Coral Coast, Fiji, 157
Corned beef, 20, 41, 60, 77, 82,
    123, 207
Counter meals, 172
Creative cuisine, 180
Creole cuisine, 136; creolization, 156
Crest Company, 71
Crisps, 75

Crocodile, 179

Crosby, Bing, 168

Crustaceans, 10, 91; crab, 14, 73, 97, 133, 189; crayfish, 12, 73

Cucumber, 157

Cuisine magazine, New Zealand, 53

Cuisine of the South Pacific, The, 108

Culinary hybridization, 144

Culture: exchange in markets, 143; meaning of food, 104

Curaçao, 168

Curry, 72, 75; curried cassava, 64, 121; curries, 103; curry houses, Fiji, 165; curry leaves, 52

Custard apple, 138

Cut, 98

Dairy products, 58, 75; dairies, New Zealand, 172; Tonga, 73

Dalmatians, immigration to New Zealand, 172

Dalo [Fijian], 58, 122

Damper, 194

Dampier, William, 193

Dampierland, north western Australia, 49

Daw daws, 49

Dargeville, New Zealand, 145

Davies, William, 19

Deadly Tucker, 215

Deer, 134, 138

Degustation menus, Australia, New Zealand, 112, 178

Delicatessens, Australia, 172

Denny, Martin, 169

Derrett, Rod, 81

Diabetes (Type II), Pacific region, 197, 200, 206, 211; Australasia, 210; Hawaii, 200

Dietrich, Marlene, 169

Dining etiquette, 27, 122, 152

Dinner, 124; Australia and New Zealand, 129; Indian Fijian, 124

Disease, 23, 24, 41; diet-related illness, 198

Diversification of food products, Australia and New Zealand

Diversity: Australasia, 82, 171; Pacific Islands, 170

Dog, 6, 12, 137

Dole, James Drummond, "pineapple king," 36

Domino's Pizza, 177

Donn the Beachcomber, 168, 169

Doughnuts, 126; Hawaii, 167

Dried foods, 85, 87, 97–98, 185; fish, 74

Drinking, Australasia, 173–75

Duck, 134

Duruka, 70, 162, 188

Earth ovens, 85, 90–95; Australian Aborigines, 91. *See also, Umu*

Easter, 28

Easter Island, 4, 8, 13, 59; coconut, 66

Eastern European immigrants, Australia, 51

Eating out as entertainment, 177

Eco-hangi, 113

Economic influences, 104; economic downturn, 176

Ecotourism, 38, 157

Ecuador, 35

Edward, Prince of Wales, 146

Eel, 73

Egalitarianism in food culture, Australasia, 148

Eggplant, 70, 75, 157

Eggs, 15; imported, 71

Ellis, William, 28

Emu meat, Australia, 109, 135; earth oven cooking techniques, 91

English and Australian Cookery Book: Cookery for the Many, as well as for the "Upper Ten Thousand," 109

Environmentalism and food, 157

Europeans, 17–18, 19, 20; food
    practices, 26
Evening meals, 120

Fair Trade foods, 212
Farmers markets, Australia and
    New Zealand, 111, 212
Fast food, 58, 127, 155, 176, 177,
    202; Australasia, 176; Pacific
    Islands, 152, 153; fast food outlets,
    127, 128, 154, 211
Fasting, Kiribati, 185
Fat (oils and dairy food), 58, 201, 211
Feasts and feasting, 2, 17, 27, 28,
    66, 73, 88, 90, 95, 98, 119, 137,
    138–39, 149, 190, 191, 195, 200,
    207; and religion, 208; Barossa
    Valley, 141; Chinese, 164;
    family reunions, 186; Pacific
    Islands, 183–87;
Fergusonina nicholsoni, 49
Fermentation and fermented food,
    6, 66, 67, 69, 85, 87, 98, 99,
    118, 126, 133, 134, 200;
    advantages, 99
Ferns, 9, 47, 49, 179, 200
Festivals, 141, 147; Chinese, 164;
    Tahiti, 164
Fiji, 3, 4, 5, 8, 9, 18, 22, 29, 30, 34,
    57, 58, 103, 107, 131, 133, 134,
    155, 157, 158, 164, 180 n.4, 186,
    188, 189, 197, 205; Anglo-Saxon
    culinary legacy, 127; breakfast,
    123; brewing, 75; cassava, 63, 121;
    chicken production, 71–72;
    coconut, 67; cookbooks, 108;
    diseases, 24; fire customs, 88;
    fishing concessions to the US, 74;
    fruit, 70; imported foods, 125;
    Indian food, 30, 165; land use,
    125; meat consumption, 72;
    missionaries, 27; plantain, 65;
    population, xi; potato, 70; raw
    fish, 126; rice-growing, 87; SPC,

33; table manners, 122; taro
    exports to New Zealand, 61; taste
    for chili, 76; tourism, 170; water,
    37; wedding meal, 152; worms,
    188; yams, 62
Filipino plantation workers, 24
Fire, 85, 90; methods of creating and
    tending, 88–89; symbolic use, 88
Fish and chips, New Zealand, 171
Fish and fishing, 10, 12, 15, 25, 58,
    73, 90, 91, 97, 102, 103, 119, 124,
    125, 131, 133, 137, 138, 143, 156,
    158, 162, 185, 189, 200;
    barbecued, 194; canned, 207;
    consumption, Australasia, 79–80;
    farming, 6; fish fingers, 77; fish
    head delicacy, 188; Australian
    Christmas fare, 193; fish hooks, 5;
    industry, 38; sauce, 108; treaties,
    74; Tuvalu cooking methods, 100
Fishers food company, 118
Flavor, Pacific Island foods, 87; *umu*
    cooking, 97
Flax: cooking baskets, New Zealand,
    93; seeds, 144
Fleurieu Peninsula, South Australia,
    142
Fluoridated water, 210
Food: access, 75; aid, 201; and cash
    economy, 155; and gender, 105,
    110, 120, 124, 153, 188, 194;
    and poverty, 117, 212; and social
    rank, 11, 12, 119, 120, 122, 188;
    and traditional obligations, 75;
    costs, 72, 104, 129, 152, 158, 160,
    162, 175, 178, 184, 202–203;
    food culture, decline, 41; habits,
    Australasia, 77–80; presentation,
    178; preservation, 13; sacred food,
    12; social aspects, 2, 10–12, 119,
    124–25, 144, 152–53, 175, 211;
    staples in the Pacific, 12, 120;
    symbolism, 186; trade, 15, 18–20;
    twenty-first century, 43–44

Food choices, 126; Australia, 113; New Zealand, 113

Food consumption, Micronesia, 73; Tonga, 73

Food Lover's Guide to Australia, The, 141

Food of Paradise, The, 108

Food Safari, 141

Foundation for Rural Enterprises 'N' Development, 39

France, commercial power, 31

French cuisine, 167, 171; influence of, 108, 110; in New Caledonia, 138; Tahiti, New Caledonia, 32, 127; on Australian and New Zealand food, 50

French Polynesia, 4, 8, 33, 131, 133, 167; *umu,* 91

French-Chinese Tahitians, 164

Fresh food, 118; Australia and New Zealand, 127

Fried foods, 58, 124, 201, 203

Fruit, 15, 20, 70, 119, 121, 128, 136, 158, 162, 169, 187, 200; juice, 177; soup, 123; stone, South Australia, 142

Funeral feasts, 185

Furo, 65

Fusion cuisine, 53, 159; Hawaii, 137; New Caledonia, 138

Futuna Islands, 8, 33

Galangal, 52

Gantt, Ernest, 168

Gardener, Mark, 149

Gardening, 5, 6, 12; and lunar calendar, 15; seasonal planting, 16

Gary, Lamora S., 76

Gastronomic tourism, 38, 140; New Zealand, 144

Gauguin, Paul, 168

George Tupou I, King, 27

Germany, coconut plantations, 26

Giant clam, 73, 189

Gilbert Islands, 21

Ginger, 52, 108

Globalization, 35, 39, 160, 170, 201, 204; and Australasian food, 79; and social differentiation in diet, 179

Global recession, 197, 129

Goat, 134; goat cheese, 142

Gogodala communities, 204

Gold Pudding, 107

Goroka, earth oven, 96

Gourds, 70, 133

Gourmet Traveller magazine, Australia, 53

Grapes, South Australia, 142; Australasia, 174

Grated taro pudding recipe, 61

Graters, 102

Grazing meals, 118

Great Council of Chiefs, Fiji, 125

Great Depression, 168

Greek immigrants, Australia and New Zealand, 50, 51, 128, 172; Greek cuisine, 110

Green vegetables, 70

Groper fish, 179

Grubs, 135

Guam, 31, 33; fast food, 154; fish consumption, 74; Guamanian population in the United States, 42

Guava, 70, 157

Ha'amonaga 'a Maui Trilithon, 16

Haliotis iris, 73, 147

Hands, use of for eating, 100, 101, 122, 187

Hangi cookery, New Zealand, 69, 113

Hapuka steak, 179

Hare soup, 171

Haupia, 64

Hawaii, 4, 8, 13, 18, 19, 22, 24, 31, 58, 59, 69, 77, 100, 131, 136, 137–38, 154, 155, 159, 164, 168,

184; barbecue sauce, 76; breadfruit, 64; Chinese immigrants, 164; cultural diversity, 137; diet related illness, 199–200; diseases, 24; ethnic restaurants, 167; fast food,154; fish consumption and production, 74; food culture, 12, 108; *imu*, 95; introduced foods, 14; Japanese influences, 76; migrant influences, 167; monarchy, 6; pigs, 70; population, 6; raw fish, 126; *umu*, 91; taste for chili, 76
Hawaiian population in the United States, 42
Heart disease, 207; Australasia, 210; Hawaii, 200; Pacific region, 197
Hearth cookery, 8
Heiva, 164
Heliconia leaves, 98, 99
Herbal lore, 38
Herbs, South Australia, 142
Heterofermentation, 99
Heyerdahl, Thor, 168
Hibiscus, 70, 122, 200
Hima'a, 90
Hindu traditions, 186
Hivoa, 20
Hoho, 62
Holothurian, 19
Horopito, New Zealand, 144
Hospitality and visitors, 2, 17, 18, 42, 186, 190, 191
Hotel dining rooms, 172
Hot rocks, 91, 93, 101, 102
Houma, 16
Hughes, Howard, 169
Hybrid cuisine, 77, 156, 170
Hypertension, 197, 200, 211

Ice cream, 41, 126, 172; Tonga, 73
I coi, 120
Ika mata, 133
I-Kiribati, 14

Imported food, 106, 125, 198
Imu, 90
Inamona, 133
Inanga, 9
Indenture system, 29, 30
Indian food, 165; breadfruit, 65; curry, 127; Fiji, 30, 100, 124, 135
Indian migrants, 76; Australia, 51; population of Fiji, 134; workers, 29
Indian plants, 70
Indigenous foods, Pacific Islands, 156
Indonesia, 3; pineapple production, 37
Industrialization, Australasia, 78
Ingredients, Pacific Island cuisine, 57
Innovative Chef of Year, New Zealand, 144
Inocarpus fagiferus, 98
Insects as food, 15, 81, 135
International food, 156, 175
Internet cafes, 159
Ipomoea batatas, 4, 62
Ipu, 102
Iremonger, Mrs. Thomas Lascelles, 106
Islands of the South Pacific, 208
Italians, 110; food in the Pacific, 166; immigrants, Australia and New Zealand, 50, 51, 128, 172; restaurants in Sydney, 173
Itinerant Europeans, 19

Japanese fish imports, 74, 176; food exports, 72; influence in Hawaii, 76; influences on food, 76; in the Pacific, 167; restaurants in Sydney, 173; soy sauce, 127

Kadavu Island, 157
Kaffir limes, 52
Kahuna, 184
Kai, Maori food, 25, 57

*Kaikai Aniani: A Guide to Bush Foods,
    Markets and Culinary Arts of Paua
    New Guinea*, 108
Kaikoso (*Anadara antiquata*), 67
Kai raurau, 70
Kakana dina, 57, 120
Kaleve vi, 67
Kamali, 204
Kamehameha I, II and III, Kings, 6,
    31, 184
Kanac people, 97
Kanak people, 10, 32, 61, 138;
    use of fire, 88
Kanavata, 152
Kangaroo meat, 80, 109, 112, 179,
    215; earth oven cooking
    techniques, 91
Kao, 102
Kapauku people, 70
Karajarri people, Australia, 49
Karengo, 179
Katsuwonus pelamis, 73
Kau kau, 62
Kava, 21, 119, 188–89; ceremony,
    184, 189; shops, Pacific
    Islands, 152
Kawakawa, New Zealand, 144
Kayasa festival, 187
Kebabs, barbecued, 194
Keradek Island, 16
KFC (Kentucky Fried Chicken), 112,
    153, 154, 176, 204
Kikkoman (soy sauce), 76;
    New Caledonia, 139
Kina, 57, 73, 113, 133, 145
Ki plant, 69
Kippered salmon, 171
Kiribati, 7, 14, 21, 33, 72, 133, 184,
    185; coconut, 66; fishing
    concessions to the United States,
    74; tea consumption, 73
Kokoda (Fijian fish dish), 67,
    126, 133
Kon Tiki, 168

Koso, 101
Kosrae, 7; yams, 62
Koua, 90
Kouka (cabbage tree hearts), 82
Ku, 184
Kukui nut, 133
Kumala, 62
Kumara (sweet potato), 9, 25, 59, 62,
    81, 95, 191, 205
Kumete, 102
Kuru papa, 132

Labor market, 21, 22
Laksa, 111
Lamb: Australasia, 78; chops,
    barbecued, 194; flaps, 72, 203,
    209; Limestone Coast, South
    Australia, 142; Maori
    consumption, 81; roast,
    and mint sauce, 148;
Lamingtons, 148
Lanai, 36
L&L Hawaiian Barbecue, 124
Langa Langa people, 15
Lapaha, 16
Lapita, 8; cultural complex, 5–7;
    people, cooking pots, 86
Larvae, 135
Latvian immigrants, New Zealand, 51
Laudan, Rachel, 108
Laulau, 102, 184
Lautoka, Fiji, 39, 199
Leaves, 15, 162; leaf vegetables,
    135–36, 205; fermentation
    process, 98; leaf wrapping for
    food, 89
Leftovers, 119, 120, 124, 187
Lei ika, 133
Lemongrass, 52
Lemon myrtle, 112, 179
Lemons, 133, 157
Leodice viridice, 188
Leptomeria acida, 47
Lettuces, 157

Lever Brothers, 26
Levuka, 164
Liliuokalani, Queen, 31
Lime, 108, 133, 138
Limpet, 73
Line Island, 16, 72
Living Waters, 157
Lizard, 15, 91
Lobster, 12 , 97, 133, 185
Loco moco, 167
Lolo fala, 68
Lomi lomi, 167
London Missionary Society, 27, 34
Los Angeles, 167, 168
Lovo, 90
Lua'i masi, 98
Luau, 58, 136, 167, 184; Samoa,
    138–39
Lunch, 119, 123; Australia and
    New Zealand, 128; luncheon
    meat, 77; Fiji, 119
Lu pulu, 131

Macropiper excelsum, New
    Zealand, 144
Madrai ni viti, "bread of Fiji," 99
Madrai, 99
Magabala fruit, 49
Magiti, 189
Mahimahi, 189
Mai kana, "come and eat," 122
Mai tai, 168, 169
Maize, 63
Malasadas, 167
Malaysia: food in New Zealand, 111;
    Malaysian immigrants, Australia,
    51 pineapple; production, 37
Ma, mahi, madrai, mahr, 65, 98
Mana, 189–90
Manaaki, manaakitanga, 191
Mandarins, 157
Mango, 49, 70, 132, 157
Mangosteen, 49
Manihot esculenta, 62

Manioc, 57, 62, 121
Maoli, plantain, 65
Maori, 9, 18, 59, 62, 69, 133, 135,
    145, 167, 211; chiefdoms, 6;
    culture, 191, 204, 206, festivals,
    113, fishing rights, 38, 146;
    food, 81–82, 144, 179; food aid,
    214–15, food and the Internet,
    113; food culture, 48; hangi 90,
    95; New Zealand restaurants, 112;
    population, 7; trade, 25; tutu berry
    juice extraction, 105; use of
    indigenous ingredients, 53
Mara, 99
Maratan, 98
Mariana Islands, 4, 7, 16, 33, 59,
    145, 197
Marinating, 89; raw fish, 67, 74, 125,
    133, 163
Market, 60, 62, 69, 76, 123, 125, 135,
    141, 143, 152, 177
Marlborough region, New Zealand,
    53, 174
Marmite, 128
Marquesas islands, 4, 5, 19, 98, 137;
    diseases, 25; missionaries, 27; pigs,
    70; plantain, 66
Marshall Islands, 7, 124; fishing
    concessions to the United
    States, 74
Martinborough, New Zealand, 53
Masi paste, 65, 102; *masi* pits, 98
Matai plates, fast food, 124
Mata mata, 135
Matangi, 180 n.4
Matava resort, 157
Mats (laulau), 102
May, R. J. 108
McCafe, 176
McDonald's restaurants, 105, 152,
    153, 154, 155, 176
McLaren Vale, South Australia, 142
Meals, Australia and New Zealand,
    127–29

Meat pie, Australia and New Zealand, 148; pie carts, 172

Meat, 58, 70–73, 90, 124, 129, 131, 186, 200; fresh, imports, 77; frozen processed meat imports, 77; refrigerated exports, 171

Media, influence of, and cooking, 110; and regionality, 141

Meika, 70

Melanesia, 7, 8, 9, 14, 59, 70, pot culture, 86; recipes, 105; taste preferences, 97

Melbourne, 175

Melons, 157

Methodist missionaries, 27

Metroxylon sagu, 64

Micronesia, Federated States of, 3, 4, 7, 8, 10, 23, 33, 57, 64, 97; breadfruit, 65; coconut, 66; Japanese influences, 76; kava, 189; 27; missionaries, pot culture, 86; rice-growing, 87; yams, 62; recipes, 105

Microwave ovens, 85

Middens: Lapita people, 5; Australian Aborigines, 91

Migration, 3, 6; Chinese in the Pacific, 164; foods introduced through migrations, 12–14; laborers, 42; migrant foods in Australia, 148

Milk, 75, 58; Maori consumption of, 81; milk bars (Australia), 172; milkshakes, 172; powdered milk, 58

Mincers, 102

Missionaries, 26, 101, 198; and cookbooks, 106; and influences on food, 27

Miti, 124

Mitiori, 133, 134

Moca [Fijian], 123

Modern Australian cuisine, 51, 142, 180

Moe 'ese 'ese, 135

Mokoia Food Tour, 144

Molecular gastronomy, 178

Molluscs, 14

Moonfish, 133

Moror, 126

Motu, 90

Mozzarella, Australia and New Zealand, 78

Mt Hagen, New Guinea, earth oven, 96–97

Muffins, 75

Multicultural food, Australia and New Zealand, 111

Mumu, 90, 95

Murray River cod, Australia, 80

Musa paradisiaca, 65

Mussels, 73, 133

Mutton birds, 113

Nadi Bay Resort Hotel, Fiji, 108

Namandi, 65

Nambo, 97–98

Namu, 124

Nanuya Levu, 156

Native spinach, New Guinea, 49

Nauru Island, 33, 50, 161, 186; fishing concessions to the United States, 74

Netherlands, SPC, 33

Neutraceuticals, 49

New Caledonia, 3, 5, 9–10, 14, 17, 32, 33, 61, 64, 88, 90, 97, 108, 127, 138, 167; Chinese population, 164

New Guinea, 5, 8, 133; kava, 189. *See also* Papua New Guinea

New York World's Fair, 168

New Zealand, 4, 8, 13, 18, 31, 33, 43, 51, 59, 71, 82, 111, 131, 145, 164, 214; breakfast, 128; chefs, 111; cuisine, 52–53; fishing concessions to the United States, 74; dinner, 129; foodways post

World War II, 77–79; lamb
    export, 72; lunch, 128; Maori
    hangi, 95; multicultural food, 111;
    New Zealand Society, 146;
    population, 42; pudding, 132;
    regionalism, 53; restaurant
    cuisine, 111–12; Samoan
    population, 61; steam cooking,
    102; taro consumption, 61;
    tourism, 144; *umu*, 91; vegetable
    exports to Pacific Islands, 75;
    wine, 48
Ngali (*Canarium* species), 98
Ngaua, 90
Nipa palm, 49
Nita, 70
Niue Island, 4, 16, 33, 55 n.33, 103,
    125, 133, 186; fishing concessions
    to the United States, 74;
    population, 42
Noni fruit, 70; noni juice, 39
Noodles, 61, 74, 166, 201;
    Hawaii, 137
Norfolk Islands, 16
Northern Territory, Australia, 52
Noumea, 32; Chinese food, 163;
    fast food, 154
Nouvelle cuisine, 52
Nuku'Alofa: bread consumption, 74;
    fast food, 154
Nuts, 15, 98

Obesity, 154, 199, 200, 201, 203–5,
    206, 208; Australasia, 210;
    Australia, 212; Pacific region, 197
Octopus, 133, 189
O'Donoghue, Ben, 149
Oils, 75, 203; Australia and
    New Zealand, 78, 142
Oka i'a, 133
Oki (Tahitian chestnut), 98
Okinawa, 24; influence in Hawaii, 76
Okolehau drink, 69
Olives, South Australia, 142

Oral tradition, 105
Orange juice, China, 35
Orao ra, 133
Oregano, 157
Organic foods, 170, 212, 213;
    Australia and New Zealand, 111,
    127, 143; in restaurants, 157
Organization for Economic
    Co-operation and
    Development, 214
Ota, 120, 133
Ota ika, 133
Ota miti, 163
Our Daily Bread, 106
Outrigger canoes, 6
Overeating, 204–5; Australasia, 210
Oxalis species, 47
Oyster, 73, 133, 147; Coffin Bay,
    South Australia, 142; oyster
    sauce, New Caledonia, 139

*Pacific and Southeast Asian
    Cooking*, 108
Pacific Cookbook, 1968, 109
Pacific Hostess Cookbook, The, 76
Pacific Islanders: chicken, 71;
    contemporary cooking
    techniques, 100; diet, 58; food
    aid, 214; migrants to New
    Zealand, 51; pudding, 132
Païta beans, 138
Pakeha, 81
Palau, Republic of, 4, 7, 33, 124;
    fishing concessions to the United
    States, 74
Palm fronds, 97
Palm lily, 49
Palolo, 188
Palusami, 60, 62, 77, 82, 107, 131,
    185, 186
Pandanus (*Pandanus tectorius*), 3, 4, 9,
    10, 12, 48, 52, 67, 69, 101, 185
Papaya, 49, 64, 132
Paphies australe, 73

Paphies ventricosum, 145
Papua New Guinea [PNG], 3, 9, 33,
    34, 59, 70, 131, 134–35, 164, 212;
    Chinese immigrants, 164; earth
    oven, 90, 95; fishing concessions
    to the United States, 74; food
    plants, 49; introduced foods, 14;
    pigs, 70; potatoes, 70; sago, 64;
    sweet potatoes, 62; *umu*, 91
Parkinson, Susan, 107
Passion fruit, 49
Pasta, 74, 166; pasta restaurants,
    Australia, 51
Patu aruhe, 9
Paua shellfish, 73, 147
Pavlova, 148
Paw paw, 49, 70, 157, 188
Peaches, 142
Pearl Harbor, 31
Pe'epe'e, 99
Penu, 68
Pepper shrub, 188
Periwinkle or "cats eye," 73
Peru, 24, 188
Philippines, 3, 4
Phoenix Islands, 16, 72
Phonpei, vanilla, 25
Phosphate mining, Nauru, 50
Pi, beans, 70
Pia, 64
Pickled oysters, 171
Pigs, 6, 12–13, 20, 25, 70, 90, 95,
    106, 131, 134, 185, 187, 188,
    184; bride-price, 134–35; cultural
    importance, 70; husbandry, 5;
    suckling, 73
Pikopiko fern, New Zealand, 144, 179
Pineapple, 22, 25, 30, 34, 36–37, 70,
    77, 132, 136, 157; production,
    New Caledonia, 139
Pinot noir grapes, 53
Pioneering colonists, cookbooks, 106
Piper methysticum, 188
Pipi (shellfish), 73, 113; steamed, 145

Pipi kaula (dried beef), 167
Pitcairn Islands, 8, 16, 33
Pit storage of food, 6
Pit-style ovens, 90
Pizza, 167; pizza restaurants,
    Australia, 51, 177
Plantain, 57, 65, 123, 137;
    fermented, 98
Plantations, 25
Plate lunch, Hawaii, 137
Po'e, 64
Poe (Hawaiian fruit pudding), 132
Pohnpei, 7; yams, 62
Poi, 12, 61, 98, 100, 102, 137, 167
Poingo banana,
Poisson cru, 90, 126, 133, 138, 163
Poke (version of marinated raw fish),
    64, 126, 132, 133, 137, 167
Polynesia, 3, 8, 14, 71, 137, 211;
    arrowroot, 64; hospitality, 184;
    kava, 189; missionaries, 27; pot
    culture , 86, 88; pudding, 102;
    recipes, 105; taste
    preferences, 97
Polynesians, 8, 42; in New Zealand,
    97; obesity, 199; processed meat
    consumption, 77
Polystichum richardii, 144
Pomme-cannelle (custard apple), 138
Ponape, 98
Pork, 106, 131, 134, 186, 202; early
    export, 22; fat, 202 ; method of
    cooking, 159; ritual
    celebrations, 70
Port Lincoln, South Australia, 150
Port Moresby, Papua New Guinea,
    fast food, 154; yams, 62
Portuguese sausage, Hawaii, 167
Portuguese, 62
Potatoes, 20, 25, 60, 70, 137
Pot culture, 5–7, 28, 85; Australia,
    194; decline in the Pacific, 87–88;
    Melanesia, 105
Poverty, 82, 126, 214, 215; Fiji, 197

Prawns, 176, 189; barbecued, 194;
    recipe, 126
Preserving techniques, Pacific
    Islands, 13, 85, 98
Prestige and food, 60, 207
Processed foods and preferences,
    77, 129
Project Ma'alahi, 209
Pseudowintera colorata,
    New Zealand, 144
Pteridium esculentum, 47
Pteris aquilina, 9
Pudding, 102, 103, 107, 123, 131,
    132, 137, 187
Puha, 82
Puha and Pakeha, song, 81
Puha porirua, 81
Puha rauriki, 81
Puha tio tio, 81
Pumpkin, 64, 157, 187; scones, 148
Pupu, 145
Pupu, Hawaii, 136
Pupus, 160, 170

Qalu, 103
Quangdongs, 112
Queensland, Australia, 22, 52
Qumu, 90

Rabaul [PNG], earth oven, 96
Rarauhe, 9
Rare Fruit Council International
    (1991), 108
Rarotonga, 10, 35, 40, 43, 75, 123,
    132, 133, 154, 158, 159, 160, 166,
    186; brewing, 75; chickens, 71;
    diseases, 25; Rarotongan food, 60;
    Rarotongans, 34
Ratatouille, 195
Rats (*Rattus exulans*), 12
Raw food, 85, 89, 90; raw fish salad,
    90, 167
Red snapper, 189
Reef fish, 73

Regional economic decline, 33, 40
Regionalism, 131; New Zealand, 53;
    Australasia, 139–50
Restaurant cuisine, Australia,
    New Zealand, 111–12
Restaurant culture, Pacific
    Islands, 152
Restaurants, 77, 127, 155, 159, 168,
    171, 172, 180; Australasia, 140,
    176; Chinese, 164; Hawaii, 167;
    menus, 178, 179
Reymond, Jacques, 156
Rice, 3, 4, 57, 58, 60, 61, 63, 74, 121,
    124, 125, 166, 203; cooking
    techniques, 87; Hawaii, 137;
    imported, 72
Roadside stalls, Pacific Islands, 152
Roasting, 195; New Zealand, 111;
    roast lamb and mint sauce, using
    skewers, 103
Rome Declaration on World Food
    Security 1996, 214
Rou rou, 60, 120
Roussettes (flying foxes), 138
Royal, Charles, 144
Rukau, 60, 123
Rum, 168, 173
Ryeberries, 112

Saccharum edule, 70
Saffron, 52, 138
Sago, 3, 4, 9, 48, 63, 64; palm, 49,
    135, pancakes, 64; sago grub
    satay, 135
Sahul, 3
Sake, Hawaii, 137
Salad, 129, 195
Salmon, 80, 167; barbecued, 194
Salt, 87, 124, 211
Salvation Army, 214
Samoa, 3, 4, 14, 90, 97, 98, 125, 133,
    138–39, 186, 189, 206;
    Anglo-Saxon culinary legacy,
    127; breadfruit, 64; brewing, 75;

Chinese restaurants, 164; diseases, 26; fast food, 154; fishing concessions to the United States, 74; fruit, 70; grubs, 135; missionaries, 27; pot culture, 88; taro exports to New Zealand, 61; Samoan culture, 204; population in New Zealand, 42, 61; population in the United States, 42; Samoans, 183, 188

Sandalwood, 19, 22, 20, 24, 34

Sandwiches, 123, 128

Santa Cruz Islands, 5

Sarcocornia quiqueflora, 47

Sarsaparilla, 47

Sashimi, 134, 167, 177

Sausages, 148, 194

Sauvignon blanc, New Zealand, 48, 53, 174

Scurvy, 47

Seafood, 19, 47, 58, 73, 113, 126, 133, 145, 156, 158, 162, 170, 175–76, 187, 189; New Zealand, 144–48; and restaurant trade, 155

Searle, Philip, 52

Seasonal planting, 16

Seawater salt, 102, 123

Seaweed, 14, 73, 133, 179

Secretariat of the Pacific Community (SPC), 32, 33, 157, 184

Seeds, 162

Sepik River region, 135

Serbs, immigration to New Zealand, 172

Shallot onions, 75

Shao-hsing wine, 52

Sheep, South Australia, 142

Shellfish, 10, 74, 91

Shell utensils, 102, 103

Shepherd's pie, 129

Sherry, 173

Shiraz, South Australia, 48, 142

Shoyu, 76

Sigatoka, 189

Skinner, Gwen, 108

Slavery, 23, 24, 30

Smilax glyciphylla, 47

Smoking foods, 97, 135

Snack food, 41, 75, 118, 119, 123, 126, 202

Snake, 91

Snapper, 73, 133

Society Islands (French Polynesia), 4, 137; missionaries, 27; *umu*, 91

Solomon Islands, 3, 8, 9, 15, 24, 33, 90, 134–35, 164, 185; fishing concessions to the United States, 74

Sonchus asper, 81

Sonchus oleraceus, 81

South Africa, 52

South America, 4; breadfruit, 65; sweet potatoes, 62

South Australia, gastronomic tourism, 140, climate, 142

South Pacific Commission, 32, 33

South Pacific musical production, 168

Soy sauce, 76, 108, 139

Spam, 41, 77

Sri Lankan cuisine in Australasia, 165

Staple foods, 25, 58, 74, 80, 187

Starvation strikes, 205

Steak and kidney pudding, 148

Steak, barbecued, 194

Steam cooking, 102, 103

Stews, 129

Stir-frying, 111, 165

Stirring techniques, 101–2

Stone boiling, 102

Sugar, 22, 25, 28, 29, 30, 34, 35, 36, 58, 72, 74, 124, 201, 211; sugar cane, 4, 49, 119; sugar industry, labour conditions, 29

Sumatra Kula, 168

Sunda, 3

Sunday food, Pacific Islanders, 28, 29, 183

Sun-drying foods, 97
Supermarket, 75, 153, 154, 155;
    Australia and New Zealand, 78
Surfing the Menu, 149
Sushi, 74, 101, 167, 177
Suva, 69, 154
Sweet potato, 4, 9, 10, 25, 57, 61, 62,
    86, 95, 97, 103, 137, 185, 209
Swordfish, 74
Sydney, 175
Syrah, South Australia, 142

Tacca leontopetaloide, 64
Tahiti, 4, 8, 10, 18, 22, 24, 58, 64, 69,
    90, 132, 133, 168; Chinese
    immigrants, 164; dynasties, 16;
    festivals, 164; French culinary
    style, 127; missionaries, 27;
    standard of health, 17; Tahitian
    apple, 70; Tahitian chestnut, 98;
    raw fish salad, 74
Taiwan, 4
Tapioca (*tavioka*), 57, 63, 121
Taro, 3, 4, 5, 6, 11, 13, 44, 49, 58, 59,
    81, 86, 90, 97, 98, 102, 103, 107,
    119, 120, 121, 123, 131, 137, 159,
    162, 185, 187, 188, 203, 205, 209;
    fermented, 98; consumption,
    New Zealand, 61; cultivation, 9;
    plantations, 198; preparation
    of, 60; taro leaf soup, 163; taro
    leaves, 100, 107, 122, 200; taro
    paste, 98; taro pies, 152
Tasman, Abel, 45
Taste preferences, 88
Taufa'ahau Tupou IV, King of Tonga,
    27, 154, 187, 209
Tea, 72–73, 123, 175, 194, 202; tea
    shops, 172
Television and food practices,
    77–78, 198
Terminalia catalpa, 98
Terminalia ferdinandiana, 49
Terroir, 53, 143

Tetragonia tetragonioides, 47
Texture, Pacific Island
    foods, 87
Thai food, 165, 173, 110, 111
Thailand, 132; pineapple production,
    37; rice exports, 125
Thanksgiving, 97
Tiki culture, 167–70
Tikopia, 16
Time-Life cookbook series, 108
Tio para (Maori shellfish), 73
Tiostria chilensis, 147
Ti plant, 69, 99
Tobacco, 21, 25
Toddy, 14, 21, 119, 152, 185;
    ceremony, 184
Tofu, 137, 166
Toheroa, 73, 113, 145–46
Tokelau Islands, 4, 10, 14, 33, 67,
    119, 125, 149, 186; coconut, 66,
    67; meals, 118; population in
    New Zealand, 42, 97
Tolaga Bay, 9
Tomatoes, 34, 70, 75, 122, 133, 157;
    tomato sauce, 194
Tonga, Kingdom of, 3, 4, 5, 8, 13, 16,
    18, 33, 62, 70, 72, 74, 90, 125,
    131, 133, 183, 186, 187, 206,
    207, 209; Anglo-Saxon culinary
    legacy, 127; Chinese restaurants,
    164; fast food, 154; feasts, 16, 188;
    fishing concessions to the United
    States, 74; grubs, 135;
    missionaries, 27; population in
    the United States, 42; pot
    culture, 88; standard of
    health, 17; Tongan culture, 204;
    Tongans in New Zealand, 97;
    whaling, 208
Tonga Room, Fairmont Hotel,
    San Francisco, 169
Tongatapu, 16, 75
Tourism and food, 34, 38, 39, 75,
    109, 125–26, 131, 136, 138, 139,

143, 155, 156, 158–59, 160,
161, 169, 170, 191; Australasia,
139–40
Trade, power and influence on
food, 29
Trader Vic's Cookbook, 169
Trader Vic's restaurant, 109, 168
Tradewinds and Coconuts, 108
Transculturalism, 72
Trevally, 189
Trobriand Islands (Melanesian
New Guinea), 187
*Tropical Fruit Recipes: Rare and Exotic
Fruits*, 108
Truk, 7
Ts'ai, a Chinese meal's flavour
component, 5
Tuamotu Archipelago, 4, 10, 64, 70,
73; missionaries, 27
Tua tua, 113, 144–45
Tuatua, 73
Tuava, 70
Tuffery, Michael, 207
Tuhoe Maori tribe, 135
Tui Tonga dynasty, 16
Tuna, 38, 73, 74, 133, 150,
176, 189,
Tunu, 90
Tupou IV (king of Tonga), 209
Turtle, 12, 21, 73, 185; turtle
eggs, 15
Turtle Island, 156
Tutu berry, 105
Tuvalu, 14, 15, 23, 33, 100, 102;
fishing concessions to the US, 74;
taro pudding recipe, 61

Ubai, 131
Ufi (yams), 188
Umu (underground oven), 6, 17, 29,
44, 62, 65, 66, 69, 85, 86–97, 99,
102, 118–19, 123, 124, 131, 134,
137, 183, 186; cooking method, 8;
gender roles, 122; social

importance, 97; spiritual
importance, 187
*Under the Mango Tree . . . The People,
the Palate, the Pleasures*, 108
*Unforgettable: A Coconut
Cookbook*, 108
United Kingdom, 33
United States, 31, 33, 42, 52, 72,
74, 136
University of Hawaii, 184
University of the South Pacific, 184
Urbanization, diet and cooking, 89,
152, 200
Uto, 66
Uvea (Wallis Island), 16
Uvi, ufi, or *uhi*, 62

Vaihu tamoko, 67
Vakalavalava, 132
Vakalolo, 131; recipe, 132
Valavalava, 103
Vanilla, 25, 34
Vanua Levu, 29
Vanuatu, 3, 5, 24, 25, 33, 70, 90, 137,
164; concessions to the United
States, 74; kava, 189; worms, 188
Vatulele Island resort, 155
Vegemite, 128
Vegetables, 121, 158, 166, 187, 194;
storage for feasts, 187
Vi, 70
Vietnamese immigrants, Australasia,
51, 52, 111, 165
Vi kavakava, 70
Viti Levu, 29, 37, 180 n.4
Vogue Entertaining magazine,
Australia, 53

Wahou, 73, 189
Waibulabula (Living Waters), 157
Waiheke, New Zealand, 143
Waikiki Wedding, 168
Wairua, 206
Wakes, 183–84

Wallis Island, 8, 16, 33
War Economy Cookbook, 132
Warfare and food supplies,
    17, 18
Warrigal greens, 47
Water, bottled, 37
Watercress, 49, 200
Watom Island, 5
Wedding, Fiji, 186
Western adoption and adaptation of
    Australian Aboriginal foods, 81;
    of Pacific banquets, 185; of Maori
    foods, 81
Western cultural influence, 2, 21, 26,
    32, 58, 80, 85, 161, 162, 203, 137,
    152, 153, 200
Whale meat, Tonga, 207–8
Whaling, 18, 34, 19, 20,
    21, 22
Whangaroa, New Zealand, 28
Wheat and wheat flour products, 25,
    57, 63, 74, 142
Whitebait, 25; New Zealand,
    147–48
Williams, John, 28
Wine production and consumption
    in Australia and

New Zealand, 140, 142, 143,
    173–75, 195
Witchetty grubs, 80
Wombat, 109
Wood sorrel, 47
Wooden utensils, 87, 103
Wood-fired ovens, Australia and
    New Zealand, 78
World War II, 31, 48, 200
World War II, Australians,
    pandanus, 68
Wrapping food, 99, 108

Xanthosoma, 59

Yakara Valley, 37
Yams, 3, 4, 10, 20, 49, 58, 61–62, 86,
    90, 97, 103, 120, 185, 188, 191,
    203, 205, 209; cost, 121;
    storage, 62
Yap, Island of, 7, 23, 62
Yaqona, 119, 188, 189
Yarmouth bloaters, 171
Yasawa Island, 180 n.4
Yoghurt, 128, 177
Yugoslavian immigrants,
    New Zealand, 51

About the Author

ROGER HADEN is Lecturer in Gastronomy and Director of the Research Centre for the History of Food and Drink, University of Adelaide, Australia.

Recent Titles in
Food Culture around the World

Food Culture in Mexico
Janet Long-Solís and Luis Alberto Vargas

Food Culture in South America
José Raphael Lovera

Food Culture in the Caribbean
Lynn Marie Houston

Food Culture in Russia and Central Asia
Glenn R. Mack and Asele Surina

Food Culture in Sub-Saharan Africa
Fran Osseo-Asare

Food Culture in France
Julia Abramson

Food Culture in Germany
Ursula Heinzelmann

Food Culture in Southeast Asia
Penny Van Esterik

Food Culture in Belgium
Peter Scholliers

Food Culture in Scandinavia
Henry Notaker

Food Culture in the Mediterranean
Carol Helstosky

Food Culture in Central America
Michael R. McDonald